The
Accidental
Librarian

D1553356

Pamela H. MacKellar

Information Today, Inc.
Medford, New Jersey

First printing, 2008

The Accidental Librarian

Copyright © 2008 by Pamela H. MacKellar

Library of Congress Cataloging-in-Publication Data

MacKellar, Pamela H.
  The accidental librarian / Pamela H. MacKellar.
    p. cm.
  Includes bibliographical references and index.
  ISBN 978-1-57387-338-3
  1. Libraries science--United States--Handbooks, manuals, etc. 2. Libraries--United States--Handbooks, manuals, etc. I. Title.
  Z665.2.U6M33 2008
  020.973--dc22

                                                        2008036937

Printed and bound in the United States of America

President and CEO: Thomas H. Hogan, Sr.
Editor-in-Chief and Publisher: John B. Bryans
Managing Editor: Amy M. Reeve
Project Editor: Rachel Singer Gordon
VP Graphics and Production: M. Heide Dengler
Book Designer: Kara Mia Jalkowski
Cover Designer: Ashlee Caruolo
Copyeditor: Pat Hadley-Miller
Proofreader: Dorothy Pike
Indexer: Beth Palmer

www.infotoday.com

This book is dedicated to the success of the
Corrales Community Library

Contents

Chapter 11: Library Policies 173

Chapter 12: Library Management Essentials 185

Figures and Tables

Foreword

Through most of my career, I have been fortunate to work closely with "Accidental Librarians"—library directors, managers, and staff without an MLS degree. In Montana, where I was State Librarian, most public library directors do not have an MLS, and in Idaho, where I was the State Library's consultant for the 10 northern counties, most libraries are run by men and women who accidentally became library directors. In these sparsely settled states where rural economies sometimes do not allow communities to hire librarians, Accidental Librarians face the same challenges as their MLS counterparts in more prosperous communities. Yet, in most cases, these important public servants have little or no formal training.

Beyond the limited training, I've found that Accidental Librarians share two characteristics: an overwhelming eagerness to learn everything they can about library science, and a dedication to providing exceptional library services to their communities. I recall that the public library in Libby, Montana, was one of the very first in the state to offer Internet access, while the Boundary County public library in Bonner's Ferry, Idaho, received the prestigious National Medal for Museum and Library Service award from the Institute of Museum and Library Services. The Accidental Librarians in charge of these two libraries showed the rest of us how to provide exemplary library service.

State and regional libraries try to help fill the training gap by providing multiple education opportunities and in some cases, one-to-one assistance, but tight budgets and limited time often prevent this assistance from reaching Accidental Librarians when and where they need it the most. That's where this book will provide invaluable assistance, and, just as important, calm reassurance. Pamela MacKellar offers information and practical advice on all the fundamentals of running your library, from understanding the role of the library board to ordering library materials.

It's apparent that Pamela not only understands library fundamentals but respects and values the important work of Accidental Librarians. All you need to add to this wealth of knowledge is your own dedication!

Karen Strege, PhD
Director, Library Support Staff Certificate Program,
American Library Association
Former Montana State Librarian

Acknowledgments

This book would not have been possible without all the accidental librarians I have met and worked with over the years. Thank you for your hard work and dedication to our profession and for the very existence of some of our best libraries. I have learned more from you than you will ever know. Thank you to Joanne Berglund, Susan Halloran, Martha Liebert, Nancy Madigan, and Carmen Weinreich for gently introducing me to accidental librarianship so many years ago. A special thanks to my good friend, Stephanie Gerding, who suggested that I write this book to reach more accidental librarians who are eager to learn. Thanks to Bill Katz, an outstanding teacher, who was the first to suggest I publish. Rachel Singer Gordon, editor extraordinaire, it is a real pleasure working with you. And lastly, I am grateful for Bruce, my life partner, for supporting me in everything I do and for accepting me as I am—especially during the past year.

About the Website

www.accidentallibrarian.com

This book explains the basic principles and practices of library and information science for accidental librarians. It is intended as a starting point—a place where you are introduced to some new ideas and encouraged to think about others with which you are already familiar. You will no doubt want to pursue some of these concepts by reading further and investigating topics of particular interest.

I have provided many links to resources in this book, but there is always something new to read or learn. All the links in this book will be updated on a companion web page, www.accidental librarian.com, which will also include additional resources and information for accidental librarians. Please take advantage of this site and email me at pam@accidentallibrarian.com with your ideas, input, suggestions, and contributions. I look forward to hearing from you!

Disclaimer

Neither the publisher nor the author makes any claim as to the results that may be obtained through the use of this website or of any of the Internet resources it references or links to. Neither publisher nor author will be held liable for any results, or lack thereof, obtained by the use of this page or any of its links; for any third-party changes; or for any hardware, software, or other problems that may occur as the result of using it. This website is subject to change or discontinuation without notice at the discretion of the publisher and author.

Introduction

Did you become a librarian without planning on it? Maybe you volunteered at your local library and were so good at doing library work that the director encouraged you to apply for a paid position as a librarian. Perhaps your town library was searching for a music librarian, and, as an accomplished musician with extensive music education, knowledge, and experience, you thought you were as equipped as anyone to do the job. As a young mom, you may have offered to read at your library's story hour and assist with children's craft programs. Then, after your children were in school, you applied for the Children's Librarian position and were offered the job, even though you had never worked in a library before or even finished college. Maybe you stepped forward when your synagogue was looking for someone to organize its extensive collection. Before you knew it, you were the librarian at your synagogue. The possibilities are endless.

Many of you took on the task of librarianship when there was no one else to do the job. Some of you volunteered to start the first libraries in your communities or organizations and even bought books for the library with your own money. Without you, your communities, organizations, churches, synagogues, schools, and associations wouldn't *have* libraries. Often, communities that cannot afford to hire a librarian with a master's degree in library and information science are delighted to hire someone with a high school diploma or undergraduate degree to fill a librarian position. A church, organization, or school may be happy just to have a library and someone to run it at all. We are fortunate to have people who step up to the plate when the job of librarian needs to be filled.

The traditional route to becoming a librarian is to attend an American Library Association (ALA)-accredited school of library science and earn a master's degree. Depending on the school, this degree might be a Master of Library Science (MLS), Master of Library and Information Science (MLIS), Master of Science in Information Science (MSIS), Master of Science in Library Science (MSLS), Master of Arts in Library and Information Science (MA in LIS), or Master of Information Science (MIS). The debate about whether librarians must have one of these degrees to practice librarianship has been going on for decades. Some insist that a librarian without an MLS is not a "real" librarian. However, according to the report, *Public Libraries in the United States: Fiscal Year 2004* from the National Center for Education Statistics, 32.1 percent of all librarians practicing in public libraries in the U.S. do not have ALA-MLS degrees. [1] This percentage is likely comparable in special libraries and may be even higher in school libraries.

So, who makes up this third of librarians, if they are not "real" librarians? For the purposes of this book, accidental librarians are librarians without a formal education in library and information science, librarians with no professional library experience prior to becoming librarians, those who didn't set out to be librarians through the traditional channels. If this sounds like you, you are probably an accidental librarian.

Since becoming an accidental librarian, you may have done your best to learn about librarianship by reading books and journals about libraries and librarianship, joining library associations and chapters, meeting and talking with other librarians about the profession, attending library conferences, watching other librarians do their work, asking questions, or taking classes and workshops. Even under the best of circumstances, it is challenging to learn the basics of librarianship while working a demanding job in a small rural school or a public library, or as a solo librarian in a special library.

Some of you may think it has been pretty easy to learn all there is to know about librarianship. You are confident that you've picked up all the skills you need "on the fly" and that there's nothing new you can learn. I hope this book will change your mind. Many librarians understand that there is always something to learn about librarianship, especially at this time of immense change when technology is having such an impact on libraries and the profession overall.

Our society holds so many misconceptions about librarians that we must be assertive in educating people about the work librarians do, our value, and the value of libraries in our communities, schools, organizations, and corporations. To do this, we must all be certain about our role and know the value of libraries. We must know what we are doing, where we are going, and why. We must lead our libraries into the future with purpose and show by example. Many people assume that librarians spend their time buying bestsellers, checking out books, socializing, surfing the web, and reading. Some people think that everyone working in a library is a librarian, and, based on what they see, they deduce that anyone can be a librarian. It is our job to change that perception.

Some libraries will probably never have funding to hire an MLS librarian; some librarians aren't ever likely to pursue an MLS. If all librarians, though, have a common understanding of the foundations of our profession; are clear about the role of libraries in our communities, centers, organizations, churches, and corporations; know with certainty our value and the value of libraries in the lives of the people we serve; competently perform our jobs; and are sure of what we are doing and where we are going, then together we can take the risks and make the continuous changes necessary to ensure that our libraries not only succeed, but thrive.

This book provides a straightforward introduction to basic library principles and practice for accidental librarians. If you are practicing librarianship, it is essential that you understand:

- The fundamentals of what librarians do and why

- The basic theories behind and functions of information acquisition, collection, organization, retrieval, and dissemination

- Your place in the changing role of libraries in society today

Part I, Basic Library Principles, discusses how people become accidental librarians and provides some inspiring stories. Chapters cover the function of libraries in our society, including the relationship of libraries to the people they serve, and outline the evolution of librarianship, highlighting the influence technology has had on libraries in recent years. There is also discussion on how to understand the people libraries serve and determine their needs and how to use the library's vision, mission, and plan to guide you in your work. Part I establishes a big picture of librarianship that will facilitate your understanding of the basic library practices covered in Part II.

Part II, Basic Library Practice, begins with a discussion on developing a library's collection based on the needs of the people served. Subsequent chapters detail the basic functions of acquiring information, organizing information, and information retrieval and dissemination—including why it makes sense for librarians to do these things, and tools to help you do them. Other topics covered include library services, such as programs for all ages, reference, readers' advisory, and more; essential library policies, their purpose, and how to write them; management, including leadership, personnel, communication, working with boards, your relationship to the larger organization, library budgets, and volunteers; and marketing, including your library's public image and brand, ways for librarians to inform the community about library news, services, and programming, and methods for attracting new users. The section concludes by outlining common barriers faced by librarians and suggesting how to move beyond them. Part II gives an overview of basic library practices to help build a foundation for those new to the field and serves as a way for all librarians to focus on our primary practices.

Part III, Technology and the Library, covers public access computers, automated catalogs, online reference tools, and Library 2.0. Highlights include how to maintain and manage PACs, selecting integrated library systems, using online reference tools such as Internet reference sites and online databases, and the opportunities Library 2.0 has introduced (including library websites, blogs, and social software). Part III provides information about how technology impacts the work of librarians, shows how we can use technology to enhance what we do, and gives some guidance on selecting appropriate technology for your library.

Part IV, Career Development, suggests ways for librarians to connect with and support each other through library associations, state libraries, library systems and consortia, electronic discussion lists and blogs, and conferences. Librarian certification, continuing education, distance education, library science degree programs, certificate opportunities, and web-based tutorials are listed. Part IV encourages readers to move forward in their careers by connecting with other librarians, staying informed, and finding support, and to learn more about the profession by taking classes, becoming certified, or earning degrees.

Appendix A contains some sample library policies, including a Weeding Policy, Computer Use Policy, and Donations Policy. Appendix B provides LIS education resources, and Appendix C covers some library issues and legislation such as the Library Bill of Rights, the Freedom to Read Statement, the Copyright Law, the USA PATRIOT Act, and the Children's Internet Protection Act. These appendices include policy samples, educational resource lists, and supporting documents that will help you in your daily work and in pursuing librarianship as a career.

While reading this book, I hope you will open your mind to learning something new that could help you in becoming the best librarian you can be and in becoming an active participant in the future success of libraries. Stay connected and keep learning by visiting www.accidentallibrarian.com.

Endnotes

1. Adrienne Chute, Patricia O'Shea, Terri Craig, Michael Freeman, Laura Hardesty, Joanna Fane McLaughlin, and Cynthia Jo Ramsey, *Public Libraries in the United States: Fiscal Year 2004* (Washington, DC: National Center for Education Statistics, 2006), 62.

Part I

Basic Library Principles

Chapter 1

What Is a Librarian?

In his book *Our Enduring Values: Librarianship in the 21st Century*, Michael Gorman defines a librarian as a person who earns a master's-level education at an accredited school and receives on-the-job training, as well as carries out one or more of the following tasks:

- Selects materials and electronic resources
- Acquires the selected materials and resources
- Organizes and gives access to them
- Preserves and conserves them
- Assists library users
- Instructs library users
- Administers and manages the library, library personnel, services, and programs[1]

Many librarians, though, perform these duties with neither a master's-level education in library and information science (LIS) nor school library media specialist credentials. Some of these non-degreed and noncredentialed librarians are even certified by their states as librarians or library directors. Aren't they librarians?

Why We Become Librarians

Why do we choose librarianship? Some people know they want to become librarians from a young age. They were read to as toddlers, attended library story hours, learned to love reading and discover the hidden joys in books, felt comfortable in the children's room of their local library, loved attending children's and teen programs as they were growing up, and maybe found a mentor in a librarian.

People interested in technology may aspire to be systems librarians. Inquisitive types may strive to be reference librarians, desiring to help people find information by using electronic databases, while others might long to contribute to the educational role of libraries as centers of lifelong learning in their communities. Future leaders in our profession may see themselves playing an instrumental role in the acquisition, collection, organization, retrieval, and dissemination of information. When *American Libraries* editor Leonard Kniffel asked a class of library school students at Dominican University what made them choose librarianship, he found that "they were attracted by the books, the place, the people, and the need to find a job worth doing."[2]

How We Become Librarians

How do we become librarians? Those determined early on to become librarians proceed straight through school, graduating from high school and college and going directly to graduate school. Although this is the most straightforward path to librarianship, it is not the most common way people become librarians. For most of us it is a much longer and more circuitous road—in fact, librarianship may not even be our first career choice. Some people may earn their bachelor's degrees only to find out that there are no jobs available in their field or that they are not suited to that particular field. Those with bachelor's degrees in English, history, philosophy, religion, or fine arts, for example, often require advanced degrees to secure a job in their field, which are limited primarily to college or university teaching, research, or scholarly publishing positions. If you aren't interested in a lifetime of teaching or scholarly research and publishing, you might start looking for another career. Librarianship attracts people with education, interests, and backgrounds in all subject areas. No specific undergraduate program of study is required for acceptance into library school, so people from many disciplines enter LIS graduate programs.

According to the *Occupational Outlook Handbook,* librarian positions in most public, academic, and special libraries, as well as in some school libraries, require a master's degree in library science (MLS) or library and information science (MLIS). The U.S. government requires that the librarians it employs have an MLS or the equivalent in education and experience, while other employers often require librarians to be graduates of the more than 50 schools accredited by the American Library Association (ALA).[3] The ALA website (www.ala.org) states that the educational requirements for a librarian position can span a large range:

- Four-year undergraduate degree in any field
- Master of library science (MLS) degree
- MLS degree from an ALA-accredited school
- ALA-accredited MLS degree plus a teaching certificate (often the case in school libraries) or an ALA-accredited MLS plus a second degree, for example, a law degree[4]

School media specialists (also known as school librarians or teacher-librarians) can pursue either an ALA-accredited master's degree or a master's degree in education with a specialty in school library media from an educational unit accredited by the National Council for Accreditation of Teacher Education (NCATE).[5]

Library School Education

Melvil Dewey founded the first library school in 1887 at the Columbia School of Library Economy in New York. Dewey pioneered the education of librarians, believing that the best way to prepare people for library work was through classroom instruction combined with practical work in a library. He helped to set standards for the profession of librarianship in terms of education, ethics, and the role of the librarian in society. Columbia admitted women to its first class, which was a point of contention with the trustees. This disagreement eventually resulted in the school's closing two years later and its move to the state library in Albany in 1889. The curriculum in early library schools emphasized technical subjects such as cataloging and bibliography.

Graduate-level education for librarians wasn't introduced until 1926, when the Graduate Library School at the University of Chicago opened. The Carnegie Corporation provided funding for the school to create an advanced, research-oriented library school; its first graduates accepted positions as academic librarians, library school teachers, and deans. The need for this level of education was slow to be accepted by librarians; however, several important works and conferences on library education between 1936 and 1948 led to the consensus that professional librarians needed a graduate degree. Library education thrived in the 1950s and 1960s, when federal funding supported libraries, library schools, and students of librarianship to a greater degree than ever before. Libraries improved, the demand for librarians increased, and library school recruiters were busy enrolling new students. The 1970s were not so favorable for the profession, and in recent decades a number of library schools have closed.

Over the last 60 years, library science education has continuously adapted to the changing needs for library and information services. The increasing importance of library automation, electronic information systems, and online access to information has caused some changes in library school curricula, but ALA's Standards for Accreditation of Master's Programs in Library and Information Studies does not include a core curriculum. The standards mention that curricula "encompass information and knowledge creation, communication, identification, selection, acquisition, organization and description, storage and retrieval, preservation, analysis, interpretation, evaluation, synthesis, dissemination, and management."[6] However, since these 14 elements aren't defined, and the standards don't mention which ones require greater emphasis, there are wide differences among ALA-accredited schools in how these areas are covered and what MLS librarians need to know.

Due to this lack of a common core curriculum in LIS education, graduates from ALA-accredited LIS programs aren't mastering comparable skills. Some schools cover in a week what others take a semester to teach. This inability to define a core curriculum contributes to the difficulty in maintaining the status of librarianship as a profession. Other professions, such as medicine, nursing, dentistry, law, architecture, and real estate, have clearly defined standards, comparable certification exams from state to state, and minimum requirements for continuing education.

You can earn undergraduate and graduate degrees in library science, associate's degrees, and certifications as a library assistant or library technician. Some states certify library media specialists, public librarians, and library directors. Continuing education, online education, and distance education opportunities have become more important than ever as a way to keep up with constant change, learn new skills, and acquire degrees and certificates. Today, you can earn LIS degrees and certifications wherever you may live.

Kinds of Librarians

Librarians are generally categorized according to the type of library in which they work:

- *Public librarians* work in public libraries.

- *School librarians, library media specialists,* and *teacher-librarians* work in school libraries or media centers.

- *Academic librarians* work in college, university, or post-secondary school libraries.

- *Special librarians* work in specialized information centers such as corporate libraries, government agencies, military libraries, law libraries, art libraries, museum libraries, or medical libraries.

In larger organizations, librarians may specialize in technical services, administrative services, electronic services, or user services. In small libraries, librarians typically perform duties encompassing all aspects of librarianship. Some librarians choose to work with specific groups such as children, young adults, students, adults, or special populations.

What Is an Accidental Librarian?

ALA itself recognizes that the educational requirements for librarian positions do vary, including a four-year undergraduate degree in any field. In states where an MLS is not required to practice public librarianship, librarians—even library directors—without MLS degrees are common. Many smaller libraries, especially those in rural areas, have a difficult time filling librarian and library director positions. They often hire people with other degrees or equivalent experience. In many rural areas throughout the U.S., there is no MLS librarian to be found for miles. Even if there were, most small towns cannot afford (or are not willing to pay) an MLS librarian's salary. Many small communities cannot afford librarians with college degrees, much less those with graduate degrees in library science.

How I Discovered That Not All Librarians Have MLS Degrees

If you live in a part of the country that requires an MLS to be a librarian, it may come as a surprise to you that many librarians don't hold this advanced degree. I grew up in Massachusetts and New York, where it was commonly known that the way to become a librarian was to go to library school and earn an MLS. Before deciding to pursue librarianship as a career, I worked as a paraprofessional in a public library where the librarians all had MLS degrees. No one without a professional degree would consider calling herself a librarian. When I moved to New Mexico, I met many librarians; however, outside of the university it was rare to find one who had been to library school. There wasn't (and still isn't) a library school in New Mexico, and online degrees didn't exist at the time. Most of the librarians I met came to librarianship out of a love for their communities; they valued books and reading, recognized the power of information, and supported education and lifelong learning on behalf of their communities. Many of these librarians founded the first libraries in their communities, volunteering their time to do so, and some even used personal funds to purchase books for the libraries they started.

Librarians without MLS degrees are essentially accidental librarians—increasingly being hired as frontline librarians in libraries of all kinds and sizes, performing duties that were formerly carried out exclusively by professional librarians, while MLS librarians can be found working behind the scenes in management and administrative positions, including technical services, marketing, systems administration, and personnel. It is not uncommon to see advertisements for librarian jobs in large city systems that require a four-year degree in any field plus library experience, while an ALA-accredited MLS degree is listed only as being "preferred." A recently posted Assistant Librarian position in my area required only a high school diploma or GED, plus two years of postsecondary education.

Throughout this book, successful accidental librarians (such as Linda Hardy Dydo in the sidebar on this page) share their stories of how they found success and what they do in their jobs. I hope they will motivate, inspire, and encourage you to learn more about librarianship as you move ahead on your chosen path.

Linda Hardy Dydo, Assistant Library Director, Los Gatos (CA) Public Library

I had recently moved to San Jose, and I was looking for a job. I went to the EEOC (Equal Employment Opportunity Commission) to look at the job boards and to CETA (Comprehensive Employment and Training Act), a federal employment program that was just starting. I registered, and they sent me out on interviews.

My first interview was with the police department as a record keeper. Before the interview, I sat down on the curb and cried. I was a secret anarchist, an anti-war protestor, a free-love proponent. How could I work for the cops? I wiped my face and went into the station, but it was too late. Someone else got the job. Yahoo!

My second interview was with the library department. I got hired two minutes after the oral interview. I didn't even make it to the elevator. I was a library aide! Promotions followed—to clerk, then library assistant (leaving the CETA program and entering civil service at this point). Librarian tests were scheduled, and no degree was necessary, so as not to disqualify all the students from San Jose State library school (which was having accreditation challenges at the time). I placed high on the list, and I was respected for my work ethic, attitude, and skills. I worked my way through Children's Librarian, Teen Librarian, Branch Manager, Head of the IT Department, and Head of Reference at Main. I was part of the team that established the agreement between San Jose Public and San Jose State to occupy and run a new eight-story library together, and part of the team that implemented this merger.

Thirty-two years later, here I am, the Assistant Director at Los Gatos Public Library. I am proud of myself and proud of a profession that could look beyond credentials.

The Facts About Accidental Librarians

Accidental librarians may be more numerous—and important—than you think:

- For decades, great research libraries have hired scholars over degreed librarians for director positions.

- Many deans of library school programs do not hold MLS degrees.

- No special qualifications are prescribed by law for Librarians of Congress, who have come from the varied professions of newspaperman, novelist, poet, physician, and diplomat. In 1899, at the urging of the ALA, President McKinley appointed the first experienced librarian, Herbert Putnam, to the position of Librarian of Congress. L. Quincy Mumford, Librarian of Congress from 1954 through 1974, was the first Librarian of Congress to have graduated from library school.

- The Council on Library and Information Resources (CLIR) offers postdoctoral fellowships in research libraries to humanities scholars to develop meaningful linkages between disciplinary scholarship, libraries, archives, and evolving digital tools. Study in the area of LIS is not a requirement for this fellowship.

• The Virginia code does not require the state librarian to have an MLS. Sandra Treadway served as Deputy State Librarian at the Library of Virginia for more than a decade and became the Virginia State Librarian before she had a library degree. Treadway "learned about library operations the old-fashioned way—climbing the ladder to the top one rung at a time." She never intended to do library work.[7]

As you can see, many accidental librarians are both accomplished and prominent.

According to *Public Libraries in the United States,* only 67.9 percent of FTE (full-time equivalent) public librarians in the U.S. hold ALA-accredited MLS degrees.[8] Table 1.1 lists the states in which less than half of the total FTE public librarians have ALA-accredited MLS degrees. Table 1.2 lists the states where more than half of the total FTE public librarians hold ALA-accredited MLS degrees.

As you can see, the situation varies considerably between Montana, where 20.9 percent of FTE public librarians hold an ALA-accredited MLS, and Hawaii, where 99.7 percent hold such a degree.

In most states, school librarians (also known as teacher-librarians or school media specialists) are not required to have MLS degrees. School librarians are usually required to have an undergraduate degree in education, with a school library media specialist certification. This certification requires coursework in library science or passing a qualifying test. School librarians are certified at the state level, and each state has its own requirements.

Often an organization or corporation will add a librarian's duties to the job of a secretary or administrative assistant when materials

Table 1.1 States in which less than half of public librarians have ALA-accredited MLS degrees (Data from Public Libraries in the United States: Fiscal Year 2004. National Center for Education Statistics: Washington, DC, 2006.)

State	Total FTE Librarians (percentage)
Montana	20.9
Wyoming	21.5
North Dakota	22.6
Kentucky	23.8
Iowa	25.6
Mississippi	26.3
Vermont	26.9
Nebraska	27.2
West Virginia	27.2
South Dakota	28.9
Oklahoma	33.6
Idaho	33.7
Kansas	36.8
New Hampshire	37.2
Alabama	38.4
Arkansas	40.3
Louisiana	41.2
New Mexico	43.2
Maine	45.6
Tennessee	49.4

Table 1.2 States in which more than half of public librarians have ALA-accredited MLS degrees (Data from Public Libraries in the United States: Fiscal Year 2004. National Center for Education Statistics: Washington, DC, 2006.)

State	Total FTE Librarians (percentage)
Delaware	50.7
Maryland	52.0
Utah	53.5
Wisconsin	53.6
Missouri	55.0
Alaska	58.1
Illinois	62.8
Massachusetts	64.9
Indiana	65.0
Minnesota	65.5
Pennsylvania	67.7
Michigan	68.0
Colorado	70.0
Nevada	71.8
Texas	71.8
Ohio	73.3
Oregon	75.3
Connecticut	76.3
Arizona	78.3
South Carolina	78.9
Florida	83.4
Virginia	83.9
New York	84.0

Rhode Island	85.5
District of Columbia	88.5
California	93.2
Washington	94.3
Georgia	95.1
North Carolina	95.4
New Jersey	99.6
Hawaii	99.7

purchased for shared use by employees have accumulated to the point that they are no longer accessible. In such a case, management realizes the need for someone to organize and manage the collection, track usage, and retrieve information. They may not recognize that this is a "librarian" position, or that the job requires any special skill or knowledge.

Other special librarians, such as church or synagogue librarians, often begin as volunteers. Many prison librarians are not required to hold MLS degrees; some hold the title of Library Aide or Library Technician, but are actually running their libraries single-handedly.

Because academic librarians work in an environment that values the degree, postsecondary, college, or university libraries are less likely to hire librarians without MLS degrees, making it less common to find accidental librarians in academic situations.

Mary McKinley Ingraham, University Librarian at Acadia University in Nova Scotia, driving force of the Maritime Library Institute and editor of its *Bulletin,* said in a 1939 editorial, "There is no doubt that specialized training is a necessity for most of us who would work in libraries, but is there any absolute norm by which we may determine the method or content of that training? Despite the unquestioned value of the many schools of library service, we have to admit that the greatest librarians in the world, from

Zenodatus at Alexandria to Putnam at Washington, were not graduates of library schools." She was careful to stress that librarianship requires education and training, calling it a "learned profession," but suggested that this training can take place in many contexts and by diverse means.[9]

What Makes a Librarian?

By now you can see that there really are no universal criteria in the U.S. for determining what makes a librarian. It's no wonder that librarians have such varying levels of education, experience, and knowledge about library and information science. Librarians come from all subject backgrounds and educational levels, and have varying degrees of library experience.

Eileen Gilbert, Director, Boscawen (NH) Public Library

I'm so glad this author has acknowledged the fact that not everyone working in a library has an MLS! I would like to earn mine fairly soon, but I'm enjoying my work without it. I am 26 years old and the Library Director in a town of around 3,500. I worked as a page at a different library in high school and as a student aide in my college library. I really enjoyed both jobs and when I graduated with a degree in English I knew I didn't want to teach. In my current job I plan programming, work the circulation desk, order and process books, and shelve.

Although some states and schools have established standards, with very few exceptions these are voluntary or optional. Some state standards can easily be met with very little education, experience, or training, and it may be possible to be certified as a librarian or library director in your state with no library education or experience. If you don't qualify as a librarian in one state, you can go to another state and easily become certified as a library director there. Some people assume that passing their state certification test is equivalent to an MLS, but even if you have an MLS there is no common basic foundation of knowledge you are required to master in graduate school. Confused?

The lack of national standards in the U.S. for qualifying librarians creates a chaotic professional atmosphere. Disagreements about who is and isn't a librarian abound. We engage in ongoing discussions about the state of LIS education and our profession, "illegal librarians," and what makes a "real" librarian. In this atmosphere, insisting that someone has to have an MLS to be a librarian is unrealistic: There are plenty of practicing librarians who do not have the degree.

Unfortunately, when nondegreed librarians reject learning from MLS librarians because they feel threatened by them, and when MLS librarians reject nondegreed librarians because of the belief that they are not "real" librarians, they overlook some of their greatest opportunities to learn from each other, advance our profession, and improve our libraries. Misunderstandings on both sides of this issue abound, causing our profession to be fragmented. We cannot afford a "librarian vs. librarian" mentality. We are facing some of the most challenging and exciting changes in our field, and this is the time to join together and move forward. Degreed and nondegreed librarians alike are responsible for creating and upholding the standards of our profession, and for valuing librarianship and each other.

What Do Librarians Do?

The primary functions of a librarian are to:

- Collect information

- Acquire information

- Organize information

- Retrieve information

- Disseminate information based on the needs of the populations we serve

These five functions create a foundation for the practice of librarianship, and understanding them as such helps librarians stay focused on our main purpose. As our profession rapidly changes and evolves it is essential for us to be grounded in a set of core functions that we can easily apply to new developments in the information field. Brief descriptions of these functions follow, and each will be covered in detail in Part II of this book.

Collect Information

Librarians develop collections to meet the information needs of their communities. They must constantly assess their community's changing information needs and collect, as well as deselect, materials and resources based on those needs.

Acquire Information

Librarians evaluate, select, and purchase or lease materials and information resources to meet the information needs of the populations they serve.

Organize Information

Librarians organize information by (1) classifying it according to subject, and (2) cataloging it by describing it in a way that makes the information easily accessible. Librarians also make library resources, services, and programs available electronically in a way that users can easily access and utilize.

Retrieve Information

Librarians find information to meet the needs of library users. This involves analyzing users' needs to determine what it is they want and at what level, and searching for and extracting information in multiple formats from multiple sources. Librarians also assist people in finding the information they need.

Disseminate Information

Librarians play an important role in facilitating the transfer of knowledge and ideas from the sources of the knowledge and ideas to the people who need and want the information. Librarians do this by synthesizing and delivering information to people who request it in a form that is useful to them.

What Else Do Librarians Do?

In the process of acquiring, collecting, organizing, retrieving, and disseminating information, librarians also:

- Assist and instruct

- Provide services and programs

- Utilize technology

- Preserve and conserve library materials

In the process of doing our work, librarians are also responsible for upholding the basic principles of intellectual freedom, or the right of every individual to both seek and receive information from all points of view without restriction. ALA's Library Bill of Rights affirms that all libraries are forums for information and ideas and articulates basic principles to guide their services. Librarians support the Freedom to Read and the Freedom to View under the Constitution of the United States, and we are responsible for advocating for these rights.

Additionally, we must be aware of legislation that affects libraries or that may threaten these basic rights. We need to take responsibility for acting in support of the freedom of information on behalf of libraries and the citizens of our country. We are expected to protect the creators of works being shared in our libraries by seeing to it that the Copyright Act is observed (see Appendix C).

Assist and Instruct

Librarians play an instructional role, which includes teaching users how to access information, synthesize it, and use it. They also teach users how to effectively use library tools, technology, and resources. The desired result is for users to be able to search for information, analyze it, synthesize it, and use it on their own in the future. Librarians also develop content and design materials for instructional purposes.

Provide Services and Programs

Librarians plan, budget, and manage programs such as story hours, literacy skills classes, book groups, programs for all ages, and educational classes based on the needs of the community. Other services librarians provide include reference service and readers' advisory service.

Utilize Technology

Because technology has become such a large part of information storage and delivery, librarians evaluate information technologies; develop, design, and manage digital access and content; use technology appropriately and effectively; administer and manage computer systems; and train users on using technology to retrieve information and for other purposes.

Preserve and Conserve

Librarians are responsible for maximizing the life of library materials by preserving and conserving them.

What Do Librarians Need to Know?

Librarians need to know the following to be successful:

- The philosophy, theory, principles, and techniques of acquiring, collecting, organizing, retrieving, and disseminating information and how to apply them and adapt them to constantly changing environments

- The role of computers, the Internet, and emerging technologies in libraries

- Basic library materials and resources in all formats and how to use them

- Methods and techniques for researching, analyzing, synthesizing, and delivering information

- Reference interviewing techniques

- Community needs assessment methods

- Library planning processes and methods

- Budgeting methods

- Policy creation and development methods

- Management methods

What Skills Do Librarians Need?

In recent years, the LIS field and the practice of librarianship have undergone tremendous changes due to the growth of information technology and the resulting changes in the methods of acquiring, collecting, organizing, retrieving, and disseminating information. There has been a fundamental shift in libraries from ownership to access, and a corresponding shift in the skills librarians need.[10] Today, librarians not only need to understand the basics of managing and disseminating information, they also need to:

- See the big picture
- Make things happen
- Remove barriers
- Create vision and mission
- Work independently and on teams
- Exercise initiative and independent judgment
- Think creatively and innovatively
- Create partnerships and alliances
- Evaluate, select, and apply new technologies
- Troubleshoot technology
- Communicate clearly and effectively verbally and in writing
- Seek additional funding to meet unmet community needs
- Write grant proposals
- Develop new systems and adapt old ones to new situations
- Work with diverse populations
- Teach

What Are the Characteristics of Librarians?

Librarians are:

- Change agents
- Proactive
- Creative

- Inquisitive

- Initiators

- On the leading edge

- Customer service oriented

- Collaborators

- Risk-takers

- Active communicators

- Flexible

- Advocates

- Continuous lifelong learners

- Leaders

- Networkers

- Visionaries

- Team players

- Analytical thinkers

- Strategic planners

(This list is inspired by SLA's Competencies for Information Professionals, www.sla.org/content/learn/comp2003/index.cfm, and ALA's Accreditation Draft Core Competencies, www.ala.org/ala/accreditationb/Draft_Core_Competencies_07_05.pdf.)

Don't be shocked if you are beginning to realize that there is much more to librarianship, what librarians do, what they need to know, and the skills and qualities they need to possess than you previously thought. You aren't alone. Perhaps you haven't had a positive librarian role model or mentor, you didn't work in a library before becoming a librarian, or you were never in a position where you learned what is really involved in librarianship. You came into this profession accidentally, or as a second career, without the benefit of education or professional experience, easily meeting your state's qualifications (if any!) to practice librarianship. You thought, "The state certified me, so I must know all there is to know about being a librarian." Although this is not uncommon, it is a mistake to think that passing a certification test or meeting your state's qualifications to be a library director is the same as earning a graduate degree in library and information science. It's not quite that simple.

When you accepted your job as a librarian for your municipality, school, organization, or corporation, you became professionally obligated to perform your job competently and to continue to learn about librarianship. Most of you have taken this responsibility seriously and have worked hard to live up to the standards of our profession. A few of you, though, may find it easy and safe to keep doing what you've always done, resisting change and new ideas proposed by staff members. Over the years you may have surrounded yourselves with supportive friends, volunteers, and library users who praise you for the good job you are doing—but do they know what librarians do? You might attend your state library association conference every year and an occasional local workshop to fulfill continuing education requirements, but do you challenge yourself, apply new concepts, or plan to change? Do you wonder why you should put in all that hard work to become a better librarian when things are fine just the way they are?

If this sounds at all like you, it is time to take notice. You have an obligation to an entire profession and to the people you serve to take the next step. Librarianship is a dynamic, exciting, and challenging profession with room for many great librarians. By joining together to establish a common understanding of our profession and our role as librarians, we will all help ensure the survival of librarianship and libraries.

Exercise 1.1

Answer the following questions:

What are the 5 primary functions of a librarian?

What other things do librarians do to support these functions?

What skills and characteristics must librarians have?

Have you ever learned anything from an MLS librarian that helped you in your job?

If you were to make one improvement or change as a librarian, what would it be?

Endnotes

1. Michael Gorman, *Our Enduring Values: Librarianship in the 21st Century* (Chicago, IL: American Library Association, 2000), 14.
2. Leonard Kniffel, "What Turns You into a Librarian" (Editorial), *American Libraries* 35:5 (2004): 29.
3. Bureau of Labor Statistics, U.S. Department of Labor, *Occupational Outlook Handbook*, 2006–07 edition, www.bls.gov/oco/ocos068.htm
4. American Library Association, "What Librarians Need to Know," www.ala.org/ala/hrdr/librarycareerssite/whatyouneedlibrarian.cfm

5. American Library Association, "Education & Degrees," www.ala.org/ ala/education/degrees/degrees.cfm

6. American Library Association, "Standards for Accreditation of Master's Programs in Library and Information Studies," www.ala.org/ ala/accreditation/accredstandards/standards_2008.pdf

7. Gary Robertson, "Learned Librarian Keeps State's Treasures," *Richmond Times-Dispatch*, July 29, 2007, www.inrich.com/cva/ric/ news.apx.-content-articles-RTD-2007-07-29-0191.html

8. Adrienne Chute, Patricia O'Shea, Terri Craig, Michael Freeman, Laura Hardesty, Joanna Fane McLaughlin, and Cynthia Jo Ramsey, *Public Libraries in the United States: Fiscal Year 2004* (Washington, DC: National Center for Education Statistics, 2006), 62, nces.ed.gov/ pubs2006/2006349.pdf

9. Greg Bak, "The Greatest Librarians of the World ... Were Not Graduates of Library School," *Libraries & Culture* 37:4 (2002): 373.

10. John Philip Mulvaney, and Dan O'Connor, "The Crux of Our Crisis: We Must Pinpoint What Every New Librarian Must Learn, Lest We Lose Our Professional Way," *American Libraries* 37:6 (2006): 3.

Chapter 2

What Are Libraries?

Although the traditional concept of a library is that of a place that houses books and printed materials, today's libraries are portals—no longer limited to buildings—for accessing information in multiple formats, as well as vital and dynamic community information centers offering resources, staff, and space. Library buildings are still important for holding print materials, microfilm and microfiche, CDs and DVDs, video recordings, audiotapes, and other resources that do not exist in electronic formats. In library buildings, customers use public access computers, seek face-to-face information services, take advantage of computer and technology training, use meeting places, enjoy exhibits, and attend programs for all ages. People continue to visit libraries to borrow books, browse collections, peruse the latest periodical issues, do research, and use print materials. But libraries are more than buildings: They are the physical and virtual information centers in our communities.

Library customers can now use computers to access many library resources remotely, in many cases making a visit to the physical library building unnecessary. Library customers can search online catalogs, electronic periodical databases, and other online reference resources from home, school, or work. Their information needs are emerging as they become accustomed to the ease of finding information on the Internet. Library patrons are used to Internet businesses that serve their online customers by recommending new products that may interest them based on their previous purchases or views. Libraries must adapt using similar techniques—plus inventing a few of our own—to create places people want to go for online information.

As information centers, libraries must stay on the forefront of information technologies, applying the tools that will help them to fulfill their role of meeting the information needs of the people they serve. The future of libraries depends on their relevance. If people can satisfy their information needs more effectively in other places, they will go other places.

Libraries are no longer expected to possess, house, or subscribe to all the materials and information resources needed by their communities. They do, however, need to provide easy access to necessary materials and information, even if these are accessed through other libraries, cooperatives, consortia, state libraries, or public online resources. Libraries without adequate funding to purchase all the materials necessary to meet the needs of the communities they serve can take advantage of programs and resources made available to them by state libraries or regional library systems, collaborate and partner with surrounding libraries, and otherwise be creative problem-solvers. Technology has made this possible.

Libraries are responsible for meeting the information needs of their communities—whatever the makeup of that community. Because every municipality, organization, association, school, university, hospital, and law office has different needs, the ways that libraries meet those needs will be different. Depending on the people you serve, your library could provide the following and more:

- Bookmobile service

- Computer games

- Consumer health information

- Educational support

- Genealogical resources

- Historical documents

- Literacy support

- Outreach to senior citizens

- Popular reading materials

- Research support

- Town government archives

A library today cannot isolate itself—ignoring the importance of new technologies, remote access to resources, collaborative resource sharing, outreach to the underserved, and the use of online social tools—and continue to survive as a library. To be valued in our communities, libraries must change with the times, using the latest methods and technologies to fill their roles as community information centers.

Types of Libraries

America's approximately 123,291 libraries fall into these major types: public, school, academic, and special, differentiated primarily by the kinds of communities they serve:

- *Public libraries* serve members of a municipality, defined geographical area, or physical jurisdiction. There are more than 9,000 public libraries in the U.S., which serve the general public in communities of all sizes and types. They serve people of every age, income level, race, religion, ethnicity, and physical ability, and are usually publicly funded.

- *School library media centers* serve students, teachers, and staff in a school or school system. They support curricula, reading, and literacy initiatives in a school. There are more than 99,000 school libraries in the U.S., which are typically funded by a school or school district.

- *Academic libraries* serve the students, faculty, and staff in colleges, universities, junior colleges, and community colleges. There are more than 3,600 academic libraries in the U.S.

- *Special libraries* offer information services within specialized environments like corporations, hospitals, law offices, museums, churches and synagogues, associations, and businesses. There are more than 9,000 special libraries in the U.S.

- In the U.S., *armed forces libraries* number approximately 300, and *government agency libraries* more than 1,000. *Armed forces libraries* serve military and nonmilitary personnel and their families on military bases, ships, schools, training institutes, and academies. *Government agency libraries* serve federal, state, and local government employees and, in some cases, residents of their jurisdictions.

- *State library agencies* often serve as repositories for public information, as a research arm of the state government serving their state legislators, and as a resource for other libraries in their states.[1]

Who Uses Libraries?

In the survey "Households' Use of Public and Other Types of Libraries: 2002," results show that 31 percent of households used a public library, 19 percent used a school library, 10 percent used a college or university library, and 4 percent used a workplace library in the month preceding the survey.

Households varied in their use of public libraries by income and education. Sixty-one percent of households with incomes in the top 20 percent used a public library in the past year, compared to 33 percent of households with incomes in the lowest 20 percent. Twenty-one percent of households in which the highest education level was less than a high school diploma used a public library in the past year in comparison to 66 percent of households in which the highest education level was an advanced degree. Sixty-six percent of households with children under 18 and 36 percent of households with retired persons used a public library in the past year.[2]

America's public libraries see increased demand as the sole source of free public access to the web and hands-on computer use. According to the survey "Public Libraries and the Internet 2007: Study Results and Findings," 73 percent of public libraries report that they are the only provider of free public Internet access in their communities.[3] In a recent report from the Pew Internet & American Life Project, 13 percent of the adults surveyed reported going to a local public library to consult sources of information when they needed to solve problems. Of those, 62 percent used computers, 58 percent used reference books, and 42 percent used newspapers and magazines.[4] Interestingly, the highest rate of usage among users of public libraries is by those who have high-speed Internet access. The dialup group is a potential core group for the nation's public libraries.[5] "Many more people consider going to libraries than actually do. This suggests that libraries should try to untangle the complex web of reasons why different groups of people—even those who might profit most from using the library—don't in fact use the library, and in some cases, actually shun using it."[6]

Library Standards

Public library standards are determined by each state, but about 10 states have no formal standards. Most states provide these as suggestions; compliance is voluntary. In a few states, public libraries do not qualify for state aid if they fail to comply with state standards. The American Library Association (ALA) and Public Library Association (PLA) do not themselves set standards, but rather "advocate an outcomes-based assessment process set forth in a series of books on planning and assessment. The reason for this is that each library serves a different community with different needs."[7] Many librarians are unaware of these planning and assessment tools, do not understand the importance of planning and assessment, or are not inclined to investigate this alternative to meeting standards.

Without formal or mandatory standards, many libraries drift along without creating meaningful assessments and plans. Most librarians are doing their best, yet many consider themselves too busy and overworked to embark on an outcomes-based assessment process. Even in states where complying with minimum standards is required to qualify for funding, a library director can complete paperwork and submit plans that have little to do with what is really going on at the library. This lack of standards and accountability has not helped librarians navigate the dynamic changes we face in our libraries today. Creating standards, or making a concerted effort to accurately meet voluntary standards, will help us to move forward together and position ourselves ahead of the information technology curve.

The Future of Libraries

Opinions on the future of libraries vary widely, from "Libraries are doomed!" to "This is the most exciting time ever for libraries!" Many people believe that they no longer need libraries to find information: Google has all the answers. Will municipalities, schools, universities, corporations, and other organizations continue to pay for our libraries if they have outlived their usefulness in the eyes of the people they serve?

Jo Haight-Sarling, Director of Access and Technology Services, Denver Public Library, says that people are using the library virtually but also coming in to borrow books, do research, and attend programs. Tom Frey, Executive Director of the DaVinci Institute, thinks that the traditional library is not doomed but that it must change dramatically. He projects that the way we access information will continue to change, and libraries will need to keep up with technology to provide access.[8]

In October 1999, Stanford University president Gerhard Casper remarked to the university community at the dedication of the Bing Wing of the Cecil H. Green Library: "Even the most futuristic of thinkers would have to admit that we are likely to have physical libraries and paper books for decades to come. We are far from the point where everything we need is on the web or where the web is the preferred method of distributing and receiving knowledge."[9] Yet, in October 2007, the headline "Closing the Books: Sandia National Laboratories Cuts off Access to Hard-Copy Content in Its Technical Library" was splashed across the front page of the *Albuquerque Journal*. The accompanying full-color photo, occupying most of the space above the fold, depicted a staff member shelving books that "may never leave the library again." In the foreground, a sign such as the one in Figure 2.1 was posted at the end of the stacks.

The article explained that Sandia was cutting off access to hard copy content in an effort to reengineer library services and save money. An independent study had revealed that researchers were not coming into the library to look at hard copy, but instead did research from their desktops. Some chagrined researchers, insisting they needed to access books, maps, and printed journals, voiced their opinions.[10] This decision to close the book collection at Sandia has since been reversed;[11] however, this may be a preview of what is to come if we don't educate the people in power about the value of libraries—both physical and virtual.

BOOK COLLECTION CLOSED!!!

NO CHECKING OUT

Figure 2.1 Sign similar to the one that appeared at the end of the stacks in the Sandia Laboratories' Technical Library one day in 2007

In Sarah Long's Longshots podcast (2007) on the future of libraries, ALA Senior Associate Executive Director Mary Ghikas projects that we will see library buildings and librarians far into the future. Ghikas asserts that libraries are extremely healthy and librarians are doing innovative things. People have the need to connect with each other and library materials, and libraries are the places to do that. Although library environments will become almost exclusively digital, users will need librarians to access and interpret digital information. It is important to recognize that libraries are not in a single solution environment; solutions must be optimized for our varying purposes, and we will continue to see new and creative approaches.[12]

In the same series, Brad Baker, President of the Illinois Library Association and Dean of the Library and Learning Resources at Northeastern Illinois University, predicts that academic libraries will lease more electronic resources and acquire fewer print materials in the future. Libraries will provide more online reference services, so we will need to find new roles for ourselves and reinvent ourselves. We must think more broadly, be proactive and partner, let go of old ways that are not useful any more, and experiment more. It will be necessary to see where the users are and market ourselves to them where they are. Libraries must change with their changing communities.[13]

While it is clear that in this virtual world we will continue to need librarians to acquire, collect, organize, retrieve, and disseminate information, what about libraries as physical spaces? An entry titled "Library as Place," on the Library Garden blog, points out that people are using the Internet in the privacy of their own homes for activities that were previously carried out in public spaces—shopping, banking, talking, writing, doing research, listening to music, reading, and watching movies, for example. Americans are socially interacting less often and are increasingly disconnected from their families and friends. They have a greater need for shared spaces and social interaction than ever before, but they also have more options for how and where they choose to spend their free time. Businesses have become "destinations" that compete for the attention of consumers. If libraries are to survive they must ensure that they are destinations of choice.[14]

Libraries as Community Centers

In an effort to stay relevant in their communities and ensure their survival, many public libraries are assuming a larger role as community centers, providing a wide range of entertaining activities and programs for people of all ages. Libraries, as the one place where everyone gathers, are truly the "hearts" of their organizations, institutions, centers, schools, and associations. Cutting across the lines of departments, disciplines, specialties, and positions, libraries are neutral territory. This unique position, in combination with the emergence of new technologies, offers libraries a rare opportunity to become more than "places where the books are." It is wise for librarians to take advantage of this opportunity; however, what is successful in one library will not necessarily be the answer in another. This is not as simple as turning into a community center, offering gaming, or opening a café.

Part of the solution for your library may be to collaborate and partner with nearby community centers and recreation centers. Small communities are constantly looking for ways to save money, so your community leaders will lend their support to joint projects. Seek grants for common projects with community centers, schools, recreation centers, clubs, and other organizations that already provide recreation and entertainment.

Expanding library programs and services to attract new customers and accentuate the role of libraries as community centers can be exciting, but before getting carried away, ask yourself these questions:

- How will you fund the new ideas, services, and programs?

- Will funding for other services or programs be decreased?

- Does the new initiative address the information needs of the community?

- Does the new program support the mission of the library?

- Are you duplicating an activity already provided in your town's recreation or community center?

Remember the core purpose of libraries as information centers, focus on meeting the information needs of the people you serve, and stay true to your mission and vision. If you build on that foundation, the sky is the limit. This is a time of great change, and we can incorporate whatever new technology and innovation comes our way to help us accomplish the work of libraries.

Endnotes

1. American Library Association, "Number of Libraries in the United States," ALA Fact Sheet 1 (Chicago, IL: American Library Association, 2008), www.ala.org/ala/alalibrary/libraryfactsheet/alalibraryfactsheet1.cfm

2. Mark Glander and Thuy Dam, "Households' Use of Public and Other Types of Libraries: 2002" (Washington, DC: National Center for Education Statistics, 2006), 3, nces.ed.gov/pubs2007/2007327.pdf

3. John Carlo Bertot, Charles R. McClure, Susan Thomas, Kristin M. Barton, and Jessica McGilvray, "Public Libraries and the Internet 2007: Study Results and Findings" (Chicago, IL: American Library Association and The Bill and Melinda Gates Foundation, 2007), 10, www.ii.fsu.edu/projectFiles/plinternet/2007/2007_plinternet.pdf

4. Leigh Estabrook, Evans Witt, and Lee Rainie, "Information Searches That Solve Problems," in *Pew Internet & American Life Project*, 31 (Washington, DC: Pew Research Center, 2007), vi, www.pewinternet.org/pdfs/Pew_UI_LibrariesReport.pdf

5. Estabrook, 29.

6. Estabrook, 31.

7. American Library Association, "Public Library Standards," 2007, wikis.ala.org/professionaltips/index.php/Public_Library_Standards

8. Neal Conan, "If a Library is Bookless, What's in It?" *Talk of the Nation*, United States: National Public Radio, 2006, www.npr.org/templates/story/story.php?storyId=5235518

9. Gerhard Casper, "Who Needs a Library Anyway?" in *Stanford Online Report* (Palo Alto, CA: Stanford University, 1999), news-service.stanford.edu/news/1999/october13/libtext-1013.html

10. John Fleck, "Closing the Books," *Albuquerque Journal*, October 22, 2007, 1–2.

11. John Fleck, "Sandia Allows Access to Books after Outcry," *Albuquerque Journal*, December 4, 2007.

12. Sarah Ann Long, "Longshots Podcast: Future of Libraries Series #65," 2007, www.sarahlong.org/podcast/Podcasting20070923.mp3

13. Sarah Ann Long, "Longshots Podcast: Future of Libraries Series #66," 2007, www.sarahlong.org/podcast/Podcasting20071002.mp3

14. "Library as Place" on the *Library Garden* blog, October 3, 2006, librarygarden.blogspot.com/2006/10/library-as-place.html

Chapter 3

The People Libraries Serve

Libraries are meant to serve all the people within a defined population. These people can be members of a community, county, or region; students and teachers in a school; employees of a business or corporation; students, faculty, and staff at a university; or members of an organization.

Who are the people your library serves? Some librarians make the mistake of thinking the people they serve are the people who use the library. Unless 100 percent of the people your library is intended to serve use the library, this is not true. The people who use libraries are often only a fraction of the populations these libraries serve. What about the others?

Librarians are responsible for building collections and providing services to meet the vast information needs of diverse community members. A library must provide a broad range of programs and services with the goal of addressing the information needs of everyone in a community. All library staff members must understand that this is the library's purpose—to serve an entire population—and that the information needs of the community are constantly evolving. Once you have established who your library serves, you can determine their information needs, make a library plan, develop the collection, create useful policies, and provide beneficial programming and services for your whole community.

Who Does Your Library Serve?

Public libraries generally have the broadest user base, because any resident of a city, county, village, or town has access to their collections and services. Users range from preschoolers to retired professionals, from rich to poor, from users with disabilities and those with specialized reading interests to those who may have literacy challenges. Some people may have circumstances that prevent them from using the library in traditional ways; some may read at different grade levels, or their first language may not be English. In public libraries, the people you serve are likely to have varying information needs and to be from different socioeconomic, cultural, and educational backgrounds.

School libraries usually serve the students and teachers in a school or school system, supporting the needs of the curriculum and promoting reading and literacy. Some private school libraries may also serve students' parents and families. Although both are school libraries, the communities they serve are different. The private school library may offer the latest fiction bestsellers and children's board books to meet the needs of parents and toddlers, whereas you would probably not find an adult bestseller or a children's board book in a public middle school library.

Academic libraries focus on serving the students, faculty, and staff at an academic institution. Some academic libraries serve people in the surrounding community as well. Large universities often have multiple libraries for different subject areas, which serve different communities. For instance, the medical library serves medical, nursing, and pharmacy students and faculty, and the information science library serves the students and faculty of the school of library and information science. The medical library might also serve the surrounding community by providing consumer health information; however, the school of library and information science primarily serves only university students and faculty.

Special libraries serve employees in a corporation, business, law office, hospital, or government agency—but which employees? A research and development company library may address the information needs of engineers and scientists; a newspaper library might serve editors, copywriters, and staff reporters; a law firm library may serve the lawyers and paralegals in a practice. Hospital libraries often consider people in the surrounding community to be their customers in addition to hospital medical staff and employees. An information center may serve people with disabilities and their families across an entire state.

Identifying and learning about the population you serve, continuously assessing their information needs, and determining how to meet them are some of the most important things librarians do. You cannot do your job well if you aren't clear about who you serve.

Exercise 3.1

Who are the people your library serves? School children? Seniors in an assisted living center? Everyone in your county? Your town administration? State legislators? Toddlers at daycare centers? People with disabilities and their families in your state? Think about each separate element of the population you serve and define them in the space below.

Your Community's Profile

Begin with a description of your community, including the people your library serves (from Exercise 3.1). Your community profile should include the characteristics of the people you serve while also defining unique community characteristics:

- Ages

- Cultural diversity

- Disability status

- Economic data

- Educational level

- Employment status

- Families and households

- Geographic area

- History

- Income levels

- Industry

- Population statistics

- Recreational information

- Transportation information

Be careful about making generalizations or coming to quick conclusions based on how long you have lived in your community, how well you know everyone in your community, the characteristics of your own neighborhood, stereotypes about the nature of your community, or who comes into the library on a regular basis. We already know that less than one third of all households use public libraries. Remember, the people who visit the library do not include *all* the people you serve—you serve your entire community. The people who aren't coming to the library must also be included in your community profile.

Your municipality, school district, academic institution, or organization may already have a community description that has been prepared for grant applications, government reporting, or other requirements. Request this information from your town administrator, school district administrator, university administration office, or organization headquarters. Find out when it was last updated. If it needs updating, if it lacks some important information about an additional element of a population the library serves, or if you want to know more information about the community you serve, this is the time to find out.

Check with your local Chamber of Commerce, tourism office, economic development office, school district, or state for the information they have already compiled about your community. Community profiles are readily available on many state websites, for example: Arizona (www.azcommerce.com/SiteSel/Profiles/Community+Profile+Index.htm), New Hampshire (www.nh.gov/nhes/elmi/communpro.htm), and Alaska (www.dced.state.ak.us/dca/commdb/CF_COMDB.htm). If your state has already compiled a profile for your community, you are fortunate because

Figure 3.1 Alaska's community database online

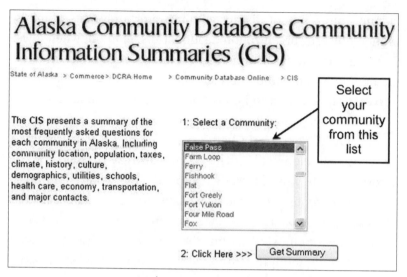

Figure 3.2 Selecting a community from the list

most of the work has already been done for you. Alaska's site, for instance, is comprehensive and easy to use (see Figures 3.1 through 3.4).

The U.S. Census Bureau website (www.census.gov) is another very useful tool for retrieving population statistics, area profiles, and fact sheets on your community. Its Population Finder, Area Profile with QuickFacts, and American FactFinder tools (Figure 3.5) will all help you generate a thorough community profile. While you are looking through census information, compare numbers from the last few censuses to see how your community has changed. Include these trends in your community profile, and, if there is projected census information available, use that as well. Using the American FactFinder, you can generate a handy fact sheet on your community, like this one for Baton Rouge, LA (Figure 3.6).

Look Around Your Community

In addition to using local and online resources, you can collect additional information by looking around your community,

Alaska Community Database Community Information Summaries (CIS)

State of Alaska > Commerce >DCRA Home Page   > Community Database Online   > CIS   > Results

False Pass

For Photos of False Pass click here

For a Map of False Pass click here

Current Population:	54 (2006 DCCED Certified Population)
Incorporation Type:	2nd Class City
Borough Located In:	Aleutians East Borough
Taxes:	Sales: 3%, Property: None, Special: 6% Bed Tax; 2% Alcohol Tax; 2% Raw Fish Tax (City); 2% Raw Fish Tax (Borough)

Location and Climate

False Pass is located on the eastern shore of Unimak Island on a strait connecting the Pacific Gulf of Alaska to the Bering Sea. It is 646 air miles southwest of Anchorage. The city owns approximately 66 square miles of land and water. The community lies at approximately 54.853940° North Latitude and -163.408830° (West) Longitude. (Sec. 34, T061S, R094W, Seward Meridian.) False Pass is located in the Aleutian Islands Recording District. The area encompasses 26.8 sq. miles of land and 41.4 sq. miles of water. False Pass lies in the maritime climate zone. Temperatures range from 11 to 55. Snowfall averages 56 inches, with total annual precipitation of 33 inches. Prevailing southeast winds are constant and often strong during winter. Fog is common during summer months.

History, Culture and Demographics

The name False Pass is derived from the fact that the Bering Sea side of the strait is extremely shallow and cannot accommodate large vessels. The area was originally settled by a homesteader in the early 1900s, and grew with the establishment of a cannery in 1917. Natives immigrated from Morzhovoi, Sanak Island and Ikatan when the cannery was built. A post office was established in 1921. The cannery has operated continuously, except for 1973 - 1976, when two hard winters depleted the fish resources. The cannery was subsequently purchased by Peter Pan Seafoods. It was destroyed by fire in March 1981, and was not rebuilt. The City was incorporated in 1990.

A federally-recognized tribe is located in the community -- the False Pass Tribal Council. The population of the community consists of 65.6% Alaska Native or part Native. The community is primarily Unangan. Fishing, fish processing and subsistence activities are the mainstays of the lifestyle. The sale of alcohol is restricted to the package store. During the 2000 U.S. Census, total housing units numbered 40, and vacant housing units numbered 18. Vacant housing units used only seasonally numbered 2. U.S. Census data for Year 2000 showed 41 residents as employed. The unemployment rate at that time was 0 percent, although 25.45 percent of all adults were not in the work force. The median household income was $49,375, per capita income was $21,465, and 8 percent of residents were living below the poverty level.

Facilities, Utilities, Schools and Health Care

Water is derived from a nearby spring and reservoir, is treated and stored in a 60,000-gallon tank. Most homes are connected to the piped water system. Residents use individual septic tanks for sewage disposal; the City operates a septic sludge tanker and sludge disposal site. All homes are fully plumbed. Wastewater from seafood processing flows directly into an outfall line. Water system improvements were recently funded, including an enlarged dam and a second 60,000-gal. water tank. The City collects refuse twice a week. There are two diesel fuel tanks containing 30,000 gallons. Electricity is provided by False Pass Electric Assoc. There is one school located in the community, attended by 12 students. Local hospitals or health clinics include False Pass Health Clinic (907-

Figure 3.3 Sample community profile summary

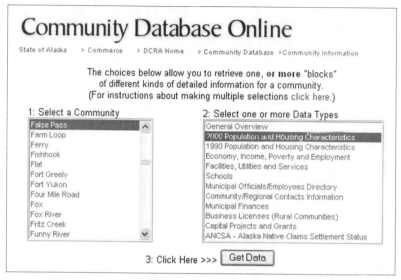

Figure 3.4 More detailed community information is available here

Figure 3.5 U.S. Census Bureau website

interviewing community leaders and business people, holding community forums, researching public records, and performing field surveys. Who and what did you miss? Has there been a surge in business development since the last census or state report? Has a large population of immigrants recently relocated to your community? Has the factory that employs most of the people in your

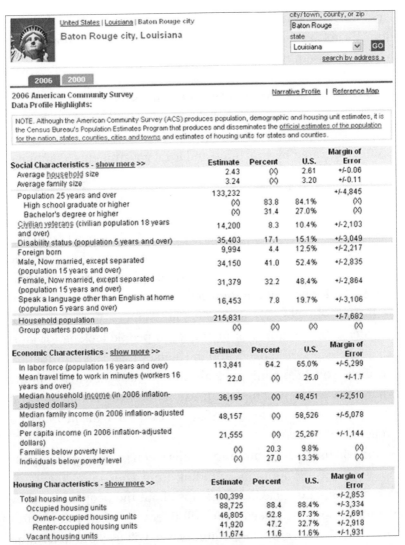

Figure 3.6 U.S. Census Bureau fact sheet

community recently closed? Is there a large home-schooled population? How many households have high-speed Internet access?

Get out into the community. Take part in meetings, serve on boards, talk to business people, attend Chamber of Commerce meetings, and be an active and visible community participant.

Don't forget about the community members who never use the library. Look around for them and make sure they are represented in your community profile.

Create a Community Profile for Your Library

Spend some time gaining a clear understanding of the demographics of your community from census data and the community profiles prepared by your state and local governments, combined with what you have learned from getting out and looking around your community. Make some preliminary observations about the facts and write them down.

Prepare a community profile for your library using all these elements. Create charts or graphs as visual representations. Include maps, photos, and graphics if they will help portray your community. Include details about information that is especially pertinent to library services, for example, the number of people with Internet access, number of unemployed people looking for jobs, what languages are spoken, and the literacy rate. This information will help you in planning, establishing goals, and determining what you want to accomplish. It will remind you about who you serve when you begin to think that you only serve the people who come into the library.

You will use your community profile when preparing grant proposals, justifying additional funding from your municipality or corporation, and speaking to groups about the people served by the library and their needs. You will refer to it when you want to know who isn't coming to the library. You will use it to determine what library programs and services to offer. Once you have a community profile in place, you will be amazed at how often you will use it. Don't forget to regularly update this profile to reflect your changing population.

Exercise 3.2

Read both A and B. Which attitude or approach will best serve the needs of the people in this community? Why?

A. I have lived in this community for 30 years and I know everyone here. I know that the children have the greatest information needs in my community, so I don't need to conduct a needs assessment. Years ago my village was isolated and rural. Many young families with children lived here, and I knew most of them. In recent years this community has been built up and many retirees have moved in, and it is now surrounded by large metropolitan areas on all sides. The library's priority is children's materials and children's programming because libraries are for children. There is not enough space in my library for adult programming. The addition we recently built on the library is for young people.

B. Because we live in such a fast growing and quickly changing area, I cannot even rely on last year's needs assessment to know the information needs of my community. Even though I have lived here for 30 years, I am always interested to see what the needs assessment will reveal. It helps me to discover the changing needs of our village's population and to be aware that it isn't the same community it was 30 years ago. The last census revealed that the demographics are shifting away from families with small children toward older people. I am considering providing more adult programs for this part of our community in the future. We have lots of room thanks to the new addition. This is what makes library work so fun and challenging.

Chapter 4

Determining the Needs of the People Libraries Serve

You must know the information needs of the people you are serving before beginning to design services, programs, and projects to meet their needs. This only makes sense: How can you provide library services and programs to meet community needs when you don't know what people need? Unfortunately, this happens more often than you might think. Librarians who are confident they know their community inside out, without ever assessing the needs of the people they serve, usually miss major segments of their community, organization, corporation, school, or institution. It is impossible to know everything about all the people you serve and their information needs—year in and year out—simply based on intuition or your impressions of those who regularly visit the library.

Once you know who makes up your community (see Chapter 3), you can ask them directly about their information needs. In most cases your population will be in continual flux, so you will have to assess their needs periodically to stay on top of what they require. In public libraries, communities change; at school and academic libraries, students graduate and faculty come and go; memberships in organizations and associations fluctuate; and corporations, law offices, businesses, and hospitals see constant personnel turnover.

Community Needs Assessment

A community needs assessment will tell you about your community and their information needs, how well you are currently meeting these needs, and how you can improve in meeting their needs in the future. Because (1) communities change dynamically and much more swiftly than in the past, and (2) the resources and tools available to us for meeting information needs are constantly changing, it is important to continually assess our community's needs. By doing so, we can select the most appropriate resources and tools for meeting our customers' needs. As librarians, we must stay in touch and be ahead of the curve when it comes to knowing who we serve and what they need.

A library staff member or consultant can oversee the community assessment. Library staff, volunteers, or consultants can carry out the work of gathering information from people in your community. This can be either a very large or very simple project, depending on your resources. Think about using a consultant to design the assessment, or a staff member or volunteer from the community with experience in assessment design. Don't overlook the talents of staff who have something to offer in this area.

Decide What You Want to Know

There are different ways to approach community needs assessments. You might want to perform a broad study or one focused on a particular aspect of your community. Consider doing a SWOT (Strengths, Weaknesses, Opportunities, and Threats) analysis to determine the challenges and opportunities facing your particular community. A SWOT analysis is a tool used to create an awareness of your current environment—both internal (library) and external (community)—that helps maximize the potential of strengths and opportunities while minimizing the impact of weaknesses and threats. It has two main components: issues that are internal (strengths and weaknesses), and issues that are external (opportunities and threats). This simple process involves listing the strengths and weaknesses of the library, as well as the opportunities and threats facing the community. The SWOT analysis will reveal potential needs in your community. It will also reveal the library's strengths and resources, which you can use to meet those needs.

This information will help you identify broad community needs. Careful examination will show some information needs that emerge directly from the community's broader needs. For instance, if a large employer in your town has recently closed, your community is probably home to many unemployed people who may need information on:

- How to use the Internet to find jobs

- How to create a resume

- Interviewing skills

- Educational opportunities for learning a new skill

If you want to clarify these hunches, ask about them in the needs assessment process.

Decide what you want to know going in; ask only what you want to know and what you are prepared to address. Don't waste people's time with pages of irrelevant questions. You will alienate them, and they will avoid you when you are doing your next community assessment. Don't waste your own time thinking up irrelevant questions, compiling the results, and then deciding you can't do anything with the information. Carefully choose the questions you wish to ask.

What issues did the SWOT analysis reveal? Do you want to focus on a few specific issues, or investigate the larger, broader information needs in your community? Once you get in the habit of doing community needs assessments, this won't seem like such a large undertaking. You can focus on different issues in successive assessments; you don't have to find out everything all at once. Community needs assessments aren't a one-time event.

Assessment Tools

Do some groundwork in advance of doing your community assessment to find out where to reach people and what assessment tools might be most appropriate for your particular population. Use the data you collected in your community analysis (see Chapter 3) to verify reading levels, education levels, and languages spoken. How many households have children in school? How many retired people are there? Are most people working full time outside the home? How many people are unemployed? How many households have high-speed Internet access? Are there people with disabilities?

Remember, your task is to find out about the information needs of your *entire* community. To reach a broad cross-section of your community, you may have to provide an online survey, interview people at the senior center, distribute surveys through the schools, and maybe provide them in three different languages.

Needs assessment tools include surveys and questionnaires, focus groups, community meetings, and interviews. You can use one or all of these methods. Using more than one method will increase your chances of reaching more people and will give you a more accurate cross section or "picture" of the people you serve. Some people who won't complete surveys may be willing to take part in a focus group, for instance.

Surveys

You can use surveys and questionnaires to ask individuals in your community about their library and information needs. You can mail or email surveys, do telephone surveys, post questionnaires on the library's website, use an online survey service, or conduct surveys in person. You might distribute surveys in several classes at the local high school or ask people survey questions outside the grocery store or in the mall.

Again, keep surveys and questionnaires short and make them relevant. Ask only questions that you can address. People can tell if you haven't put much thought into a survey or if you are asking questions just to ask questions. They will be much more likely to participate if they can see that their answers could make a difference in what the library provides.

Some survey tips:

1. Survey the entire population you serve, or a representative cross section.

2. Ask only questions that will help you to plan and develop library services.

3. Keep it brief and be specific.

4. Keep the demographics of your community in mind. Address varying education and reading levels by providing the questionnaire in multiple languages and formats.

5. Use clear and concise wording that cannot be misinterpreted.

6. Avoid double negatives and positives.

7. Use an easy-to-understand response system or scale.

8. Use an even number of response choices so answers cannot be neutral.

9. Use clear formatting and readable fonts. Make the survey easy on the eyes with adequate white space.

Consider using an online version of your survey to reach people on the Internet. Here are some online survey tools that provide free options and reasonably priced services:

- SurveyGizmo, www.surveygizmo.com

- SurveyMonkey, www.surveymonkey.com

- Zoomerang, info.zoomerang.com

Focus Groups

Focus groups bring together groups of six to 10 community members to discuss a few "focused" topics regarding their information needs. Groups are run by a facilitator and usually last one to two hours. Focus groups can elicit the types of spontaneous reactions and ideas that surveys miss. They are designed to encourage conversation among participants and to find out people's attitudes, feelings, and opinions about a topic. Members of a focus group usually share common characteristics such as age, gender, educational background, or ethnicity to facilitate easy conversation. Although focus groups can be labor-intensive, they can reveal valuable information that you would not discover using other assessment tools.

Community Meetings

Community meetings are group events open to the entire population you serve. These meetings can be very active, lively, and supportive of the library; however, most of the people motivated to attend community meetings for the purpose of assessing their information needs will probably already be regular library customers. You cannot rely on community meetings alone as a method of determining the information needs of the people you serve. They can be a good way, though, to get feedback from regular library users who are not shy about speaking in public, and they can be a good way to supplement the information you gather using other assessment tools.

Interviews

Interview individual community members to find out about their specific information needs or their impressions of community information needs. You might ask questions similar to those on your surveys, but this format allows people more time to elaborate on their responses. You can gather important information by interviewing community leaders representing different groups in your community, such as labor unions, ethnic groups, or religious groups. You will be limited by time as to the number of interviews you can conduct, so use these as a supplementary source of information in combination with other assessment tools.

Sample Questions

Design surveys, questionnaires, interviews, focus groups, and community meetings to ask questions that will get to the bottom of the information needs of the people you serve, where they go for information, why some people aren't using the library, and what you can do about it. Here are some sample questions to consider. Think about more specific questions to ask your own community, as no one template will suit all situations:

- What information have you had to learn, find out, or know in the last six months that affected your quality of life? Give examples.

- What was the most important question you had to answer?

- Was the question related to family, work, school, health, or education?

- Where did you go for the answer?

- Where did you find your answer or help?

- What form was the answer in? Book, newspaper, magazine, online article, verbal, etc.?

- Were you satisfied with the answer or help you received?

- Do you use the library?

- How? By coming in, online, telephone call?

- What kind of information do you get at the library?

- Would you like to see other kinds of information at the library? What?

- Would you like to see other programs or services at the library? What?

- What is your demographic information? Give choices re: education, age, race, sex, income, etc.

Customer Satisfaction Surveys vs. Needs Assessments

Librarians often confuse customer satisfaction surveys with community needs assessments. Many templates and examples that are available for librarians to adapt as their library's community needs assessment are actually customer satisfaction surveys. This kind of survey is fine if you want to know the satisfaction level of your customers and supporters, but, for the most part, they don't assess community information needs.

Measuring the satisfaction level of regular library customers or library supporters and determining the information needs of the people in your community, school, corporation, or institution are two different things. Customer satisfaction surveys will tell you if the people who visit and support the library are happy with the library environment, the hours the library is open, or the way they are treated by library staff. Remember, though, about two-thirds of the people in the U.S. don't use libraries—so, how can asking only current customers (about one-third of your community) if the library is comfortable, if the library is open at convenient hours, or if library staff members are pleasant be a *community* needs assessment?

Librarians understandably continue this practice because it usually yields positive results. People in the library are, for the most part, satisfied return customers. Library supporters are by nature satisfied with the library, and those likely to complete a library satisfaction survey are those who like the library. When you ask satisfied customers about their satisfaction level, guess what?

The survey will reinforce doing what you have always done, and assure you that you are doing a good job. There are few things more dismaying than when a librarian concludes, based on a customer satisfaction survey, that there is no need for change, innovation, or growth, or that all the community's information needs are being met satisfactorily. Even more discouraging is when a librarian uses these results to document her high job performance for administrators and the community. While everyone in the library is congratulating each other on a job well done and having the best library in the world, the majority of the community may have given up on the library long ago—because their information needs are not being met.

What about all the unmet needs, all the people who are dissatisfied with the library, those who stopped coming to the library out of frustration, those who don't have enough patience to wait for the library's web page to come up, or the people who never come to the library or visit the library's site at all? It is your business to find out about them and their information needs. Remember, you are responsible to your entire community, not just to your return customers and staunch supporters.

Analyzing the Data and Sharing the Results

It is useful to analyze data separately for each demographic group, because each group may have different needs. Look at each group to determine their information needs, their top information priorities, whether the library is meeting their information needs, how often and when do they use the library, and whether they use the library's website and for what. Synthesize the data and prepare a document or online product that illustrates the results in an easy-to-read format for all to see.

Share the results first with library staff and members of the board. Ask them for feedback on the results and the way you have presented the data. Next, share the results with the library's stakeholders and funders, and then with your entire community. Post the results on your library's website and in the library, issue press releases, and publish an article in the local newspaper.

Using the Results in Library Planning

Now that you know your community and have determined their information needs, you are equipped to proceed with the library's vision, mission, and plan. The planning process will focus on real needs, and you can proceed with clarity and confidence by creating library services and programs that meet those needs.

Tamara Sandia, Director,
Jemez Pueblo (NM) Community Library

Author's Note: Based on my interview with Tamara Sandia.

Tamara Sandia has loved libraries since she first visited one on a second-grade field trip to the Albuquerque Public Library's Main Branch. She was amazed that she was being encouraged to take a book home. After asking the librarian numerous times if it was really true that she could borrow a book, she selected one, checked it out, and has since repeated the process many times over. From that moment on, Tammy was hooked on libraries.

As a student worker in a college library, Tammy gained experience shelving and repairing books. She was a "regular" in her community college library, where she earned an associate's degree in Business Administration. Tammy worked in several administrative assistant positions in Albuquerque before she moved back home to Jemez Pueblo 10 years ago.

When Tammy was searching for a computer she could use on the pueblo, Tammy's mother suggested going to the library. The library? Tammy didn't know that there was a library on the pueblo. But to her surprise, she discovered not only the Jemez Pueblo Community Library, but a computer inside she could use. She visited the library often, and before long she was hired as a library assistant. She helped the library director with administrative duties, library services, and programs—and when the director resigned, Tammy and another library assistant found themselves responsible for co-directing the library. Together they studied for the librarian certification exam and passed it, becoming qualified as library directors in a community of their size. They visited other libraries to find out what services and programs were being offered, and they made connections and found support from other librarians.

As library director, Tammy is responsible for operating the library and acquiring grants and other funding to support library services, programs, and operations. In her work, Tammy is guided by these principles:

- Warmly welcome everyone who enters the library

- Help everyone who needs help

- Remember the library is here for everyone in the community

- Include all library staff in library decisions

- Never create a program just because you want to create it—it has to be for the community

- Be direct

Her success is evident through the growth of the library, its popular and highly attended programs, and high usage.

Tammy believes one role of the library is to promote literacy, and she demonstrates this by providing book clubs, story times, summer reading programs, and an early reading project for newborns. She places high importance on getting out into the community and finding out from the people what they need.

Tammy fosters successful partnerships with community agencies and schools, and participates in providing information in conjunction with the Diabetes Program, holding parents' nights in association with the Social Services Department, assisting clients from the Vocational Rehabilitation Department with computer use, preparing resumes and job searches, and providing historical information about the pueblo to the Jemez National Monument. She coordinates with the schools by working with teachers on how to support children with school projects and science fair projects.

Helping people is the most rewarding part of librarianship for Tammy. Being creative and designing innovative programs to meet the needs and interests of the community and opening her mind to new ideas is both fun and challenging. Writing proposals to secure the funding needed to operate the library is a challenge when she is so busy with her daily duties.

Tammy's future plans for the Jemez Pueblo Community Library include gaming for teens, recording oral histories, and organizing historical photographs. Some day Tammy may complete her bachelor's degree and pursue a master's degree in library science; however, until that time comes, she is satisfied knowing that she is making a difference for the people in her community.

Exercise 4.1

These are some preliminary questions you might consider including in your library's next community information needs assessment. Check the ones that will help you to do your job in meeting information needs. There are no "right" answers, because every community is different. Only you will know what questions to ask in *your* community.

_____ Are the bathrooms in the library clean?

_____ Do you use the library's online databases to find magazine and newspaper articles?

_____ Is the library furniture comfortable?

_____ If you have visited the library (building or online) in the past year, what was the reason? (Give multiple choices.)

_____ If you have not visited the library (building or online) in the past year, why not? (Give multiple choices.)

_____ Do you find the information you want when you come to the library building?

_____ Are the librarians pleasant?

_____ How easy or difficult is it to search the library's online catalog? Do you usually find what you need?

_____ Do you ever use the reference books in the library's collection? If so, can you find the information you need in the library's reference books?

_____ Are the librarians well-groomed?

Chapter 5

Letting Your Vision, Mission, and Plan Be Your Guides

You can create a vision, mission, and plan for your library without an MLS. In fact, many library schools don't require students to take courses in library planning. Most librarians learn about library planning the hard way—on the job, out in the real world, and after wasting time and effort on library projects that didn't meet community needs.

All organizations, not just libraries, need a vision, mission, and plan to know what their purpose is, where they are going, why they are going there, how they are going to get there, and what they want to look like in the future. Without these important elements, an organization aimlessly floats through the days, weeks, months, and years with no purpose or direction. Very little is accomplished, no real progress is made, and things stay pretty much the same. The information needs of communities change and evolve over time, and, in these times of great change and evolving information technologies, a library without a vision, mission, or plan will lose its way. Yes, the library building may be charming, reminding longtime residents of the values of the past. It might be a refuge for those who long for the smell of old books and the familiar experience of fingering frayed catalog cards; people who have vowed never to use a computer feel right at home there. But libraries without a real commitment to serve the changing information needs of their community make a choice to stay behind while the rest of the world races ahead. The information needs of people served by libraries like this are surely being met elsewhere.

Does Your Library Have a *Real* Vision, Mission, and Plan?

Every library needs basic navigational tools. Our function and roles are changing rapidly and information technology is emerging at lighting speed. Not enough staff, time, or money to do the hard work of planning, you say? Any library today without a *real* vision, mission, and plan is in fact *wasting* time and money by working inefficiently and failing to serve their community well. This means that *you*—the library director, staff, board, and community stakeholders—need to create these tools specifically to guide *your* library in meeting the information needs of *your* community.

All too often librarians say, "Oh, yes we have a vision, mission, and library plan," when what they really have is a generic template they have adapted to their library. Sometimes, in order to receive funding, librarians are required to submit a vision, mission, and strategic plan to their state library agency or parent organization. They may copy or adapt another library's vision statement, mission statement, or library plan, merely substituting their library's name and occasional words or facts specific to their library or community. Don't be tempted to do this. A vision, mission, and plan are useless unless they are *yours*. Generic templates are useful for getting ideas, but they are no substitute for your own plan.

This is one of the most important points in this book: *Your library must have its own vision, mission, and plan.* If you do nothing else, read this chapter and take action. These tools are the foundation upon which your library operates. Without them your library will not function well, and you will be unable to develop policies, plan relevant services and programs, seek funding, attract quality personnel, or even make daily decisions that benefit the people you serve. When you don't have a vision, mission, or plan, you will find it difficult to attract funding—and may even lose funding.

Not sure if your library's vision, mission, and plan are "real"? Let's find out. Are you experiencing any of the situations in your library presented in Table 5.1? If these situations sound familiar to you, the diagnosis may be that there is nothing to guide your library. In the absence of a vision, mission, and plan, your library operates based on personal opinions, influences, interests, and preferences; influential groups and powerful community members; or how the director is feeling on any given day. A lack of foundation, structure, and direction for the organization allow these kinds of influences to take over.

Libraries without direction fail to fulfill their role of meeting the information needs of the people they serve. If you work in a library like this, it is your professional responsibility as a librarian to take action. If you are a director or a board member, see to it that a vision, mission, and plan are developed for your library. If you are a staff member, advocate for developing a vision, mission, and plan. The success of your library depends on it. This can be very difficult to address as a staff member if the director is resistant to change or becomes threatened by your insight. The bottom line, though, is that this is the only way to survive as a viable library. Ignoring the problem is not an option. These tools help staff know what needs to be done, understand priorities, and work together toward common goals. Your library will make progress, you will meet information needs, you will work more efficiently and cost-effectively, you will be able to create functional teams, you will be prepared to seek funding, and you will have *more fun*!

Table 5.1 What is the status of your library's plan?

SITUATION	YES	NO
The director cannot produce the library plan when you ask to see it.		
The plan says one thing, and library staff is doing another.		
The director tells you that a priority appearing in the plan is not really a priority.		
The only one who can make decisions in your library is the director.		
The director is easily swayed by new ideas and changes his mind frequently.		
You wonder why you are doing what you are doing.		
It seems like you never accomplish anything.		
You are always doing busy work and putting out fires.		
The library isn't working on goals that meet community information needs.		
Library staff members work independently on projects that interest them personally.		
There is no teamwork.		
There are no common goals.		
Policies change and exceptions are regularly made based on a library customer's influence in the community or their relationship with a library staff member.		
Opinions vary widely among staff about what some library policies are (e.g., appropriate behavior or computer use).		
The library employs new technologies for the sake of employing new technologies.		
The library is often in crisis mode.		

Common Reasons Why Libraries Don't Have a Vision, Mission, or Plan

Common reasons given by librarians as to why they don't have their own specific and real visions, missions, and plans include:

- The templates work just fine for meeting state requirements.

- We are a small library, and small libraries don't need these things.

- Plans are too confining.

- It's common knowledge what libraries do.

- We are too busy and don't have the time.

- It is such hard work.

Planning can be time-consuming, but it doesn't have to be. Libraries of all sizes need direction. With some planning and preparation, small libraries should be able to develop drafts of these tools in a daylong retreat. If you don't think you can do this because you have little or no staff, think of all the time and energy you will save if you know where you are going and what you are doing. One of the reasons you are so busy is that you are running around feverishly, without goals.

There has been a great deal of discussion about the future of libraries in recent years. Some people say that libraries will all disappear. Others can see that those libraries that resist change and work without direction will be the ones to disappear—they will become obsolete and abandoned by their communities. Make a choice for your library's future by creating a vision, mission, and plan.

You can find books, articles, and websites on how to create a vision statement, mission statement, and library plan (see the Recommended Reading section at the end of the book). You can attend workshops, take continuing education classes, and use web tutorials on developing these tools. Take responsibility for educating yourself. Be very clear where you want the library to go, and you can start going there. Include community members, business leaders, school personnel, and library staff in this process. Appoint a leader or facilitator, ideally someone who is not participating in the process, so they can focus on seeing that the group produces the tools necessary for an effective library.

The Vision Statement

A vision statement is a clear, motivating message about what your library wants to become in the future. The vision statement articulates a desired outcome that resonates with all staff members and helps them feel proud and energized about the library becoming something more; a vision statement is a great team-builder and motivator. A vision stretches the imagination and the capabilities of the library's image. It gives shape and direction to the future of the library and creates a mental picture of what you want the library to become. At the same time, it must be short, realistic, and possible to accomplish.

Answering these questions will help you develop your library's own vision statement:

- What can your library become?
- Can you describe the ideal version of your library?
- What will your library look like when it is successfully meeting community information needs?
- What will your library look like in the future?
- Can you describe what your library would be like if money were no object?

Sample Vision Statements

The State Library of Pennsylvania will positively affect the workings of Pennsylvania state and local governments and improve the quality of life for all Pennsylvanians through its staff, services, and collections. (www.statelibrary.state.pa.us/libraries/cwp/view. asp?a=2&Q=40190)

Madison [WI] Public Library is a leader in building and sustaining a literate citizenry, transforming lives through knowledge and information and enhancing Madison's high quality of life. (www.madisonpublic library.org/about/mission.html)

As an integral part of Moraine Valley Community College, we will be a leading-edge library that empowers our learning community by providing quality resources, responsive services, and effective information literacy education. (www2.morainevalley.edu/ default.asp?SiteId=10&PageId=707)

By the Year 2020, the [Georgetown] University Library will be recognized as an "icon of transformation" for Georgetown University, empowering its communities to surpass their own aspirations and to have a global impact. (library.georgetown.edu/geninfo/mission.htm)

The [Albany (CA) High School] Library is a vital part of the school that provides access to information and ideas, helps to develop effective and responsible users of ideas and information, and creates lifelong readers and learners. The library program participates in the school wide mission to foster the development of healthy, academically prepared, self-directed learners who appreciate the arts, are problem solvers, effective communicators and responsible navigators to the future. (www.albany.k12.ca.us/ahs/resources/library/vision_policies.htm)

The Mission Statement

A mission statement articulates the purpose of your library. It informs you, and lets people know what your library does. For your work as a librarian to be meaningful and relevant, you must have a clear understanding of your library's purpose or mission to guide you. The mission statement serves as the basis upon which any successful organization makes its decisions.

In recent years libraries have diversified, becoming destinations for entertainment and social activities, cafés, gaming, and computer centers. Now more than ever, it is important to have mission statements to keep us grounded in our work. For many libraries, this rapid change means revising and reworking mission statements more often. Without clear mission statements, there is no way for librarians to decide which new programs and services to offer. According to Janet Balas, "We cannot hope to be successful if we are doing nothing more than reacting to the capricious and oftentimes contradictory trends in society."[1] Every member of a library's staff must understand the library's purpose. This gives individuals something to work toward and provides a framework for library staff to work together as a team toward common goals.

Without a mission statement, staff members will do what each guesses he or she should be doing. They will buy the books they personally like or want to read, have their friends present programs that don't meet community needs, and dream up fun projects for their own personal satisfaction. Libraries like this tend to drift aimlessly without direction, they are disconnected from community needs, and little of significance is accomplished.

Creating a Mission Statement

If your library already has a mission statement, review and revise it if necessary. If your library does not have a mission statement, or if you are using an example you borrowed from another library, it is time to create one specifically for your library. Investigate the mission of the larger organization, company, municipality, college, or school you serve and make sure the library's mission is in alignment with the mission of the larger organization.

Consider forming an advisory committee to help you create your mission statement. The committee should include a cross section of people representing your community, the people you serve. You want your mission statement to reflect the views, ideas, and input of a wide range of community members. Include input from library staff, community members, local businesses and organizations, and other stakeholders.

Sometimes libraries are tempted to adapt mission statements from other libraries in order to satisfy a bureaucratic requirement. Don't do this. You aren't writing a mission statement just so you can check it off a list and then forget about it. Substituting your library's name in another organization's mission statement or an example you find in a book or online does a disservice to your library, library staff, and community. There is no substitute for going through the process of developing your library's own mission statement, which lays the foundation for doing meaningful work to benefit your community. A mission statement will guide you and keep you on course, providing an essential foundation for library planning. Once you have both a vision and a mission statement, you can use these statements to create your library's plans, other policies, programs, and projects.

Keep the mission statement simple, yet unique to your library. Begin by answering these questions:

- Who makes up the community you serve?

- Why do you provide library services and programs?

- How will the library benefit the people in your community?

- What is the library trying to accomplish?

- What does the library do?

- What is the library's role?

Sample Mission Statements

The State Library of Pennsylvania provides information for State Government and citizens while collecting and preserving our written heritage through materials published for, by, and about Pennsylvania. (www.state library.state.pa.us/libraries/cwp/view.asp?a=2&Q=40190)

The Conway Public Library offers community residents of all ages access to information sources, a place to gather, opportunities for lifelong learning and personal growth, and popular materials to meet cultural, educational, and recreational needs. The library's professional staff fulfills this mission by being accessible and helpful, thus maintaining a superior quality of service. (conway. lib.nh.us/aboutus/mission.htm)

Our mission is to develop and manage convenient, accessible, and cost-effective information services that are aligned with the strategic directives of MasterCard International. We are sensitive to the dynamics within the company and the payments industry and we change our information resources as needed.[2]

The Temple Library was established to provide a well-rounded collection of resources on Judaism and the Jewish way of life for the adult members of the congregation.[3]

Schaffer Library is committed to providing excellent service to support the educational mission of Union College. Its staff is committed to intellectual freedom; building, maintaining and preserving a broad and diverse collection of information resources in a variety of formats; and offering equitable access to information and to the professional expertise of the library staff. We particularly value the traditions of Union College and the Library's role in its history and an environment conducive to intellectual and personal growth for all. (www.union.edu/PUBLIC/LIBRARY/about/about.htm)

The Library's (Library of Congress) mission is to make its resources available and useful to the Congress and the American people and to sustain and preserve a universal collection of knowledge and creativity for future generations. (www.loc.gov/about/mission)

Do You Need Both a Vision Statement and a Mission Statement?

Yes. In *Power of Vision*, a training video for organizations that need examples about how individuals and organizations use vision for their success, Joel Barker says: "Vision without action is merely a dream. Action without vision just passes the time. Vision with action can change the world. If you have just a mission, the action written—and not the vision, you will not know where you're going or if you have arrived."[4]

The Library Plan

Used as a tool to focus your energy on doing a better job, a strategic plan will ensure that library staff members are working toward the same goals, provide a benchmark for assessing and adjusting the direction you are going, serve as a map to keep you on course, and help you work more efficiently and cost-effectively. As a deliberate effort to clarify goals and objectives, roles, resources, and actions for the organization, it provides a framework for making decisions and policies, and articulates what results you desire. Strategic plans are structures that allow staff to work together as a cohesive unit, responding consciously in a changing environment.

A plan will tell you:

- Where you are now
- Where you want to go
- How you get there

If you don't have a plan, or if you just used your library's name in a template or example you found in a book or online, you are undoubtedly wandering aimlessly in your work. In libraries without a plan, library staff members typically all work independently on separate, unrelated projects of personal interest. No organizational direction or purpose drives them as a team. Often, libraries like this are chaotic.

Library directors and board members are responsible for creating library plans that address the information needs of the communities they serve, using input from a wide variety of community members, business owners, school personnel, and club or organization members. To execute library plans, librarians must be acutely aware of their communities and the information needs of the people they serve.

Your library's plan, if based in your community's real needs, will be a guiding light for you in your work. You will know what you need to do next and what needs have not yet been met. If the planning process includes diverse community members, it will provide you with partners and allies to help with library projects and programs. Attracting community members who have not used the library in the past will introduce an exciting new opportunity that you may never have imagined. Possibilities for the library will multiply and you may begin to attract funding from unexpected sources.

Elements of the Strategic Plan

Strategic plans are plans that target specific goals; define outcomes and objectives that are SMART (Specific, Measurable, Achievable, Realistic, and Time-bound); include actions and tactics designed to meet objectives, produce outcomes, and reach goals; and include crucial, important, key information about how they will be executed. Strategic plans specify within a specific time period what will be accomplished, how, when, by how much, with what resources, and by whom. They are outgrowths of the information needs of the people you serve. Because these plans are specific and focused, they make it easier to do your work. They are well worth the effort, and can be changed and adjusted for unexpected circumstances or to accommodate new information if necessary. A strategic plan must contain the following:

- Vision statement

- Mission statement

- Community and library profiles

- Community needs-assessment results

- Goals

- SMART (Specific, Measurable, Achievable, Realistic, and Time-bound) objectives

- Outcomes

- Resources available

- Actions

- Who will do the work

You can use your strategic plan to develop more specific plans, such as a technology plan or plans for programs and projects, to develop proposals for grant funds or other fundraising efforts, or to clarify your job goals. Potential donors and grant-making organizations are much more likely to donate to a specific program, project, or activity you have identified as a community need and developed in your library plan. Funders are not likely to award grants to libraries that have no plans.

Sample Strategic Plans

Full strategic plans are too lengthy to reproduce here, but many libraries have posted theirs online for their community to view. See some sample plans at:

- Evanston (IL) Public Library, www.epl.org/library/
  strategic-plan-00.html

- Glencoe (IL) Public Library,
  www.glencoe.lib.il.us/plan0609.pdf

- Parmly Billings (MT) Library, ci.billings.mt.us/
  DocumentView.asp?DID=3787

- Morse Institute (MA) Library,
  www.morseinstitute.org/PDF/StrategicPlanForWeb.pdf

In these turbulent and exciting times of changing technologies and evolving information-delivery systems, libraries need a vision, mission, and plan to know which are most appropriate to help them accomplish their goals. The tools and strategies you select will vary depending on your community needs and library plan. Without a vision, mission, and plan your library will just be reacting to technology or the latest fads, rather than responding by employing the most appropriate tool to meet the information needs of the people you serve.

Exercise 5.1

Check the statements that are true:

_____ A library plan comes from your community and addresses their specific needs.

_____ A library plan is a group effort, including library staff, community members, administration, board members, and other stakeholders, for instance.

_____ A library plan is a template you can find on the Internet.

_____ You need a library plan to get funding from your state library.

_____ A library plan is a map or a guide to your library's intentions, focus, and priorities.

_____ Our library doesn't have the time, staff, or money to develop a library plan.

Endnotes

1. Janet L. Balas, "Do You Know What Your Mission Is?" (Online Treasures)(Libraries), *Computers in Libraries* 27:2 (2007): 30(3).
2. "Spotlight on SLA Members: Trudy Katz—Special Libraries Association—Interview," Information Outlook, April 2001, find articles.com/p/articles/mi_m0FWE/is_4_5/ai_73280571
3. Ruth S. Smith, *Setting up a Library: How to Begin or Begin Again*, 2nd revised ed. (CSLA Guide, Portland, OR: Church and Synagogue Library Association Publication), 1994.
4. Joel Arthur Barker, Ray J. Christensen, Brad W. Neal, John R. Christensen, and Corporation Charthouse Learning, *The Power of Vision* (Burnsville, MN: Charthouse Learning Corp.), 1990.

Part II

Basic Library Practice

Chapter 6

Developing the Library's Collection

A library's collection may include a variety of materials in numerous formats, such as books, videocassettes, DVDs, music and books on CD, audiotapes, pamphlets, electronic resources, vertical file clippings, and municipal documents. For our purposes, "collection" will include both the print and electronic resources available in a library building and through a library's electronic presence.

Performing a Collection Assessment or Collection Evaluation

Performing a collection assessment or evaluation will tell you what your collection "looks like" right now, giving you a starting point for collection development. Collections can be assessed or evaluated using qualitative or quantitative measures. Quantitative measures usually result in numbers. Examples of quantitative measures include:

- How many items are in the collection
- How many items are in each section, such as adult fiction, adult nonfiction, children's fiction, children's nonfiction, books on CD, or movies on DVD
- How many items are in each subject
- Circulation statistics by format and by subject area

- Percent of standard titles in the collection
- Numbers of items added and deselected during a specified time period

Techniques for measuring the collection quantitatively include generating reports using your automated library system or manually counting items using the shelf list, rates of acquisition and deselection, and circulation numbers.

Qualitative measures usually result in descriptions of the quality of library materials. Examples of qualitative measures include appearance, age, formats, and numbers of standard recommended materials. Techniques for measuring the collection qualitatively include examining shelf list data, examining the physical collection, determining mean and median age of the collection by subject, and checking the collection against standard lists.

The extent and depth of the collection assessment depends on the size of your library and available staff time. Staff members may want to take responsibility for sections of particular interest or in which they have some expertise. Even if you must do this work on a small scale, make a commitment to start, in order to improve your ability to meet your community's information needs and develop a quality collection.

A Simple Collection Assessment Process

More details on each of these steps can be found in the following sections:

1. Creating or updating your Collection Development Policy.

2. Choosing a section of the library's collection and reading the Collection Development Policy relating to that section.

3. Determining use of the section by looking at turnover rate, circulation rate, and ILL statistics.

4. Visually scanning the section for appearance.

5. Performing a shelf list count for the section.

6. Determining the acquisition rate in the section for the previous year.

7. Determining the mean and median age for the materials in the section.

8. Comparing holdings in the section against a standardized list.

9. Making recommendations for acquisitions and deselections in the section.

10. Moving on to the next section.

The collection assessment can be a powerful tool. It will equip you with useful knowledge and documentation to help you defend your budget, make acquisition decisions, justify specific materials in your collection, and support funding proposals for new materials acquisitions. Decisions about developing the library's collection must be made based on real information, not on personal feelings or preferences. In order to meet the changing needs of the people we serve and to keep the information in our libraries current, relevant, and usable, we must constantly evaluate our library's collections.

Creating or Updating Your Collection Development Policy

Successful collection development requires a plan. Your Collection Development Policy will guide you in developing and managing your library's collection and information resources. Creating a policy is always the first step in the collection development process. You must create and update this policy with thought and purpose, customizing it for your library and your community. Your Collection Development Policy guides the development of the collection by telling you what should be in the collection and how to select and deselect materials based on community needs. This is a working document, applied daily by library staff, and it will change depending on your community's changing information needs.

As always, if you are tempted to simply insert your library's name and profile into another library's policy just to meet a requirement of your state library or other agency, please don't. Policies created in this way cannot be used to make decisions about developing your library's resources, because they have no relevance to *your* library and *your* community. For instance, a Collection Development Policy that states "materials will be selected based on community needs" without articulating the community needs is meaningless. A Collection Development Policy may include these elements:

- Library's mission statement
- Purpose of the policy
- Your community profile
- Your community's information needs
- Description of your library's collection
- General collection policy
  - Age of materials collected
  - Formats collected
  - Multiple copies
  - Languages
  - How materials are funded
- Selection criteria
- Suggestions for purchase

- Collection maintenance

  - Weeding policy

  - Repair and replacements

- Reconsideration of materials

- Donations

- Subject areas collected

- Collection assessment information

Intellectual Freedom

Because librarians support the right of every individual to both seek and receive information from all points of view without restriction, many libraries include the following statements from ALA in their collection development policy (see Appendix C):

- Library Bill of Rights

- Freedom to Read Statement

- Freedom to View Statement

Selection

Selection, or the process of building a well-balanced library collection to meet the needs of your community, is the backbone of collection development. To be a good selector you must:

- Have an updated and relevant Collection Development Policy to guide you

- Have a clear understanding of your community's information needs

- Stay abreast of current trends in publishing in all formats

- Be aware of current events and popular culture trends, including emerging technology trends

- Be objective

Some practical activities to help you be a good selector include:

1. Review your Collection Development Policy for currency and accuracy. Know the information needs of your community. Define a clear profile of your community by knowing the socioeconomic status of community members, their ages, education level, ethnic makeup, occupations, hobbies, interests, reading levels, and first language. What kinds of information are they seeking when they come into the library? Who is not coming into the library and why? What kind of information do they need? If you have conducted a Community Needs Assessment (see Chapter 4), you will be able to use the information you have already collected and compiled. Understanding your community's basic information needs and its other unique aspects will help you select materials to meet those needs.

2. Read reviews in a variety of publications by a wide range of reviewers. This is an essential part of your job as a collection development librarian. Good selection requires reading reviews and perusing publisher's catalogs and related publications. If you are expected to participate in collection development but are discouraged from spending time on reading reviews, you are not being provided with the resources you need to do your work. You must select based on educated choices, not on personal whims, guesses, or pretty covers. Spend time reading reviews, and, if you are a director or manager, encourage your staff to put aside time for this important activity.

3. Subscribe to *Library Journal, Publishers Weekly, Booklist, Kirkus Reviews,* and the *New York Times Book Review,* for

starters. Route these publications to staff members who can initial the reviews of materials they recommend. This is a way to compile recommendations from staff members with a wide range of experiences, interests, and contact with the community. Also, everyone will have the opportunity to read reviews as part of their job, fostering an understanding of the importance of this activity as part of selecting.

4. Consult bibliographies and core collection publications such as the *Public Library Catalog, Fiction Catalog,* and *Children's Catalog.* Many subject areas have specialized core collection recommendations, so if you are a librarian in a specialized subject library, investigate these. Browse your local bookstore for new and interesting materials, which gives you the opportunity to examine materials and read samples before purchasing.

5. Know what is going on in the world and in your community. Read the newspaper and the minutes of your town council meetings, listen to National Public Radio (NPR; visit their books page at www.npr.org/templates/topics/ topic.php?topicId=1032), and watch C-SPAN's Book TV (www.booktv.org). Stay updated about new technologies and teens' latest interests. Know what Oprah's Book Club is reading (www.oprah.com/obc_classic/obc_main.jhtml) and about the authors recently interviewed on the *Today Show* (www.msnbc.msn.com/id/3041344) and *Good Morning America* (abcnews.go.com/GMA/Books). You can be sure you will receive requests for these books.

Here are some general criteria for selection that you can use to guide you as you identify materials for your collection. Remember, your library's Collection Development Policy will establish the specific criteria for you to follow:

- Construction/recording/format quality – Is the item well made? Will it stand up to repetitive use? If the item is a DVD, CD, or audiotape, is the recording quality good? If the item is electronic, is the format easy to read, use, and navigate? If it is a book, is the binding sturdy?

- Potential use – Will your community members borrow this item? How relevant is it to your users?

- Subject matter – Is the subject matter missing from your collection, or does your collection need updating in this area? Do you need an alternative viewpoint on the topic? Does the subject matter contribute to making your collection well balanced?

- Cost – Will the level of potential use or value to providing library services justify the cost?

- Reputation and appropriateness – What did the reviews say? What is the author's reputation? The publisher's reputation? Is the item appropriate for your library?

Now that we've identified activities and criteria to help you make good selections, here are some selection practices to avoid:

1. Avoid coming to "gut" conclusions about what subjects or genres your community members are or aren't interested in. If you neglect selecting materials in certain topics or certain kinds of fiction because you think no one in your community is interested, the people who are interested in those topics and kinds of fiction will stop coming to your library. When they find very little of interest, they will leave dissatisfied only so many times before going elsewhere to meet their needs. Your notion that there is no interest in these kinds of materials is reinforced, because you don't see these people, and because the few items you have of interest to them do not circulate well (they're not going to keep borrowing the same 2 or 3 books!).

There may in fact be a large number of people interested in these types of materials, but they know not to come to your library for their information needs.

2. Abandon the "just get what you like" method. When you select materials you personally like or want to read, listen to, or watch, you will attract only community members and friends who like what you like. Before you know it you have built a collection with a narrow focus—for people like you. Circulation will be high and customer satisfaction surveys will be positive—because the library has been customized to the needs of a select group of people, who keep coming back because it has the things they like. The problem here is that you are neglecting most of your community.

3. Represent all points of view. The same principle applies when you purchase nonfiction materials compatible with your personal biases and beliefs, but neglect opposing and alternative viewpoints. A politically biased public library director fools no one when she fails to make a concerted effort to purchase library materials that represent varied and opposing political viewpoints because the majority of people using the library think like her and approve of her selections. Again, what she doesn't recognize is that people with differing viewpoints have long ago stopped visiting the library for balanced reading materials, because they know they will not find them there. By developing the collection around her own preferences and viewpoints she has created a biased library for a select group of people, a group that represents only a small fraction of the people the library serves.

Exercise 6.1

Imagine you are a newly hired librarian in your town library. You just relocated for this job, so you don't know anything about the community except where you live and where the library is. The director assigns you the task of selecting nonfiction materials, so the first thing you do is ask to see the Collection Development Policy for some guidance. She tells you that there is no Collection Development Policy and to "just get what you like." What is wrong with this approach? How will you proceed?

Donations

As long as people have books to unload, there will always be library donations. It is essential that your Collection Development Policy include a Donations Policy that outlines how to handle these. Donations can be a valuable source of materials for libraries, or they can be someone else's junk. Many libraries started with donations, and without generous donations from community members, we wouldn't have some of our best libraries. However, there comes a time when your library should no longer have to rely heavily on donations for developing the collection. If a library has been in operation for 50 years, it has had ample opportunity to become established and receive funding from the state, bonds from governments, and grants to improve the collection.

Make some guidelines for desired/undesired library donations so that, for instance, when people call to inquire about donating materials to the library you can tell them that you accept materials that are clean and in good condition, but you do not accept textbooks or old magazines. A community member on the verge of driving a truckload of *National Geographic* magazines to the library for quick disposal will have to reconsider.

Accept donations in good condition with the understanding that they may be added to the collection, sold at a library book sale, donated to a charity, or given away to anyone who wants them. Explain to donors that if materials are appropriate for the library collection as determined by the Collection Development Policy they will be added; however, make sure they understand that their donations will not necessarily become part of the library's collection.

Set aside an out-of-the-way place to store donated items until you have the time to go through them. A storage shed or back room will work. Donations should not be stored in an open area where the public is encouraged to look through them before staff has had a chance to make selections for the library. Piles of donated materials are magnets for browsers. Crowds of people looking though donations will impede the flow of foot traffic and may even inhibit the smooth operation of the library. Avoid directing donation deliveries to the entryway of a staff work area or where they may block hallways or create hazards.

Donations need to be selected because they are appropriate for the collection, in the same way new materials are selected. All new acquisitions need to make sense for the collection, whether they are donations or new purchases. Selecting appropriate materials from donations can consume a lot of time—time staff could be taking to select new materials. Thus, donations are not cost-free. They take staff time and money to select, catalog, process, cover, and label. Donations take up valuable shelf space in small libraries in the place of newer, more attractive, and more appropriate materials. Library collections dominated by excessive donations can slow a library's growth and evolution, they are unattractive to the people you serve, and they can debilitate your library.

Recruit a knowledgeable staff member, board member, or Friends of the Library member to scan donations for valuable or rare materials. These donations can turn into funds the library can use to purchase more appropriate items for the collection. If the Friends of the Library have an annual book sale, this group should have a look at the donations before they are offered to the public for sale or to charities.

Weeding

Deselecting materials (otherwise known as discarding, weeding, or deaccessioning) is part of the ongoing collection development process; a Weeding Policy should be a part of the library's Collection Development Policy. Weeding must be done continually, using a policy and guidelines, knowledge about your community and their information needs, thought, and careful consideration. Weeding eliminates inaccurate and outdated materials, materials that are in poor condition, materials that do not meet your community's information needs, and materials that are no longer in demand. It improves the collection and increases circulation. When library users see carefully selected accurate, current, attractive, and interesting materials, they are likely to borrow more.

No library has the space to continually add materials while keeping old items forever. If librarians keep adding materials and never weed, the shelves will soon become so full that you will need a crowbar just to shelve an item. Staff time is wasted jamming books on already full shelves. This is not good for the books, makes for an unmanaged collection, and discourages library use. It can even break shelves! Libraries with crowded shelves where books are jammed sideways on top of the already tightly packed books send a clear message to customers that their collections are not being managed well.

An unweeded collection turns a library into a warehouse full of old, donated, or unused materials—a junkyard for unwanted items. The better items get lost in a sea of old materials, and people are not likely to look through the junk just to find one good item. They wonder, "Is this a library, or a used book warehouse?" Ultimately the library loses credibility and will no longer be seen in the community as a vital source of current and relevant information. The physical condition of the library's collection shows library customers the value we place, not only on library materials, but on our library and our profession. Collections that consist primarily of old donations and outdated materials say volumes about the degree to which librarians understand the purpose of a library.

Weeding is an ongoing process. It is not meant to be launched in crisis mode when you cannot shelve one more book or when a shelf breaks from the weight of overcrowding. If weeding is built into regular staff duties and performed on an ongoing basis, it will seem less daunting. Schedule weeding by section, and spread the work among staff.

Weeding decisions are informed decisions. A staff member responsible for weeding a section should have some knowledge or interest in a subject; he or she must be familiar with the Collection Development Policy and clearly understand the Weeding Policy for that particular section. Staff must be familiar with the standards or classics in a section they are weeding as well as the new materials available in that subject area.

Staff members responsible for both selecting and weeding materials in the same section will be up-to-date on new materials and well equipped to do this job on an ongoing basis. Staff members responsible for weeding must also have the authority to make decisions. If your library weeds based on personal feelings, staff members will second-guess each other—one person will deselect an item, and another person will reselect it. When the director disagrees with decisions made by staff members, lots of time and energy is wasted while nothing is accomplished. Morale suffers, and the collection remains static.

CREW Method

The CREW Method was first described by Joseph P. Segal in his 1976 publication, *The CREW Manual: A Unified System of Weeding, Inventory, and Collection-building for Small and Medium Sized Public Libraries*. (A revised edition, *The CREW Method: Expanded Guidelines for Collection Evaluation and Weeding for Small and Medium-Sized Public Libraries* by Belinda Boon [www.tsl.state.tx.us/ld/pubs/crew/index.html] is listed in the Recommended Reading section at the end of this book.) CREW stands for Continuous Review, Evaluation, and Weeding, and helps librarians deselect materials. It uses the MUSTIE acronym to define weeding criteria:

Misleading and/or factually inaccurate
Ugly (worn out beyond mending or rebinding)
Superseded by a new edition or a better source
Trivial (of no discernable literary or scientific merit)
Irrelevant to the needs and interests of your community
Elsewhere (the material may be easily borrowed from another source)

When you are debating about whether to weed a book, ask yourself: "Would I like to curl up with this book myself?" If the answer is a big "NO! It smells bad and it's falling apart," you can be sure that no one else would want to either. If an item is old and worn out but of local historical value, you will likely keep it and preserve it, especially if your library serves as the town archives. If you have multiple copies of a title and none of them circulate, consider deselecting most copies. Keep one if it is a classic.

Finally, all books should be checked against a standard list before being withdrawn. We cannot all know the classics and standards in every subject. Standard lists include the *Public Library Catalog, Fiction Catalog*, and *Children's Catalog*.

Exercise 6.2

Weeding is: (Circle the ones that apply)

A. Something you do when you cannot jam one more book on the shelves.

B. Something you do when the shelves collapse due to the excess weight of overcrowding.

C. An ongoing systematic method for managing and improving the library collection so that it consists of accurate, updated, useful, and attractive materials.

D. A sin.

E. Unnecessary, because our library builds new additions and adds more shelving to handle the growing collection and alleviate space concerns.

Disposing of Materials

Beware of throwing materials out in the trash or burning them. Especially in small communities, the public can be very sensitive to what may be seen as a misuse of tax dollars. Make sure to include a section in your Collection Development Policy about how the library disposes of materials. This policy, approved by the library board, will back you up when a community member questions you about your actions.

If you put discards in the trash, community members could be less than receptive when you ask for more funding. Consider selling the more desirable materials to bring in revenue, or give them away to charities. Women's shelters, for instance, are often very grateful for children's books and women's fiction, craft books, or self-help books. Do not donate badly damaged, smelly, or moldy materials to charities, though—if the library doesn't want them, why would they? Let's not perpetuate this practice.

Reconsideration of Materials

It is important to have a policy in place in case a library customer requests that an item be removed from the collection. Part of the Collection Development Policy, the Reconsideration of Materials Policy explains how selections are made for the collection, outlines the procedure to be followed when a customer requests removal of an item, and includes a request for reconsideration form.

Preservation

Library materials will be damaged or become worn and need repair. Repair and preservation are part of collection development. Sometimes a book can be sent to a bindery for binding, or some simple repairs can be done in the library. First evaluate the item to determine whether it is worth rebinding or repairing. It may be more cost-effective to purchase a replacement, an updated edition, or a paperbound copy. Any library can do minor book repairs to save damaged books. Library suppliers provide book tape, pastes, and tools to accomplish these tasks, and classes in book repair and books on the topic are widely available.

Armed with knowledge of your community and their information needs (see Chapter 3 and Chapter 4), your library's vision, mission, and plan (see Chapter 5), your Collection Development Policy, and a collection assessment, you will be able to develop a relevant collection for your library. You will confidently select materials, acquire them, make educated decisions about donations, and deselect materials based on actual facts. In the long run, you will save time when you are clear about what you are trying to accomplish, and new staff members will get up to speed in no time when equipped with these tools. You will ensure that your library is providing reliable, current, and attractive materials that meet community information needs.

There are no right answers. The real test is whether you can quickly make confident decisions, based on your knowledge of your community and of your library's Collection Development Policy.

Exercise 6.3

Using your community assessment and Collection Development Policy, check the items you would select for your library's collection:

_____ A set of instructional DVDs on a subject the community needs more information about and the library is lacking

_____ A book donation from a prominent community member that is a classic, but smells terrible, has water damage, and is ridden with cobwebs, dust, and mouse waste

_____ A book on the Middle East that was published in 1990 by a very reputable publisher and written by a foremost authority on the subject

_____ A scholarly book on French social customs, a personal interest of yours

_____ A set of the latest *World Book Encyclopedia* to replace the well-used 1995 set now on the shelf

_____ A full set of the *National Geographic Magazine* from 1889 to the present

_____ A subscription to a conservative magazine to balance out the predominance of progressive and liberal magazines already received by the library

Chapter 7

Acquiring Information for the Library

Once materials have been selected for purchase, the acquisitions process begins. "Acquisitions forms a vital link in the cycle of publishing, selection, request and providing materials for use."[1] Acquisitions librarians must find and acquire materials effectively and economically while offering efficient and responsive service. Acquisitions work depends on establishing good relationships both inside and outside the library, with suppliers and publishers as well as financial officers and library directors.

There are various skills librarians need for acquisitions work:

- Detective skills

- Math skills

- Memory for titles

- Record-keeping skills

- Ability to work within a budget

- Ability to negotiate a license

- Ability to use multiple automated systems

- Ability to intermediate among customers, library staff, and vendors

- Ability to evaluate and analyze

- Follow-up skills

Automated Acquisitions

Acquisitions software, automated systems, and acquisitions modules have transformed the acquisition process. Computerization has simplified acquisitions, allowing this part of library operations to run more smoothly than in the past.

If your library has an ILS (Integrated Library System), you may already have an acquisitions module, or the capability to add one. Talk with your ILS vendor about the best option for automating acquisitions using your current system, look into modules from other vendors that interface with your ILS, and ask other librarians for their recommendations. Use the library automation resources listed in Chapter 17 to investigate your options.

Those without automated acquisitions can use web interfaces offered by the large library materials vendors. These allow you to place orders, review orders, run reports, and follow up online. Some online products allow you to simultaneously search multiple library material distributors for a single item. Each system, module, and software option operates differently and no single acquisitions procedure applies to them all.

Steps in the Acquisitions Process

Acquisitions procedures vary depending on your library's automation system or software and your particular library; however, the basic steps are the same.

Step 1: Gather Orders

Materials selected for ordering may be in the form of marked reviews in journals, online printouts, completed customer request forms, or pieces of information written on scraps of paper. Gather all order requests and eliminate any duplicate items.

Step 2: Search the Collection and "On Order" Items

Check the library's current catalog, "on order" files, or database to make sure an item is not already in the collection or "on order." Mark the request "Found" or "Not Found," and include the date and your initials. If your acquisitions module downloads "on order" material records to the library's catalog you can do this in one step; however, if your "on order" materials are in paper files or a database, you must also look here to avoid ordering duplicate copies. If you are using a manual system, check materials that are waiting for processing and unrecorded donations.

Step 3: Verify Accurate Publishing Information

Many large vendors and library materials distributors provide web-based databases with ordering interfaces that allow you to verify bibliographic information as you order. Here, verification and ordering can be combined in one step—but don't skip the verification process. Receiving and returning incorrect materials can become a job in itself. (If the library is responsible for the cost of returning materials, this can also get expensive!)

WorldCat (www.worldcat.org), the Library of Congress (www.loc.gov), and online retail booksellers are cost-free alternatives to large vendor databases for verifying accurate publishing information. Publishers' websites can be a good source for verifying information on hard-to-find materials and media; they are usually current. Don't hesitate to contact a publisher directly if you have questions about accurately identifying an item they publish. It is much easier to take time to do this during the preordering process than it is to return and receive credit for incorrect materials later. Subscription bibliographic databases, such as BooksInPrint.com (www.booksinprint.com), contain information about books, forthcoming titles, out-of-print titles, audio books, and videos, in addition to publisher information. These databases also include information on an item's availability at large suppliers, reviews, and author biographies.

Some materials that are trickier to verify are media, reports, series, conference proceedings, foreign language materials, and government documents. Due to the emergence and evolution of new formats, acquisitions librarians must stay current on how to identify and where to order multiple formats. Completing this step for these kinds of materials can mean going to the source, using specialized databases or directories, or knowing another language. AcqWeb (www.acqweb.org) lists various verification tools and resources.

Whatever method you use, make sure you have accurate publishing information for each item being ordered. This includes title, author/editor, publisher, format, edition, year of publication, price, and ISBN (International Standard Book Number) for books or ISSN (International Standard Serial Number) for serials. You don't need every piece of information for every item you order; however, ISBNs are crucial in the ordering process, because they are unique identifiers. If you have the wrong ISBN or ISSN you will get the wrong item or edition. ISBNs are also important to record correctly because they can be used as control numbers in automated systems.

Step 4: Choose a Source

Materials can be purchased directly from publishers, retail bookstores, online booksellers, library material vendors, suppliers, distributors, or jobbers. When evaluating and selecting a source for acquiring library materials, consider its:

- Accuracy
- Alerting service
- Automated system
- Cost/discount

- Customer service

- Ease of use

- Hit rate

- Range of supply

- Reliability

- Speed

Library Materials Vendors, Suppliers, and Jobbers

One of your jobs as an acquisitions librarian is to get the best possible price and service from your suppliers. Although you can purchase from a variety of sources, first consider suppliers that specialize in selling and distributing materials to libraries. Advantages to working with specialized library suppliers include: efficiency, discounts, waived shipping and handling fees, deposit accounts, and extra features like bibliographic databases, online ordering, processing, MARC record downloading, and collection development support. These vendors may also include special services such as locating out-of-print materials, supplying media, standing orders, electronic licenses, and periodical subscription services.

Investigate purchasing through your consortium, regional library system, or state library's purchasing contract. Their pooled purchasing power usually results in better prices and services, because vendors offer their best deals through contracts with large organizations.

Determine your requirements, identify the suppliers that meet your requirements, and then evaluate them. For instance, if you want MARC record downloading and processing for books, identify the vendors offering those services, and then look into the quality of books, records, and processing they supply. Does the vendor have a contract with your library system? If you want an easy-to-use web-based ordering interface, test vendors' websites, looking carefully at how they are organized and their ease of use. Think about the kinds of materials you order most often and check their availability with a vendor. What kind of fill rate do they claim? Ask colleagues in libraries like yours for recommendations.

In the end, one vendor probably won't be able to fulfill all your orders and meet all your specifications all the time, but it is convenient to have one main source that meets the bulk of your requirements. If you work with a primary vendor, you can easily check all in one place what you have spent, what materials are on order, what is on backorder, and when items are expected to ship. This can be a real time-saver in the long run.

Magazines and periodicals, media, and electronic resources are often acquired in different ways and from different vendors. A large supplier generally provides multiple formats, but be aware of their pricing and keep in mind that you may need to work with different vendors for different kinds of materials and formats. Investigate separate periodical subscription services that can handle your entire periodicals order as well as standing orders and serials. Ordering educational DVDs directly from a publisher can offer the advantage of discounts and replacement services, not usually offered by a large library materials supplier.

Online Bookstores

Online bookstores like Amazon.com (www.amazon.com), Alibris (www.alibris.com), AbeBooks.com (www.abebooks.com), and Powell's Books (www.powells.com) are user-friendly, and placing orders is easy. You can use BookFinder.com (www.book finder.com) to compare major online booksellers' prices for individual items. Use these sites to purchase new and used books, videos, DVDs, CDs, audiocassettes, periodicals, and ebooks. Shipping is often free if you purchase over a minimum dollar amount, and, in some cases, discounts can be deeper than those at library material vendors. Online stores have extensive inventories, and you can maintain a profile for your library to receive alerts about new materials of interest or items you are trying to locate. The disadvantage to using online stores for purchasing library materials is that downloadable MARC records, processing, and automated reports are usually not available. Also, online stores generally do not offer deposit accounts; in most cases you will need a credit card to purchase online.

Publishers

Large vendors and online stores often don't stock nontrade materials such as publications of professional associations, government agencies, academic institutions, small publishers, and private individuals. If you order these from your main supplier, they can be backordered for long periods of time, and sometimes your order is cancelled before it can be filled. Also, vendors usually don't discount these types of materials. If you instead order directly from the publisher, they may offer prepublication discounts and fill orders more quickly. Some publishers have sales representatives who visit libraries to discuss their new books, which can be an attractive service for busy librarians. Be careful to understand the terms of sale, including discounts and shipping charges, and beware of buying books based on viewing their covers only.

Retail Bookstores

Sometimes librarians like to buy materials at local retail bookstores. Visiting bookstores is convenient, librarians can examine materials before purchasing them, and they can quickly purchase a popular title. Ask about discounts for libraries, but be prepared to pay more than you would through a large vendor. Inventories at local bookstores cannot match a vendor's inventory, so it isn't wise to place large orders with local bookstores or use them for ongoing purchases.

Step 5: Place the Order

Generate purchase order numbers prior to ordering, even if not required to, because this can be helpful in tracing or returning orders. If you need to contact a vendor about an order or a particular item within an order, it is handy to have a purchase order number to help them track your request.

Periodically reevaluate your ordering process, especially when it comes to purchase orders. Is it working? If you generate many purchase orders for small amounts, you may create a tangle of "open purchase orders" that becomes impossible to track. Also, the materials you order on a single purchase order are unlikely to arrive all at once. Some items are backordered, some are forthcoming, and some will arrive in a separate shipment. If you wait until you have accounted for everything on the purchase order before forwarding it for payment, you will have a pile of open purchase orders, which can become a mess in no time.

Another purchase order issue that can cause problems is that, when you assign a small amount to a purchase order, it is very unlikely that the eventual cost of the order you place will match the amount you assigned. In many cases you do not know what the discount will be on an item at the time of purchase. If the finance people in your town administration or university frown when the actual amount spent does not match the purchase order amount, consider changing your process to better meet their needs. Some libraries assign one purchase order number for each category of materials with the entire amount to be spent in that category for the whole fiscal year. There are several advantages to doing this: (1) You will not constantly be trying to place orders to match small purchase order amounts all year; (2) you will have a good idea of the amount you have to spend in a year in a particular area; (3) you can see how your spending is going in each area as the year proceeds; (4) messy piles of open purchase orders can be avoided; and

(5) you will save time and money by eliminating the need to sort through paperwork.

The method you use to place an order will vary depending on the source; however, generally you can order library materials by telephone, fax, letter, order slips, email, or online. Whatever method you use to order library materials, you must provide a set of core information to the vendor when ordering (this is the information you verified in Step 3):

- Author

- Title

- Edition

- Publisher

- ISBN

- Price

- Number of copies

- Format

When using an online ordering system, start with the ISBN as a quick way to locate an item in a database. Remember, the correct ISBN is crucial. Hardback editions, paperback editions, audio books, and ebooks with the same title all have different ISBNs. A wrong ISBN can override other information in your order so you may receive the wrong item. If you are ordering by phone, fax, order slips, or email, provide complete bibliographic information for each item. Regardless of the method used to order, pay close attention to details such as the edition, kind of binding, format, and number of copies you are ordering.

Online ordering through major library vendors provides quick service, often complemented with MARC record downloading. If you choose to download material records upon ordering, you will be required to edit a cataloging record at that time. Essentially, this process inserts a cataloging function into the acquisitions process, making acquisitions librarians increasingly responsible for cataloging duties. Keep in mind that a solid knowledge of cataloging and classification is necessary to edit cataloging records. This can represent a huge savings in cost and time. Also, when you download records when an item is ordered, it will show up as "on order" in your online catalog. Customers can reserve or place holds on ordered items, and you can look for "on order" items in the library's catalog to avoid duplicate ordering.

Cathy Butterfield, Circulation Manager, The Community Library, Ketchum, Idaho

I graduated from college in 1978 with a BA in Sociology/ Anthropology. Aside from working a few hours a week at the Middlebury College Library while I was an undergraduate, I have no formal library education credits. Armed with a sociology degree, I did research for a community mental health center in Vermont, and then became a cook at a ski area. I've also worked at jobs in landscaping, archaeological surveying, ghostwriting ski articles, and in a fish cannery.

After almost 20 years of cooking and knee operations (also a common ski town phenomenon), I applied for an opening for Librarian I at the Community Library. While the pay was considerably less than what I made managing kitchens, the working conditions were stellar in comparison, and included benefits that are generally alien to the ski town service industry.

Over the last six years I've picked up staff training, cataloging, acquisitions, and collection management responsibilities, mostly through the learn-by-doing school of library science. Job titles have morphed from Librarian I to Librarian II to Circulation Supervisor to Circulation Manager.

I have found from my experience and from my staff that skills learned in other jobs translate very well into the library environment. Ordering books is not a huge jump from ordering pantry items. One has to factor in price, utility, and shelf life for both. Calculating library statistics over a certain population is not so different than calculating mental health statistics over a certain population. And good customer service is good customer service regardless of where you are. Even cannery work experience contributes to productivity in a library. I can hoist boxes of books as well as any of the youngsters.

My interests and hobbies also provided good background for library work. My reading tastes are wide-ranging, from science fiction and mystery to history and biography. I do, however, avoid the cookbook section as much as possible, these days.

I'm not saying it's been easy bootstrapping into library work, but it has been challenging and fun. The relatively fluid organizational charts at the Community Library allow for advancement that might not exist in larger library settings. We may not be considered "professional" in the technical sense, but I think we get the job done, and more.

Step 6: Keep Accurate Records

Either keep order records in an acquisitions database or holding area in your online catalog, or manually file a copy of orders placed, when, from where, and funds expended. The files must be well organized, accessible, and easy to use by all staff. If "on order" items are not indicated in your automated system, any staff member should be able to easily determine if an item is on order using your internal system. Customers will ask if a popular item is on order, and, to provide good customer service, you must be able to provide this information.

Step 7: Receive and Process Materials

When materials arrive, compare the items received to the order and immediately inspect the shipment for defects or damage. When you open packages of new library materials, first remove the invoices and packing slips, then check each item in the package against everything on the bill. Check the items received against the items ordered, making sure they match. Examine materials carefully for damage. Mark your orders "received" and record the actual cost of each item. The actual cost of the item often differs from what you expected to pay when you ordered; prices go up or discounts go down. The amount on the invoice (minus any credits for returned or incorrect materials) is the cost of the materials in the order. If your orders consist of materials in a single area or category, you can use this amount to calculate your spending progress by subtracting the invoice amount from your yearly budget balance in that area.

Some items may be out-of-print or on backorder. You will have to decide an appropriate course of action for these materials; however, you may be able to resolve out-of-print orders by ordering another edition, purchasing from an online retailer that specializes in out-of-print materials, or inquiring at a used book store. Backorders may be readily available directly from the publisher.

If you receive damaged materials or find errors in title, format, or edition, follow the vendor's instructions for returning these items. If there is any question about exchanging an item or receiving credit, contact the vendor by phone and talk to someone in person. They will usually ask for an explanation, but it is good customer service for a vendor to accommodate your needs.

Stamp accepted items with an identifying stamp, barcode, or security strip, or RFID the materials, cover them or box them, and otherwise prepare them for library customers to use.

Step 8: Pay Your Bills

Upon receipt of materials and resolving any issues concerning damaged items, returns, backorders, or missing items, clear the purchase order for payment. Pay your bills in a timely manner—as soon as possible after accepting the materials.

Approval Plans

"On approval" means that a publisher or vendor will send you materials to examine without you specifically ordering them in advance. Libraries contract with suppliers and publishers to send regular deliveries of materials based on an established library profile. If you don't want to purchase something sent to you "on approval," you can return it to the source at no charge. You can usually take a month or more to evaluate these materials; if you decide to buy, you pay on the invoice that comes with the shipment. Approval plans can include, for example, all new publications from a particular publisher, all titles in a subject range, or all titles in a particular medium.

Approval plans have an advantage in that the publisher selects materials for you based on your profile, saving you the time it would take to go through catalogs and alerts. Regularly monitor your library's approval plans for:

- Accurate materials you need

- Quality of materials

- Price of materials

- Minimum duplication

Electronic Products

Take care when purchasing electronic products to check what you are buying and what licensing is required. Periodical databases have been available for some time, downloadable audio books and music are now common, and ebooks are increasing in popularity. Electronic products are usually licensed rather than purchased, and acquiring them can involve negotiating licensing agreements. Licenses are configured in various ways and can be very complex to decipher. It is in your best interest to take advantage of licenses negotiated through your state library, regional library system, or consortium, which can provide large cost and time savings.

Ask yourself these questions before you purchase an electronic product:

- Do you already have the title in printed form? Do you need another format?

- Does the product offer the original full text with all illustrations, tables, and graphics, or is it abridged?

- Does the electronic version have the same standards as the printed version?

- Is the product easy to use?

- Will staff need training to use it?

- Is the product available at all times with reliable Internet connectivity?

- What is the time lag for accessing the latest issues?

- How often does the product need updating?

- Does the price vary depending on the number of users?

- Are there a maximum number of simultaneous users allowed?

- What are the licensing requirements?

- Can the product be networked?

- Can it be accessed remotely? What are the authentication requirements and restrictions?

- Can remote users download to any device? What are the restrictions?

- Does your library have the technical expertise to support the product?

- Are there options for acquiring the product through your consortium?

Exercise 7.1

You are responsible for acquiring the following items. Where could you purchase each?

1. *If you pause in a museum of craft.* (DVD) produced by the Public Service Broadcasting Trust for and in partnership with Prasar Bharti Corporation; directed and written by Sameera Jain. New Delhi: Public Service Broadcasting Trust, 2004.
   Source:_____

2. Kingsolver, Barbara. *Animal, vegetable, miracle: A year of food life.* New York: HarperCollins Publishers, 2007.
   Source:_____

3. "Proceeding of the conference on diameter-limit cutting in northeastern forests." Newtown Square, PA: USDA Forest Service, Northeastern Research Station, 2006.
   Source:_____

4. Lennox, Annie. *Medusa.* (CD) New York: Arista, 1995.
   Source:_____

5. *Occupational outlook handbook 2006–2007.* United States Department of Labor. Washington, DC: Bureau of Labor Statistics, 2006.
   Source:_____

Acquisitions Budgets

Acquisitions work is tied to a budget, and anyone responsible for selecting and ordering books must understand the budgetary parameters of their work. Budgets are usually split into categories for expenditure because this makes them easier to manage. Acquisitions budgets can be divided in many ways, but in the end it is essential to know how much you have to spend in each category.

The designated amounts in each category will change based on the needs of the community you serve and your library plan. For instance, if there is an influx of retired people in your community, your library plan might specify that the library will acquire more materials on aging and geriatric health, more large-print materials, and more books on CD in a given year. The dollar amounts in those categories are increased for that year, allowing more purchases to meet community needs at that time. This may mean decreasing the amounts in other categories for that year, but in future years other categories will become priorities.

Whatever your situation, selectors and purchasers must know how much they have to spend in a category in order to work within a budget and to purchase materials to effectively meet community needs. At any given time acquisitions librarians need to know:

- Overall budget for purchasing library materials
- Amount of money already spent and committed
- Budget balance

Endnotes

1. Liz Chapman, *Managing Acquisitions in Library and Information Services*, Revised ed. (London: Facet Publishing, 2004), 1.

Chapter 8

Organizing the Library's Information

As you select, acquire, and collect materials and information resources for your library's collection, your job as a librarian is to organize this information so librarians and library users alike can locate it easily. The key to one of our most important roles as librarians—organizing the library's information for easy retrieval—lies in thorough and accurate cataloging and classification.

The Importance of Cataloging and Classification

The ability to organize information using common systems is essential for librarians. Understanding and applying the basics of cataloging and classification will increase the usefulness and value of your own library, and will give you the foundation you need to navigate inevitable changes with confidence. Along with advances in electronic information and online resources, alternate methods for organizing and accessing information are constantly emerging.

Your skill in organizing materials and information will help create a positive atmosphere for library customers—wherever they are. People using your library, your online resources, and your website will be able to find the information they need quickly and efficiently. Library staff will be able to locate information with ease, making their assistance more valuable to your customers. A well-organized library is a functional and orderly information resource, with satisfied customers.

Library Catalogs

Library catalogs are organized lists of records that identify, describe, and indicate the location of materials in the library. They serve as indexes to the materials in the library collection, providing multiple access terms for each item to help guide users of library resources to materials that meet their needs. Library catalogs are only as good as the information entered into them by catalogers.

Until the 1980s, most library catalogs consisted of stacks of card catalog drawers containing 3 x 5-inch cards representing all the materials in a collection. Each item had multiple cards with different headings, such as author, title, series, and subjects, to facilitate accessing the item from multiple points. Some libraries maintained separate card catalogs for authors, titles, and subjects, while smaller libraries usually interfiled all the cards alphabetically in one large card catalog.

When computers came onto the scene, libraries began to record the information previously contained on catalog cards in machine-readable formats and to store these electronic records in computers. In machine-readable cataloging (MARC), bibliographic records were coded in a way that computers could interpret them and deliver favorable results. Computer catalogs, or online catalogs, soon replaced card catalogs in most libraries. Early on, computer catalog software was too expensive for small libraries; however, today the cost is affordable and the range of choices is varied, suiting libraries of all sizes. It is unusual to find a card catalog in even the smallest libraries with the smallest of budgets.

Providing Access to Information

The fundamental principles of cataloging are the same regardless of the format of the catalog (card, microfiche, CD-ROM, or online) or the type of library. Librarians must understand some basic rules, principles, and theories of cataloging and classification before beginning to catalog. Once you understand the basics, you can:

- Adapt and customize cataloging principles to fit your collection and better serve your users

- Simplify cataloging if your library is small or you have limited time or staff

- Customize cataloging if your library is specialized or users have unique needs

Before catalogers attempt to adapt, simplify, or customize, they must understand the basics of what they are adapting, simplifying, or customizing. People commonly think that anyone can catalog or that it is an easy skill to pick up quickly. Catalogers, though, must understand what they are doing and why they are doing it; they have to be trained, and someone must oversee cataloging and classification activities in your library. Find the time to take a class, online course, or tutorial, or read up on the subject. When cataloging is accurate and correct, people will be able to find the information they need and things will work smoothly in your library.

Cataloging

Cataloging describes an item by criteria such as author, title, edition, place of publication, publisher, physical description, and subjects. These elements serve as access points for information seekers to find the item. Sometimes when people use the word "cataloging" or the verb "to catalog," they are referring to cataloging *and* classification. Although these are two separate activities, the classification number becomes part of the catalog record. (See more on classification later in this chapter.)

Descriptive Cataloging

This is the process of recording information about an item such as author, title, editor, illustrator, publisher, place of publication, number of pages, illustrations, and measurements. In the case of media, descriptive information might include format, performers, director, and running time. The accepted standard resource for descriptive cataloging is the *Anglo-American Cataloguing Rules*, 2nd edition (*AACR2*), which contains all the rules you will need to perform this phase of cataloging. Anyone doing cataloging work must have this reference close at hand—and they must use it. *RDA* (*Resource Description and Access*) is scheduled to replace *AACR2* in 2009 as the standard for describing all types of content and media, digital and analog. Designed for the digital world, RDA is built on the foundation of *AACR2* and will provide a comprehensive set of guidelines and instructions on resource description and access, for use in libraries and beyond.

Subject Cataloging

Subject cataloging involves assigning subject headings to an item record. Subject headings are standardized words used to describe an item by the topics it covers. Users can find all of a library's materials on a specific topic by looking under standardized subject headings. The subject heading systems most commonly used in the U.S. are the *Sears List of Subject Headings* (*Sears*) and the *Library of Congress Subject Headings* (*LCSH*). Smaller libraries tend to use Sears, while medium and larger libraries use the much more detailed and comprehensive LCSH. There are also specialized subject heading lists and thesauri such as the *Medical Subject Headings* (*MeSH*) (www.nlm.nih.gov/mesh) for medical libraries, the *Art and Architecture Thesaurus* (www.getty.edu/research/conducting_research/vocabularies/aat/index.html) for art and architecture libraries, and the *Thesaurus of ERIC Descriptors* (www.eric.ed.gov/ERICWebPortal/Home.portal?

_nfpb=true&_pageLabel=Thesaurus&_nfls=false) for education libraries. Librarians select the most appropriate subject heading system for their particular library and use it consistently when assigning subject headings to materials in the collection. One library does not use several different subject heading systems, as this would cause confusion and defeat the purpose. Nor does a cataloger make up words as subject headings because he or she thinks another word would better describe an item. Inventing subject headings defeats the purpose of using subject headings—to collect all information on a single subject together under one term, facilitating access.

It is true that some subject headings sound unnatural or are outdated, and are not the words you (or your patrons) would use to describe a particular topic. Unfortunately, subject heading systems are not known for their currency or being cool and hip. But, you must still use established subject headings to help people find information.

Prior to selecting subject headings to describe an item, a cataloger determines what an item is about by examining it. For a book, this means looking at the title page and table of contents, scanning the inside flaps or back cover for a short description, reading the introduction or preface, and reading brief sections or paragraphs. Media such as DVDs and CDs are usually packaged in materials that describe the contents; however, it may be necessary to view or listen to a portion of the media to accurately assign subject headings. Assign as many subject headings to an item as there are topics covered in that item. Some libraries limit the number of subject headings they use. This is fine if you include every major subject the item covers. If a book is about several topics, and you limit yourself to assigning only one subject heading, you will limit access to that item. Your job is to maximize access to information.

To catalog:

1. Determine what it is that you are cataloging. Does it stand alone, or is it in a set or series?

2. Describe the item in the appropriate fields of the bibliographic record (i.e., title, author, edition, publisher, place of publication, number of pages, illustrations).

3. Determine what the material is about and assign appropriate subject headings.

Classification

Classification is the process of assigning a location identifier to an item. This can be a number, letter, or symbol, or a combination of numbers, letters, and symbols. This identifier tells us where the material is physically located on a shelf, in a cabinet, in a drawer, or in another container. Librarians use hierarchical classification systems to create location identifiers. Because classification systems are constructed according to subjects, using location identifiers locates similar materials in physical proximity to each other. Materials on the same subject are classified and shelved together for easy access and to facilitate browsing.

An item can only have one classification number and can be placed in only one location—even if it is about more than one topic. It is the cataloger's responsibility to determine the major focus of the item and assign it a classification number based on that focus. This classification places the item near other things in the collection focused on the same topic, but does not mean this is the only topic covered in that item.

The classification system you use to organize your collection will be determined by its size, subject matter, or your users' preferences. A special library consisting of materials solely on the topic of disabilities will use a different classification scheme than a university library, a public library, or a medical library. Some classification schemes are general, and some are specific; use the one most appropriate for your library's collection.

The two major classification systems used in U.S. libraries are the Dewey Decimal Classification System (DDC) and the Library of Congress Classification System (LC). The DDC is a numerical structure, ranging from 001 to 999, and the LC system is alpha-numerical, ranging from AA to ZZ. You can customize a classification system to suit your library and your users; however, the integrity of the system must stay intact to serve its purpose. Library policy will dictate how to handle specific kinds of materials.

As you assign a classification number to an item, check the collection to make sure the item fits into *your* collection in that place. Past local practices may have placed items on a certain subject in another place, and you will want to conform for the sake of easy access. For instance, materials on meditation and yoga could be classified in self-improvement, health and well-being, or Eastern religion. Where are these materials in *your* library? When the materials on yoga are in three different places in one library, you make it difficult for customers to find the information they need. Remember, your purpose as a cataloger is to keep like subjects together for easy access, not to be "right" about a classification number. What you think is right might be wrong to the cataloger on the next shift. Be consistent. It is essential for library policy to clarify the treatment of these types of materials.

Your collection may be divided into separate sections for easier use. For instance, you shelve the children's collection in a separate location from the music for adults, reference collection, books on CD, mysteries, and young adult materials. By adding a location letter, number, or symbol to the first line of the classification number, you can specify the section to which an item belongs, making locating the item easier.

The BISAC System

The Perry Branch Library in Gilbert, Arizona, recently rejected the Dewey Decimal System in favor of arranging library materials in broad subject areas (similar to a bookstore layout) using the Book Industry Standards and Communications (BISAC) Subject Headings. This decision was made in response to library users who said they come to the library to browse, not to find specific titles. They wanted the library to be as easy to use as a bookstore, so the library responded.[1] The BISAC system is different than the DDC or LC, but it is still a system. In deciding which classification or arrangement system to use in your library you must choose the one that best meets the information needs of the community you serve. The system is not the same for every library or for every community, and there is no one perfect system.

Copy Cataloging

If another library has already cataloged an item, it makes good sense to *copy catalog*, or to copy the existing cataloging record from another library that has already cataloged the same item and customize that record for your library. Original cataloging is rarely necessary these days. Libraries can purchase MARC records from suppliers on CD-ROM, download them when they order or acquire library materials, subscribe to a cataloging database service, purchase cataloging software, or find readily-available MARC records on the Internet free of charge. Many integrated library systems offer copy cataloging modules, which allow you to locate cataloging records, modify them, copy them, and download them directly into your library's system. Products vary widely in functionality and price, so it is worth your time to investigate them thoroughly. Test demo versions of these products, compare them, and select the one that best suits your library.

Sources for MARC Records

Many library material vendors and jobbers will sell MARC records when you purchase materials. This is an excellent option for most libraries and can be a big time- and money-saver. Usually, you set up a profile with a vendor in advance to specify your cataloging preferences, such as the classification and subject heading systems you use and your library's classification number prefixes. Records can be downloaded from a vendor site directly into your online catalog upon ordering. In this case, the acquisitions librarian ordering materials must understand cataloging, because a record may need some editing before being downloaded into your catalog.

You can also find quality cataloging on many Internet sites. The Library of Congress, many large universities, and major public libraries make their cataloging records available online. No one source will provide perfect cataloging records for your library, so you must have a basic understanding of the principles of cataloging to be able to recognize, modify, and customize records from multiple sites to fit your library. The major drawback to copying free records is that sometimes it is not possible to download MARC records or batch multiple records in a single download. Cutting and pasting can be tedious; however, if your library is small and can't afford other options, this is one way to make your collection accessible using quality catalog records.

The Library of Congress (LoC) has been assisting catalogers with creating bibliographic records since the early 1900s. Its catalog is provided online (catalog.loc.gov) as well as many other free cataloging tools. You can search the catalog by almost any aspect of the bibliographic record. MARC records are provided for almost every item in the LoC catalog, batch downloading is possible, and LoC records are authoritative. Refer to the Library of Congress Online Catalog Help Pages (catalog.loc.gov/help/savemail.htm) for instructions on downloading MARC records into your system, as procedures change periodically and vary for individual systems.

Lib-web-cats (www.librarytechnology.org/libwebcats/index.pl) is a worldwide directory of libraries. Each listing links to a library's website and online catalog. You can search for compatible library catalogs by limiting your search in many ways including type of library, size of collection, and current automation system. WorldCat (www.worldcat.org) allows you to search for specific items in the collections of thousands of libraries around the world.

Searching for MARC Records

Locate a matching record for the item you are cataloging in a database or a library's online catalog. The best search terms will vary depending on the format and kind of material you are cataloging. For a book, the LCCN or ISBN are good places to start; however, you will probably not find an LCCN on a sound recording or DVD.

Search strategies for each database or online catalog are different so you will have to work with each one to learn how to retrieve the best results. For instance:

- Does the database or online catalog recognize upper and lower case?

- Are you supposed to include hyphens in the ISBN?

- Should you enter all punctuation marks?

Once you have located a matching record for an item, examine it closely to make sure it is an *exact* match for the item you have in hand. Match the LC number, ISBN, main entry, added entries, title, edition, publisher, place of publication, and physical description.

Editing Records

When you decide that the record you have located is truly a match for the item you are cataloging you must decide if the record can be copied "as is" or if it needs editing. The matching record may come from a library that uses classification numbers or subject headings unsuitable for your library, it may be customized for another library, it may use a different subject heading system or classification system other than the one your library uses, or it may actually be a CIP (Cataloging in Publication) record. Chances are high that you will need to edit a matching record before saving it and downloading it into your library's system. "You should be aware that some knowledge of cataloging is required to match and copy records properly."[2]

You will need to edit a record if it uses:

- Pre–*AACR2* cataloging

- CIP cataloging

- Limited cataloging

- Minimal level cataloging

- Shared cataloging

- Different uses of subject headings

- Different choices of classification numbers

Check the record for errors, misspellings, or minor discrepancies and make corrections.

Even the best of catalogers can miss changes or simple errors, even with careful examination. It is a rare cataloger who can remember all the changes that have been made to MARC and *AACR2* over time. Keep *AACR2* and your classification and subject heading system tools close at hand for reference. Cataloging checker programs can be useful in catching errors.

Copy catalogers are responsible for ensuring that a record is an exact match for their particular library by editing it prior to downloading. To do this they need to understand:

- That catalogers are responsible for providing access to library materials

- That catalogers can "make or break" an information search

- How to properly place materials in a particular collection

- How to determine the content of an item or whether it is fiction or nonfiction

- Subject heading systems, why we have them, and how to use them

- Classification systems, why we have them, and how to use them

- *AACR2*, what is in it, and how to use it

- Specific subject heading system and classification system used by your library, related tools, and how to use them

- Special considerations when cataloging media

- Authority control

Copy cataloging requires analytical thinking skills and attention to detail. It is all too easy to quickly scan a record, determine it is a match, download it, and be done with it.

Authority Control

Authority control determines the "authorized" form for every entity known by variant forms. Satisfactory search results come from searching names, places, and subjects that have been created under authority control. If a person is identified by several forms of a name and one of those names is "authorized," then a search for that name will bring up all forms of the name. When authority control is ignored at the cataloging stage, various forms of the name will appear in the catalog and a search for one name will not retrieve the rest. If a work's title has different variations, a search for one will retrieve them all only if one of the titles has been "authorized." The same is true of subject headings and other controlled vocabularies. A search for one word will retrieve the authorized subject heading (including synonymous terms) for that word and lead to all materials on that topic in the collection. Without authority control, someone seeking information would have to search all the variant forms of a name, title, or subject. Because it is unlikely that everyone knows (or will remember to search under) all the variants, librarians do this work at the cataloging stage to facilitate acceptable search results.

Finding Sean Combs Using Authority Headings

These names have all been used by the same person:

Puff Daddy
Sean Combs
Puffy Combs
Puffy
Diddy
Diddy Combs
P. Diddy

The Library of Congress authority record establishes Diddy, 1969– as the "authorized" form of his name. Therefore, all records for items by or about this person use Diddy, 1969– regardless of what variant appears on the item. Cross references from variant forms of the name will lead users to Diddy, 1969– where all items by or about him will be listed in the catalog. Remember, the job of catalogers is to organize information so people can find it. Authority work plays a big part in this role.

The Library of Congress has an Authorities web page (authorities.loc.gov) where you can browse and view authority headings for subject, name, title, and name/title combinations and download authority records in MARC format for use in your library—free of charge.

The Price of Saving Money

You may save money by opting out of purchasing cataloging records or by hiring trained catalogers and delegating copy cataloging to volunteers. This can be a viable option if volunteers are trained catalogers who understand the purpose of cataloging, the basic tools required, and the principles and practices of cataloging. Cataloging isn't rocket science, but neither is it a "cut and paste" activity or busy work. Catalogers are responsible for making the materials in the library accessible, which is some of the most important work we do as librarians. Quality cataloging creates a functioning library. Without quality cataloging, library users and librarians alike will futilely search the online catalog and shelves for information the library does own. People will leave the library empty-handed, when the information they need is sitting on a shelf—inaccessible because no one can find it. This is a high price to pay for saving money.

Everyone makes mistakes, and perfection is not the goal. Occasional cataloging mistakes and a lack of a basic understanding are two different things. The ramifications of cataloging library materials when you don't understand what you are doing are far-reaching. Library users become frustrated when they cannot find materials or information they need. People who know how to use libraries and expect to have success lose confidence in the library's ability to perform its primary role. They don't think much of the librarian's ability to access information, of the competence of library staff, and ultimately the value of libraries and librarians in general. This image is hard to turn around, as users will eventually stop coming to your library for information, relate their bad library experiences to others, and give your library a bad reputation across the state. Even more damaging, people who have had bad library experiences will think twice before voting on library funding—if you are lucky.

How Is Your Library Doing?

As Miller and Terwillegar so aptly state, "If, at any stage in the search, a seeker of information becomes frustrated, the library has failed in its purpose."[3] A seeker of information in the library environment is anyone (including library staff) trying to find materials or information, either in the library itself, or remotely through the library's website. If your library's users are commonly unsuccessful in finding information, or if you and other staff members routinely become frustrated while trying to help users locate materials or information, the library may be failing in this, one of its primary roles. The level of frustration users experience while trying to locate information in your library is inversely proportional to your effectiveness in organizing the library's collection.

Exercise 8.1

Do any of these situations occur in your library?

_____ Users often cannot locate what they want using the OPAC.

_____ Users frequently have to ask for assistance in finding information.

_____ Sometimes the only people who are able to find things in the library are staff members who have worked there for a long time.

_____ The best way to find something in your library is by memory.

_____ Users have to search multiple synonyms to find everything in the library on one subject.

_____ Users have to search multiple forms of a name in the online catalog to find everything in the library by one author or about one person.

_____ Materials on the same subject often have different classification numbers.

_____ Nonfiction books are classified as fiction.

These scenarios may be indications that catalogers (1) have not had adequate training, (2) are using inconsistent or incorrect cataloging practices, (3) are not following current cataloging procedures, or (4) have inadequate oversight. It can be a recipe for disaster in the library when catalogers:

- Don't understand authority work

- Are unaware of *AACR2*

- Don't know how to use standard cataloging tools such as *Sears* or DDC

- Invent subject headings

- Copy catalog "matching" records without checking that all fields match

- Copy catalog classification numbers without checking they fit into their collection

- Have difficulty distinguishing fiction from nonfiction

- Eliminate important fields from a record because they won't fit on a catalog card

- Have no current cataloging procedures to follow

- Don't meet or communicate

Cataloging Is Not Dead

Despite assertions that cataloging is dead, that it has gone the way of catalog cards, and that keyword searching is the wave of the future, utilizing the basic principles of cataloging and classification is still the best way to provide access to information in most libraries. Some say cataloging is an archaic process that went out with the last century. They have no use for *AACR2* or standardized subject headings, and the term "controlled" gets them all riled up.

Metadata is in and MARC records are out, they say. Some library schools no longer require students to take classes in cataloging and classification, sending the message that librarians no longer need this knowledge. Recently graduated MLS librarians find they need to learn these skills on the job or take continuing education classes after graduation—so they have no real advantage here over accidental librarians.

Cataloging as we have known it is changing, as the information environment and technology change. Librarians have devised methods for organizing information to facilitate access, and our ability to apply these basic concepts is precisely what makes us invaluable in the evolving information field. In the future we will most likely see a merging of the old and the new. At this point, however, the proven methods and techniques of organizing library materials and resources for effective access, using standardized cataloging and classification methods, are still useful. These methods help us to do our job by facilitating access to information.

Abandoning quality cataloging and classification practices because they "are dead" or devaluing them as "old school" will surely impede access to information. Our challenge is to adapt to the changes taking place by applying the crux of cataloging to a new environment. Librarians fundamentally know that by creating access points of descriptive information and by utilizing authority control and controlled vocabularies to describe an item, the chances of retrieving a specific piece of information are greatly increased over keyword searching.

Libraries are also merging catalogs. Now we can search an entire system or multiple regional libraries with one search interface, making it more important than ever that we observe consistent standards to maintain the integrity of these mega-catalogs. Incorrect and illogical cataloging practice can impede the building of a vast information network,[4] and competent catalogers are essential in making this happen.

Understanding the basics of organizing information for effective access is essential if librarians are to position themselves as active participants in these turbulent times. Storing information is not enough. Librarians have something to offer regarding how electronic and online information is organized, how online catalogs are designed, and how to integrate multiple search interfaces for effective access.

Keyword Searching and Cataloging

The methods people use to access information today differ greatly from those used before computers came into play. Now keyword searching is the preferred technique for searching the Internet, library catalogs, and online databases. Keyword searching fulfills the need for instant gratification, giving long lists of immediate results. Some people are satisfied with shallow results, thinking that any results are good results. This thinking is to their advantage—because they don't have the patience for precise searching anyway. Some say that because everyone searches by keyword, it is time for librarians to give up on controlled vocabularies, cataloging rules, and authority work. But simply because our culture today values the instant irrelevant results yielded by keyword searching does not mean that keyword searching is an effective or efficient way to find information.

Although most online catalogs provide keyword searching options, this is usually not the best way to find the information you need. Those uninterested in bothering with subject, author, or title searches, Boolean searches, or limiting searches to narrow their results will spend their time sorting through irrelevant results at the end. (Boolean searching is based on Boolean logic, or defining the relationship among search terms using the operators AND, OR, and NOT.)

Endnotes

1. Brian Kenney, "Desert Storm: An Arizona Library Dumps Dewey," *School Library Journal,* August 1, 2007, www.schoollibraryjournal.com/article/CA6463500.html

2. Deborah A. Fritz, "Cataloging 101: Getting Started," in *The Whole Library Handbook*, ed. George M. Eberhart (Chicago, IL: American Library Association, 2006), 293.
3. Rosalind E. Miller, and Jane C. Terwillegar, *Commonsense Cataloging: A Cataloger's Manual*, 4th revised ed. (New York: H.W. Wilson Company), 1990.
4. Miller, 1990.

Exercise 8.2

Answer the following questions and record where you found the answer.

1. What is the authorized name for Princess Diana?

   _____

   Source _____

2. Is *The Innocent Man* by John Grisham fiction or nonfiction?

   _____

   Source _____

3. The Dewey number for an item you are classifying on the canned fish industry is 338.47664942. Is this number appropriate for this item in your library?

   _____

   Source _____

4. Mary is cataloging a book about dogs. The Sears subject heading for this book is "Dogs" but she thinks the subject heading should be "Man's best friend." What do think?

   _____

   Source _____

Chapter 9

Retrieving and Disseminating Information

Now that you have organized library materials and resources for easy access, your job is to effectively and efficiently retrieve and disseminate information to meet the needs of the people you serve.

The Library Collection

The term "library collection" has long meant the materials (mostly books) housed within the four walls of a library building. Librarians would find a particular item by searching through the card catalog by author, title, or subject. To answer a reference question, you might have gone to the reference section to search through encyclopedias, dictionaries, almanacs, periodical indexes, and other reference resources. Or, you might have browsed the circulating collection in a subject area, looking at tables of contents and in indexes to locate information. Today, a library collection consists of materials in many formats, both *owned* by a library and supplemented by electronic information and databases *accessed through* the library. In some libraries most of the collection consists of electronic information and databases, supplemented by print materials and materials in other formats.

Knowing Your Library's Collection

To retrieve information from your library's collection, you must first know what is in it. The easy part is to learn about materials in the library's physical building. Take the time to explore every nook and cranny of your library and familiarize yourself with the various parts of the collection. You might be surprised what you find—and where. The books, magazines, newspapers, books on CD, DVDs, audiotapes, and videotapes may be easy to see at first glance. But do you know if the mysteries are shelved separately from the rest of the adult fiction? Where is the science fiction? Are the books on CD and books on audiocassette in different areas of the library? How is the children's section divided? Do you understand the classification system in the children's section? If your library doesn't use classification numbers, can you easily locate nonfiction materials? Where are the back issues of magazines? Are you familiar with the contents of the vertical file?

Looking around the reference room, you may find a long-forgotten dust-covered vertical file cabinet in a remote corner that may contain unique local information. In the same room you may find a series of uncataloged college courses on DVD, some random movies on DVD, local college catalogs, and numerous uncataloged local government documents and reports on topics of potential importance to town residents. None of these items appear in the online catalog. Magazines, newspapers, and other print periodicals to which the library subscribes aren't found in the online catalog either, nor is there a list of current subscriptions—you just have to know about them. Without knowing they exist, it is impossible to retrieve them or the information within them.

If your library's new employee orientation (if any!) didn't include instruction about *all* library resources, you must take it upon yourself to learn the collection as an independent study project. Look around. Ask questions. Dig under piles. Look in cabinets. Clear the cobwebs. Put the pieces together. Develop a finding aid for these hidden materials so that other librarians won't have to resort to the "find by accident" method or not find them at all, impeding the retrieval of information.

Gaining a thorough knowledge of the library collection takes time. You need to work in a library for a while to know what it holds, and must immerse yourself in the collection to really learn it. Every collection is different; LIS education and previous experience have nothing to do with knowing what is in a particular library's collection. To help you learn the collection:

- Do work that involves working in the collection

- Do reference work

- Update the reference collection

- Spend time in public areas assisting customers to retrieve information

- Work on collection development in an area of interest

- Organize and develop vertical file materials

Information Retrieval Defined

You must know how to find and retrieve information both physically and electronically, in multiple ways. This can be a tall order if you have a combination of (1) electronic databases from different vendors, (2) an online catalog that contains data on books, DVDs, audiotapes, videotapes, ebooks, and books on CD, (3) magazines and newspapers and other print subscriptions, (4) digitized local materials, and (5) a vertical file and other uncataloged materials. The methods you use to retrieve information from each part of a collection may differ. Information retrieval requires multiple sets of complex skills that you must master to do your job well. As librarians, one of our basic roles is to retrieve information to meet the needs of our customers. Everyone whose job it is to serve library users—especially those responsible for answering reference questions—must know what is in the library collection and how to find information so that customers are not unnecessarily discouraged or turned away.

Online Catalogs

It is the business of librarians to know how to use their online catalog to effectively retrieve information from the collection. Make a point of learning how to manipulate your library's catalog to maximize search results. Every online catalog is different, so knowing how to use one product doesn't mean that you instantly know how to use all online catalogs effectively. Spend some serious time learning the basic, or default, search interface, where most people using the online catalog will start. Learn how to make the catalog retrieve relevant results. Use each search option and experiment with how each performs. To learn more, take the training classes and online tutorials offered by your online catalog vendor. Read help screens, refer to manuals, and read support documents and updates. Become an expert in using your library's online catalog.

Figures 9.1 and 9.2 show two online catalog interfaces that look and work very differently. A Subject search for "cats" in Library A (Figure 9.3) yields subject headings containing the word "cats" (Figure 9.4). Library B offers Browsing and Keyword as search choices (Figure 9.5). What do these terms mean? Subject searches for "cats" using the Keyword and Browsing options in Library B yield different results (Figures 9.6 and 9.7). Which one is more useful?

Most online catalogs also offer advanced search choices. What advantages does advanced searching offer in your library's online catalog? In what kinds of situations would you use it? Learn how to easily retrieve information from your catalog so you can help users find the information they need. Learn how it works well enough that you can instruct customers how to use your library's online catalog to their advantage.

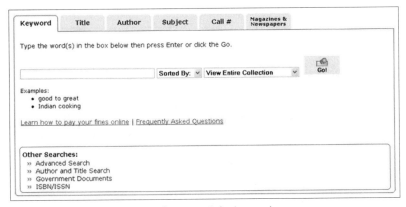

Figure 9.1 Library A default search screen

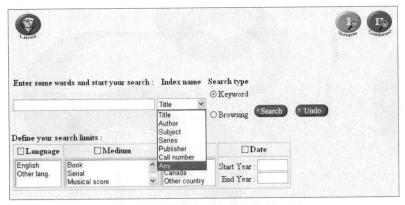

Figure 9.2 Library B default search screen

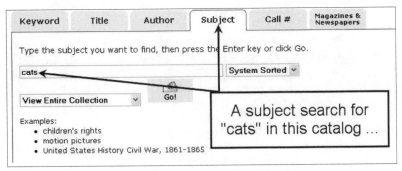

Figure 9.3 Library A Subject search for "cats"

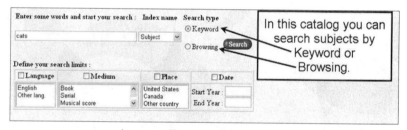

Num	Save	SUBJECTS (1-50 of 155)	Year	Entries 1766 Found
1		Cats -- 8 Related Subjects		8
2	☐	Cats		75
3		Cats Adoption -- See Cat adoption		1
4	☐	Cats Anecdotes		17
5	☐	Cats Anecdotes Juvenile Literature		2
6	☐	Cats Antarctica Fiction : Alexander, Caroline,; Fiction Alexand		1
7	☐	Cats Arizona Fiction		2
8	☐	Cats Behavior		30
9	☐	Cats Behavior Anecdotes		2
10	☐	Cats Behavior Anecdotes Juvenile Literature : Singer, Marilyn.; 636.8 Singer	2006	1
11	☐	Cats Behavior Case Studies : Dodman, Nicholas H.; 636.8 Dodman	1999	1
12	☐	Cats Behavior Juvenile Literature		6
13	☐	Cats Behavior Kenya Lamu Island : Couffer, Jack.; 599.752 Couffer	c1998	1
14	☐	Cats Behavior Massachusetts Anecdotes : Dodman, Nicholas H.; 636.7 Dodman	c2002	1
15	☐	Cats Behavior Miscellanea		2
16	☐	Cats Behavior Miscellanea Juvenile Literature		2
17	☐	Cats Behavior Therapy		2
18	☐	Cats Behavior United States Anecdotes : Chicago, Judy,; 636.8 Chicago	2005	1
19	☐	Cats Breeding : Rixon, Angela.; 636.8 Sayer	1983	1
20		Cats Breeds -- See Cat breeds		1
21	☐	Cats California Anecdotes : Leigh, Diane.; 636.0832 Leigh	c2003	1
22	☐	Cats Caricatures And Cartoons		28
23	☐	Cats Caricatures And Cartoons Juvenile Fiction : Davis, Jim,; 741.5 Davis	1984	1
24	☐	Cats Caricatures And Cartoons Juvenile Literature		17
25	☐	Cats Cleaning : Aslett, Don,; 636.0887 A835	c1988	1
26	☐	Cats Color : Crimmins, C. E.; 636.8 Crimmins	c2001	1

... yields subject headings that contain the word "cats".

Figure 9.4 Library A "cats" Subject search results

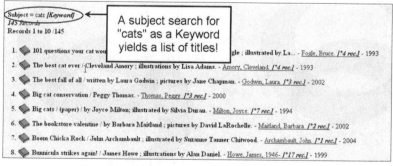

In this catalog you can search subjects by Keyword or Browsing.

Figure 9.5 Library B offers Keyword and Browsing choices

A subject search for "cats" as a Keyword yields a list of titles!

Subject = cats [Keyword]
145 Records
Records 1 to 10 /145

1. 101 questions your cat wou... gle ; illustrated by La... - Fogle, Bruce. [*4 rec.] - 1993

2. The best cat ever / Cleveland Amory ; illustrations by Lisa Adams. - Amory, Cleveland [*4 rec.] - 1993

3. The best fall of all / written by Laura Godwin ; pictures by Jane Chapman. - Godwin, Laura [*3 rec.] - 2002

4. Big cat conservation / Peggy Thomas. - Thomas, Peggy [*3 rec.] - 2000

5. Big cats / (paper) by Joyce Milton; illustrated by Silvia Duran. - Milton, Joyce [*7 rec.] - 1994

6. The bookstore valentine / by Barbara Maitland ; pictures by David LaRochelle. - Maitland, Barbara [*2 rec.] - 2002

7. Boom Chicka Rock / John Archambault ; illustrated by Suzanne Tanner Chitwood. - Archambault, John [*1 rec.] - 2004

8. Bunnicula strikes again! / James Howe ; illustrations by Alan Daniel. - Howe, James, 1946- [*17 rec.] - 1999

Figure 9.6 Library B Keyword search for "cats"

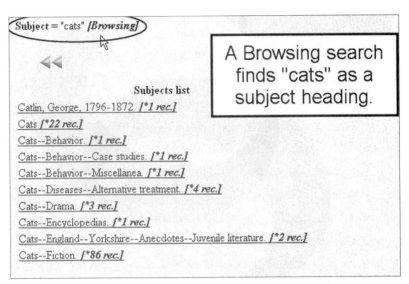

Figure 9.7 Library B Browsing search for "cats"

Databases and Electronic Resources

As a librarian, it is also your business to know what electronic resources are in your library's collection and how to retrieve information from them. Start by identifying your library's databases and electronic resources. This should not be difficult. The library either subscribes to them for a fee or receives them through a state, regional, or consortial agreement.

Once you determine the electronic resources available in your library, find out about their content. Are there reference resources, periodicals and journals, or newspapers? Is everything full text, or do some databases provide only citations? Do you know where to find the resources that are cited? Does your library offer electronic auto repair manuals, laws, or civil service tests? If you don't know what is in the resources your library has, you won't know when to go to them for information. This may sound simple, but people have been turned away from libraries only because the librarian they asked did not know to look in a database in the

Exercise 9.1

1. Search your library's online catalog for something that you know is in the collection. Try looking for it by author, title, subject, and keyword. Can you easily find it?

2. What happens when you enter a subject in the default search box?

3. Is there a better way to find items on this subject in the online catalog?

4. What limit options does your library's online catalog offer that will help you in your search?

5. Can you use Boolean searching?

6. Do you know what all the features do and how to work them to your advantage?

library's collection. For instance, if a database provides the full text of a magazine, consider that magazine as part of your holdings. You can access and retrieve the magazine through the database, often with the capability to print the image of an article within it just as it appears in the print version.

As for search techniques, repeat the process described in the previous section for the library's electronic databases. If you have access to several databases from the same vendor, this makes things a little easier; you can apply the same search strategies to all databases from the same vendor. You can often search multiple databases from the same vendor with a single search strategy. Again, vendors offer training, online tutorials, and documentation. The "Help" section of a database is usually very helpful in learning how it works. Be aware that databases from different vendors will require different search strategies, so be prepared to apply different search techniques when retrieving information from multiple databases.

Are there any other electronic resources in your library, such as encyclopedias, directories, indexes, or periodicals? Find out and make a point of learning (1) what information is contained in each one and (2) how to retrieve information from each.

Determining the Best Resource

The question will dictate the resource. When you know what resources are available to you, you can determine the best one for finding information or answering a question. If you don't know what you have available, you will be working in the dark. At times, librarians may search Google by default. This is tempting, because you know you will get results quickly, and it makes you look like you know what you are doing. But, remember three important things:

1. Everything is not on the Internet.

2. The Internet is not always the best resource for answering an information request.

3. Librarians' search expertise reaches beyond a Google search.

"Googling" has become part of our culture, and if you aren't paying attention you can find yourself searching Google for all your information needs. But librarians know better. Librarians know what other resources may be more appropriate for answering a question. Librarians know that Google searches often yield shallow and irrelevant results. Librarians know that the results of a Google search are not all from reliable sources.

There are times when Internet resources are the best place to fill information needs. Many ready reference resources on the Internet provide a quick and easy way to access information such as ZIP codes, word definitions, weather reports, census data, and tax forms (see Chapter 17). Librarians know when the best resource is the Internet, an electronic database, or a reference book.

Making It Easy for Others to Retrieve Information

As you know, the point is not to be the only one who can answer questions or retrieve information from the library collection. Do your part to make the information in your library easily retrievable and teach others how to find the information they need. Here are some tips:

- Catalog materials accurately and thoroughly (see Chapter 8)
- Add shortcuts to databases and electronic resources on desktops
- Create a web page of ready reference resources on the Internet (see Chapter 17)
- Provide good signage
- Provide information on library resources and where they are
- Make user guides available
- Clear away the clutter

Disseminating Information

After retrieving information, librarians impart or deliver that information to the people who need it. Information dissemination has taken on a different meaning in the Internet era. With the emergence of new technologies like blogs and RSS feeds, the burden of information dissemination has shifted in some cases from the librarian to the user. Information dissemination could be as simple as:

- Handing a requested book or other library materials to a library user
- Printing an article from a library database for a library user
- Making a copy of an encyclopedia article for a library user
- Distributing lists of materials about specific topics of interest
- Distributing new acquisitions lists
- Posting news on the library's website or blog
- Providing RSS feeds or email alerts
- Distributing newsletters

Selective Dissemination of Information

A more formal method of disseminating information to users is Selective Dissemination of Information (SDI), a current awareness service designed to alert the population you serve about recently published information in a topic of interest. A library customer usually registers a search profile in a system using keywords representing his or her fields of interest. When new publications matching the search profile appear, the system informs the user of them instantly, periodically, or upon request. Some systems are able to inform the user if changes in already notified publications occur.[1]

Preferred Searches

In libraries serving companies and businesses, medical institutions, or law offices, access to current information may be essential. Some online catalogs and bibliographic databases include a "preferred searches" option that allows the library user to archive

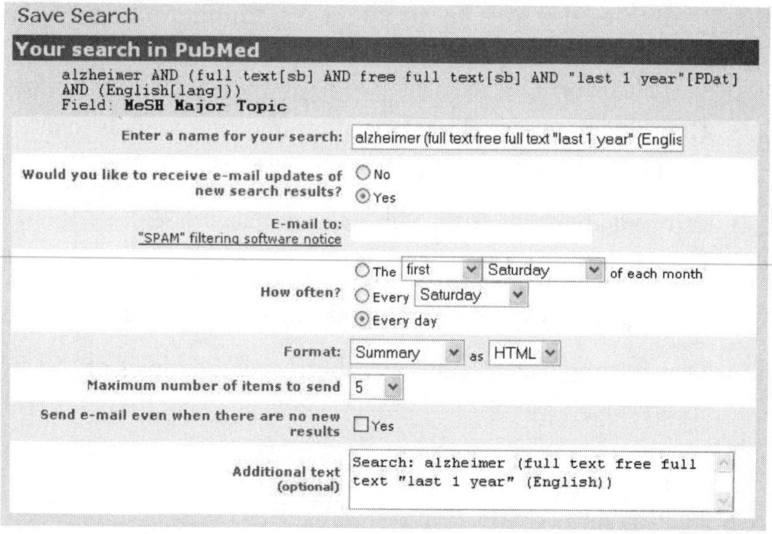

Figure 9.8 Saving a search in PubMed so that updated results are sent daily

search statements and reexecute them as needed. Others allow you to save a search, and when the databases are updated, it will automatically rerun and be emailed to the user (Figure 9.8).[2]

Tables of Contents Services

Some publishers, organizations, and societies offer a dissemination service whereby they email tables of contents to libraries or individuals whenever a new issue of a journal is published (Figure 9.9).

RSS Feeds

RSS feeds are summaries of updated headlines, web page contents, blogs, podcasts, or photo and video content from the web. To receive RSS feeds, you must first subscribe to an RSS aggregator or reader like Bloglines (www.bloglines.com), NewsGator (www.newsgator.com), or Google Reader (www.google.com/reader). Instructions for subscribing to RSS feeds vary depending on the aggregator, but you can generally set up your subscriptions

---

Free Table of Contents Alerting Services

To register for the free alerting services, simply send an e-mail to the address listed next to the journal with the word "subscribe" in the body of the message (no other words need to be in the e-mail message other than "subscribe").

To unsubscribe, send an e-mail to the same address with the word "unsubscribe" in the body of the message.

Alerting Services

J. Opt. Soc. Am. A	josaasubs-request@lists.osa.org
J. Opt. Soc. Am. B	josabsubs-request@lists.osa.org
Applied Optics	aooalert-request@lists.osa.org
Optics Letters	olosubs-request@lists.osa.org
Optics Express	opexsubs-request@lists.osa.org
J. Opt. Netw.	jontxt-request@lists.osa.org
Virtual J. Biomed. Opt.	vjbo-request@lists.osa.org

Figure 9.9 Table of contents alerting services from
the Optical Society of America

by clicking on the RSS symbols or links on your favorite websites and blogs and adding the resulting link to your aggregator. (Read your aggregator's "Help" files for additional information on how to subscribe.) If you see a subscribe symbol for your particular RSS aggregator, click on it for one-step subscribing.

Many libraries provide RSS feeds for new acquisitions, library news, upcoming events, and podcasts (Figure 9.10). New information added to those sites can be easily browsed in patrons' RSS aggregators, which automatically check for updates and display them to your readers. A publisher or database may have an RSS feed that delivers information directly to a user.

Blogs

Blogs have created new opportunities for librarians to disseminate information. No library should be without a blog. Many free services provide a place to host blogs and easy-to-use tools for creating them; two of the most popular free web-based blogging services include Blogger (www.blogger.com) and WordPress (wordpress.com). These services provide blog templates and easy-to-use interfaces that allow you to create an account and start a blog—complete with built-in RSS feed—in minutes. There is no need to know code or

Subscribe to our Free RSS Feeds

This 🔲 **RSS feed** button allows you to subscribe to one or more of our RSS Feeds. (What are RSS feeds?)

Library News
🔲 **Latest goings-on at Hennepin County Library.**

My Account
Personalized feeds of your items out and holds information. Get started at **My Account**.

Library Catalog
Make any **Catalog search** into a custom RSS feed. Watch for the 🔲 button on every search results page.

Catalog News
🔲 **News and search tips for using the Hennepin County Library Catalog**

Events & Classes
Make any **Events or Classes search** into a custom RSS feed. Watch for the 🔲 button on every search results page.

Bookspace
Most of our **book lists**, including on order titles, bestsellers and more, are available as RSS feeds. Watch for the 🔲 button.

Subject Guides
🔲 All Subject Guides – includes all the subject feeds below.

🔲 Arts & Entertainment	🔲 Language Learning
🔲 Automotive	🔲 Law & Government
🔲 Books & Authors	🔲 Libraries
🔲 Business & Investments	🔲 Magazines & Newspapers
🔲 Consumer Information	🔲 Minnesota
🔲 Countries & Travel	🔲 Music

Figure 9.10 RSS feeds offered by the
Hennepin County Library in Minnetonka, MN

any advanced computer techniques. Save time by creating one place where people can find information about library resources.

Endnotes

1. "The Free Dictionary," encyclopedia2.thefreedictionary.com/Selective+ Dissemination+of+Information
2. Joan M. Reitz, "Online Dictionary for Library and Information Science," lu.com/odlis/search.cfm

Chapter 10

Library Services

As we've learned, knowing who your library serves and how to meet their information needs is essential to providing comprehensive library services to your community, school, institution, corporation, or church. Most librarians serve various kinds of users with different needs, so services must be designed to address diverse needs and adjusted to meet the changing needs of the people you serve. Sticking with a formula that worked 25 years ago is unrealistic, because, whatever your type of library, the population you serve and their information needs are constantly evolving. Your library's community assessment (see Chapter 4) will tell you about the current makeup of the community you serve, and your library's plan (see Chapter 5) will help you focus on priorities.

Customer Service

All librarians need to understand the importance of superb customer service. This does not mean allowing customers full access to staff work areas, accepting disorderly behavior, or allowing pornographic material on public computers. It does mean that you treat all customers with respect as you perform your job. Here are a few pointers:

1. Acknowledge people who are waiting in line for service.

2. Take care of people in the library before answering the phone or handling electronic questions.

3. Create a clear and concise phone message that provides basic library information and a way to quickly leave a message. Be sure to keep it updated.

4. Create clear signage.

5. Develop tools to help you deal with routine requests.

6. Keep a ready reference shelf or web page of basic reference resources for answering quick questions.

7. Provide a way for customers to make comments and suggestions both in the library and on the library's website.

8. Create policies for dealing with difficult customers.

9. Put yourself in the customer's shoes.

The Library Building

It is important to provide a physical place that is conducive to delivering quality library services and programs. Some factors include:

- Accessibility for people with disabilities
- Book drop available outside the library
- Clean restrooms
- Designated service desks
- Easy navigation
- Flexible spaces that can change with the times
- Inviting and comfortable atmosphere
- Open design with good sightlines
- Program rooms
- Reader tables and seating
- Safety

- Sturdy library shelving
- Welcoming and user-friendly environment
- Wireless access

Here are some factors that may inhibit the provision of quality library services:

- A predominance of "Don't" signs
- Built-ins that are fixed or anchored for life
- Dust and dirt
- Harsh glaring lighting or dim inadequate lighting
- Labyrinthine pathways with places to hide
- No reference desk
- No rooms for programs
- Overcrowded shelves
- Poor signage
- Poor temperature control
- Too many entrances with no security
- Weak handcrafted shelving with limited flexibility

Online and Computer Access to Information

Now that much of the library's collection and other information is accessible online, librarians need to ensure that customers have adequate access both in the library and remotely. Are all formats equal in your library, or are the databases hidden? Does the library have a high-speed Internet connection? Is everything accessible remotely? Does your library have a strong and easy-to-use web presence? Does it meet accessibility standards? Are some computers in your library equipped with assistive technology? Is there wireless access in your library? Is it easy for customers to log in to online databases from outside the library? To provide adequate access to electronic information and remote access to the library's collection, libraries need:

- Public access computers with a high-speed Internet connection

- A user-friendly interface to electronic databases on library public access computers (PACs)

- Online public access catalogs (OPACs) in the library

- A library website with:

  - Information about the library, hours, location, services, and contact information

  - Calendar of events

  - Links to the library's online catalog and online databases

Reference Service

According to William A. Katz, a reference librarian "interprets the question, identifies the precise source for an answer, and, with the user, decides whether or not the response is adequate."[1] A reference librarian also determines what sources of information are useful or relevant based on input from the user, and may instruct a user on how to access information.

Responding appropriately and accurately to requests for information is one of a librarian's main functions, and where we really use our skills and abilities in information retrieval and dissemination. Many libraries offer reference services 24 hours a day, by email, web forms, and instant messaging (IM), as well as in person and by phone, fax, and mail. Library customers can now access a library's reference services from anywhere at any time (see Chapter 17).

The ways in which librarians handle reference requests differ depending on the type of library and the population they serve. For instance, in a corporate library, a librarian may perform exhaustive research for users, supplying them with literature searches or lists of annotated citations and resources. Librarians in smaller specialized libraries may have more time to spend researching a question, discussing results, and showing customers the resources they have located. In a school library, the reference process includes instruction in research methods, and it is usually an important part of an academic librarian's job to teach these methods. Public librarians typically answer ready reference requests promptly or help a library user locate a resource where they can find an answer to a question; however, public librarians are not usually equipped to do extensive research for users or to provide extensive instruction on research methodologies. It is important for libraries to have a policy defining the extent of the reference services they will provide, so that users have realistic expectations.

Anyone responsible for providing reference service must have adequate training or experience. Volunteers who work in your library a few hours a week, who have little knowledge about the library's resources and no training in the reference process, cannot be expected to provide quality reference service. If your library lacks adequate trained staff, consider limited reference hours. When no reference librarian is on duty, record the questions that come in and tell customers they will be contacted when the reference librarian returns. Another option is to train volunteers—providing poor reference service, though, is not an option.

Small libraries may lack the resources to answer all the reference questions that come in. Even large libraries are not equipped to answer all the technical and specialized reference questions they receive. You will sometimes need to refer the customer or the question to another source or library; however, make sure you have an understanding or agreement with other libraries to which you refer questions and customers. Here are some ideas:

1. Join a cooperative library system that provides assistance with difficult reference questions.
2. Contract with a larger library for supporting reference service.
3. Investigate what your state and national library associations offer.
4. Use contract librarians.

Never guess at an answer, brush off a customer, or turn customers away empty-handed without a referral to another library or resource. Librarians answer questions. Low-quality, inaccurate, or nonexistent reference service will undermine your users' confidence in and support of the library, and make them doubt the ability of your fellow librarians to do their jobs.

The essential elements to providing quality reference service are (1) know the resources available in your library, including print, media, online databases, and other electronic resources, (2) know the broad scope of reference resources available outside the library and how to identify them, (3) know the art of reference interviewing (see the next section), and (4) understand that your goal as a librarian is to match library users with the information they need.

The Reference Interview

Any staff member who provides reference service has to know how to conduct a reference interview. Many people do not know how to articulate their information requests clearly. Sometimes people don't really know what they want, sometimes they have not thought it through well enough to ask their question clearly, and sometimes they frame their question around a particular reference source because they have a preconceived idea about where they might find the answer. The reference librarian must avoid making assumptions based on the initial question and then interview the customer to determine the actual question.

The reference interview is an art. Reference librarians must take care not to overstep the boundaries of the customer or make judgments about a question in the process. This is a private conversation, not to be broadcast across the library for all to hear. Every question, every customer, and every reference interview is different, but here are some general suggestions:

1. Make eye contact and listen carefully to the question without interrupting.

2. Find out the context of the question.

3. Find out how the information is to be used.

4. Find out any parameters such as time, location, and dates.

5. Find out where the customer has already looked and why they weren't successful.

6. Repeat to the customer your understanding of the question.

7. Find the answer while explaining to the customer what you are doing.

8. Ask the customer if they have the information they need.

Interlibrary Loan (ILL)

Regardless of a library's size or materials budget, it is impossible for any one library to house the entire world of information within its four walls—or even electronically. Libraries depend on one another to satisfy user requests for materials they don't own or have access to. Interlibrary loan, or ILL, is an established process for libraries to share materials. This is one of the most useful services a library can provide, so promote awareness among all library staff and users. Everyone working in public areas of the library must know that ILL exists, the ILL policy, the cost (if any) to customers, and how to assist users in completing ILL requests.

Every state and major region in the U.S. has ILL networks that interface with networks in other states and regions. Usually these networks are hierarchical, so a library must first request an item from the next highest entity—often a regional or state library system. Special libraries and university libraries have their own networks and consortia. Medical and hospital libraries, for instance, request ILLs through the National Networks of Libraries of Medicine system. If you are unsure how the ILL system in your area or for your type of library works, contact your state library agency or regional library system for more information. Never tell a library user that you are unable to request materials from other libraries; this is one of the basic services that libraries provide.

Sometimes a customer doesn't want to wait for an ILL request and is willing to travel to a nearby library for the item. Search the online catalogs of nearby libraries or search OCLC's WorldCat (www.worldcat.org) to see if an item is owned by a library close to you. Libraries don't usually have agreements to share materials directly with each other, and sometimes this is difficult for users to understand. If you find that you frequently request ILLs for materials from a neighboring library, it might be worthwhile to investigate a reciprocal agreement. Remember, the idea is to get users the information they need.

Readers' Advisory

All kinds of libraries provide readers' advisory services. These services facilitate matching the library customer with the materials they want, they promote the library and reading, they encourage the concept of the library as a community center, and they can increase circulation.

Readers' advisory involves helping library customers find books, ebooks, stories, movies, music, journal articles, or any other information in the library's collection in any format that they might enjoy reading, listening to, or watching. Librarians provide readers' advisory service by making suggestions or recommending library materials to customers based on their knowledge of the customers' interests and the content of the library's collection—as opposed to reference service, which is the art of interpreting and answering specific informational questions. Librarians often provide this service without thinking about it as readers' advisory; however, providing good readers' advisory can be a challenge. No librarian can know enough about the collection and library customers to make good recommendations to everyone, all the time. The longer you work in a particular library, and the more familiar you become with its customers and their reading preferences, the better you will be at readers' advisory. Here are some things you can do to assist library customers in making appropriate choices:

- Make learning the collection—in all formats—a top priority.

- Read books, listen to CDs, read tables of contents, watch movies, and subscribe to alert services.

- Monitor bestseller lists, read reviews, and know popular reading club selections.

- Listen to author interviews and book review podcasts. For example, NPR's *Book Tour* (www.npr.org/templates/

story/story.php?storyId=10448909) presents leading contemporary authors reading from and discussing their work, and the *New York Times Book Review* podcasts (www.nytimes.com/2006/10/08/books/books-podcast-archive.html?ref=books) present recorded book reviews.

- Familiarize yourself with books and databases that help you provide readers' advisory, for example, Nancy Pearl's books, *Book Lust*, *More Book Lust*, and *Book Crush*, the *Read On* and *Genreflecting* series' from Libraries Unlimited, and NoveList, a fiction database from EBSCO.

It can be advantageous and efficient for library staff to work together to provide readers' advisory services. Share the information you have learned about providing readers' advisory in your library with your co-workers. Here are some ways to work together:

- Keep reading logs with short notes about the books you have read and feedback from library users about books they have read. This provides other staff members with valuable information about materials that may be new to them.

- Ask library customers to make comments about what they are currently reading or DVDs they recently viewed. Keep index cards for this purpose at the circulation desk, or collect comments on the library's blog.

- Use the library's website to recommend books.

- Create lists of materials similar to current bestsellers.

- Discuss new materials and the kinds of readers who might enjoy them at staff meetings.

Children's Programs

Children's programs usually focus on introducing children to reading, learning, and information. Just as with other library services, children's programs are meant to meet the information needs of the children you serve. Refer to the goals in your library's plan that can be met through children's programs and stay focused on what you are trying to accomplish.

The basic (and most traditional) form of library programming for children is story time. At one time, children's librarians believed that they were building reading and literacy skills by providing story hours. However, in recent years, research on emergent literacy and reading readiness has shown that the literacy value of a group story time is relatively small: The real value of library story hours lies in modeling for parents and caregivers how to use books with young children.[2]

More and more public libraries now offer family literacy programs as a way to build literacy skills. There are many programs available, including Every Child Ready to Read @ Your Library (www.ala.org/ala/alsc/ecrr/ecrrhomepage.cfm), Family Place Libraries (www.familyplacelibraries.org), and Prime Time Family Reading Time (www.leh.org/html/primetime.html). Each library needs to assess the needs of the people they serve, individual programs, and the library's resources when evaluating literacy programs; these vary widely. Successful literacy programs are usually implemented in collaboration or partnership with schools, agencies serving children, or other community organizations.

Public libraries also typically offer Summer Reading Programs. These usually involve a contest where prizes are awarded to those reading the most books, and certificates are given to all participants. Many libraries reward frequency of library visits or number of hours read as other measures of success. Some state libraries, consortia, and regional library systems have taken the lead in Summer Reading Programs by creating themes, producing materials, and providing promotional and marketing support for member libraries. For instance, the Collaborative Summer Library Program (CSLP; www.cslpreads.org) is a consortium of states working together to provide high-quality summer reading program materials at the lowest possible cost for participating libraries. Efforts like this make it feasible for smaller libraries to offer quality Summer Reading Programs.

Other library programs for children, including craft programs, puppet shows, animal displays and demonstrations, musical performers, and other entertainment, are designed to attract children to the library, highlight library materials, promote people and organizations in the community, and promote literacy.

There are many ideas for possible children's programs, and numerous local resources for providing them. Don't get stuck presenting the same programs and presenters, year in and year out. Ask community members to share their hobbies or experiences; education programs at local museums routinely make community presentations; local police and fire departments can show-and-tell on a number of topics; inquire at small businesses and professional offices like veterinarians, doctors, bakeries, karate instructors, newspaper reporters, artists, musicians, authors, and TV personalities for new ideas.

Young Adult Services

A Benton Foundation report found that teens are "the least enthusiastic of any age group about the importance of libraries in a digital future."[3] Thriving libraries, however, see teens as an opportunity. Teens want to create their own identity, explore being adults, and "hang out" while they build relationships and connect with each other. Young adults yearn for a space of their own that is comfortable and safe from adult invasion. Libraries that have been successful in serving teens have created separate spaces in the library for them, and have involved them in designing and creating these spaces.

Teens want change and they want to be involved. Some ways teens may want to get involved in the library include:

- Assisting library customers in using computers
- Creating library web pages, MySpace pages, and YouTube videos
- Helping with children's programs
- Reading to children
- Representing the library in the community
- Selecting library materials for peers
- Tutoring

Reaching young adults where they are on the Internet is essential. Some libraries have extensive web presences for teens where young adult programs and services are listed, such as homework help links, links to popular databases used by teens, and book reviews by their peers.

Some ideas for young adult programs include:

- Dance Dance Revolution competition
- Debates
- Fantasy book club
- Guitar Hero tournament
- Japanese anime and manga club
- Magic club
- Open mic night
- Poetry club

- PS2 (Playstation 2) events

- Short film festival

- Stock market club

- Teen fashion show

- YouTube video contest

Lita Slaggle,
Library Director,
Baylor County (TX) Free Library

It was not my intention to become a librarian when the job first opened up. I had just quit a job at the local weekly newspaper (where I worked for more than 21 years), when the county judge asked me if I would be interested in serving the county as librarian. I've always enjoyed working with children, having taught Sunday school for more than a decade, and considered myself a "people person"—so I decided to give it a try. My surprise was just how much a rural librarian has to contend with on a daily basis when she is the only employee.

Seymour is a farming and ranching community with families going back several generations. There is no industry, and many of those who leave return to settle after retirement or to care for aging parents, giving us a sort of "bedroom community" feel.

The part I love the most about being a librarian is the interaction I have with people daily. Being the only hand around each and every day, I get to personally greet and assist almost every patron that enters our library. I try to remember what most patrons like to read, and I stock those authors or subjects. When a patron finds a book that they have been searching for or I can give them a call letting them know that a title has come in, it just makes me happy.

Balancing a shoestring budget is probably the most challenging aspect of any rural library. With a smaller population
than we've had in the past and budget cuts on the county
level, the first place to suffer is the library or other so-called
luxury items. It is hard for people to perceive a library that is
many things to many people—an information center, computer work center, audio and video accessibility, games and
activities for children, free computer classes—with most
services offered free of charge. The library is one of the few
institutions that has actually changed with the times. Books
have been around for centuries and will continue to be a
source of information in the future.

When I first came to the library, there was a small box of
about 10 VHS tapes in the store room. They were still
wrapped in cellophane and were of interest to young children—no adult titles to be found, other than free health
videos from the health department. We began to fill the need
of entertainment for the community by spending a couple
hundred dollars on videos and DVDs each year to develop a
collection. The second summer of my tenure, we launched a
"Friday Night at the Movies" campaign to bring families
together the way we used to in the 1950s and 1960s: at the
drive-in movies. I secured a multimedia projector that had
been sitting in the Chamber of Commerce office collecting
dust for two years, threw a king-sized sheet up on the outside
of the library wall—and the Red Neck Drive-In was born. The
movies begin each Friday night in June and July at dusk with
concessions of soda pop, popcorn, and candy. Families bring
their blankets, lawn chairs, or whatever else is comfortable to
sit on and we camp out on the north lawn of the courthouse
to watch a movie and enjoy family time. The month of June is
geared toward our Summer Reading Program theme and the

July movies are usually something family-oriented or ani-
mated that everyone can enjoy. We never charge for the
movies, as we have a performing license, and the money raised
from concessions goes right back into movies for the library.

Most of the people that you work with in the library profession are great. They love people, they love to read, and they
believe passionately in the right to read for everyone. This is
a luxury not afforded in many areas of the world.

Adult Programs

Unfortunately, some librarians fail to provide programs for the
adults in their communities. They believe adults are too busy, are
not interested, or can fend for themselves. These librarians are so
focused on programs for children, teens, and young adults that
they forget about the importance of providing services to this segment of their population.

To provide effective adult programming, you must first know
the adults in your community. Look at your community profile and
your library plan. What is the demographic makeup of the adult
population in your community, and what are their information
needs? What are your library's goals for serving adults, and how
can programming help you to meet those goals? Don't make
assumptions. Demographics may have changed in recent years.
Does your community contain adults who have immigrated from
other countries, adults with disabilities, adults looking for jobs,
retired adults, adults trying to connect with other community
members, and/or adults who want to join a book group or learn a
new activity? Some common adult programming ideas include:

- Book discussion groups

- Classes on how to find health information

- Classes on the databases the library offers and how to use them from home

- Computer skills for people with disabilities

- Computer training in basic skills such as word processing, email, and spreadsheets

- English as a second language

- Exhibits and displays

- Knitting groups

- Local author talks

Services for the Underserved

The underserved can be defined as any segment of your population that has traditionally been neglected. In general terms, when librarians refer to the underserved, they may mean groups like people with disabilities, minority ethnic groups, senior citizens, poor people, gay and lesbian teens, or people who speak a language other than English.

If you have a community profile, you understand the demographics of the population you serve. If you have performed a community information needs assessment, you already have some of the information you need to serve these people. Census data will not reveal information about all the underserved people in your community, so you must be open and receptive to learning about them. If your needs assessment doesn't address their information needs, this is the time to find out.

There is no one formula or answer on how to serve the underserved because every community is different. The key is to be aware of their existence, to understand their information needs, to serve them as a segment of your population—and never to ignore their needs.

Jessica Fenster-Sparber,
Library Coordinator,
Passages Academy, Bronx, New York

Like others creating libraries inside detention facilities, I did not imagine that I would choose to spend my days making books available to people who otherwise didn't have them. In fact, I did not know what I wanted to do when I graduated from college. I enrolled in The New School's Masters in Teaching program and accepted a job teaching students who had been left back in the eighth grade. The first year I taught creative writing, science, and social studies in a little unheated basement in Harlem. I did not understand why students often didn't come to school, sometimes for long stretches of time—weeks, and even months, at times. I mentioned this to a veteran social worker and she laughed, saying, "Don't you know 60 percent of these kids have parole officers?"

The next year, as a literacy teacher, I learned that most of the students had great difficulty reading or proclaimed an intense dislike for it. I came to understand that the particular books made available to struggling readers will make a huge difference in their interest in reading. I wrote a successful grant proposal to form a library cooperative with the students. The program closed, and when the principal of Passages Academy invited me to teach literacy and offered to house the library at Bridges, a juvenile detention center in the Bronx, I accepted, not knowing what to expect.

The students I work with include young men and women ranging in ages from eleven to seventeen who come from every ethnic and language background in New York and are overwhelmingly poor. So many students let me know that they appreciated the library's arrival. Four years later, the library has moved to the largest room on the school floor. It holds several thousand volumes, the majority of which have been requested by the students themselves. The most enjoyable part of my job is talking with students and helping them find something that turns them on to reading.

My teacher-colleagues support the library and participate in interdisciplinary activities to promote the library and a love of reading. The principal who hired me is an extraordinary supporter of the library. Daily morning meetings are held in the library as are other events and facility meetings. Our school, which has seven other sites, is committed to developing a high-quality school media center program, and we are currently building other library spaces.

I have been fortunate to have both a predecessor and a nonprofit partner in this work. The Prisoners' Reading Encouragement Project (PREP) has supported and sustained the work through their partnership with Literacy for Incarcerated Teens (LIT) and the generous donors who fund them. During the last four years our library has received many visits from dynamic and engaging New York Public Library Young Adult librarians. I have grown such an appreciation for these librarians as professionals, youth advocates, educators, and humanitarians that I have decided to join their credentialed ranks. I am now pursing an MLS at Queens College, City University of New York.

Services for People with Disabilities

People with disabilities are a large and often neglected segment of the population who are often challenged and discriminated against. Serving people with disabilities is of utmost importance for libraries, and librarians have a legal and moral obligation to see that library services and programs are accessible to people with disabilities. Libraries can play an important role in the lives of people with disabilities by providing access to information that can make a difference in their lives.

Librarians must ensure that people with disabilities have equal access to library resources by making accommodations including extending loan periods, waiving late fees, providing books by mail, providing volunteer readers, providing materials in alternative formats, or making assistive technology or computer assistance available.

Outreach

Outreach services are appropriate for reaching people you serve who are not able to come to the library. Some examples of outreach services include:

- Bookmobile service
- Books by mail
- Homebound services
- Nursing home services
- Services for children in daycare centers
- Talking books

Endnotes

1. William A. Katz, *Introduction to Reference Work*. 8th ed., Vol. 1. (New York: McGraw-Hill, 2002), 10.
2. Noreen Bernstein, "Youth Services," in *Running a Small Library*, ed. John Moorman (New York: Neal-Schuman, 2006), 226.
3. Marylaine Block, *The Thriving Library* (Medford, NJ: Information Today, Inc., 2007), 13.

Chapter 11

Library Policies

Having some basic library policies in place will help to make your library run smoothly. Policies give you answers when there are disagreements or misunderstandings, answering questions and averting potential crises. A policy states the way the library wants things done, reflects the library's priorities, and supports the library in accomplishing its goals

Policies must apply to your particular community and to your particular library. They are enforceable only if they are in writing and formally adopted by a library board or other organizational authority overseeing the library. Everyone working in the library should know what the policies are, where to find them, and how to enforce them. Library policies are not secrets; they are for everyone to see. Library staff should be involved in developing library policies whenever possible and need to feel free to discuss and clarify policies with the library director. When a director claims that there is no policy or avoids discussing policy, trouble lies ahead.

Purpose of Library Policies

The purpose of library policies is to:

- Make the library run more smoothly and minimize chaos
- Provide a way for the library director and staff to accomplish library goals
- Ensure that library staff have the tools they need to do their jobs effectively

- Ensure that library customers know what to expect and are treated equally

- Provide documentation in the case of legal action

The Four Tests

Library policies provide a framework for library operation and the delivery of services and programs. Apply the four tests for legality, reasonableness, nondiscrimination, and measurability to make policies viable, clear, and enforceable:[1]

1. Legality – Does the policy conform to current law? State and federal laws prevail over library policy. For example, library policy cannot conflict with the Americans with Disabilities Act (ADA), Children's Internet Protection Act (CIPA), or the USA PATRIOT Act.

2. Reasonableness – Policies can be challenged if they are unreasonable. For instance, overdue fines of $20 a day, or involving a collection agency when books are one week late, could be seen as unreasonable consequences.

3. Nondiscrimination – Policies must be fair to all customers. For instance, circulation policies must be the same for everyone. Staff, board members, and volunteers should not get special treatment, and there should not be a separate policy for homeless people.

4. Measurability – Make policies quantifiable so they are enforceable. For instance, the number of DVDs a customer is allowed to borrow at one time, loan periods for different media, and the number of times a customer is warned about inappropriate behavior before a staff member calls security should be specified.

Fair and Equitable Service

It is important that every member of the community you serve knows the services and programs provided by the library are fair and equitable. Fair and equitable library service is the natural result when all library staff members, including the director, know about, honor, have access to, understand, know how to enforce, and consistently abide by the library's policies. Don't keep library policies in a binder collecting dust in the director's office or under the circulation desk. Discuss them with new employees and volunteers. Make sure everyone knows what they are. Regularly review policies. Make sure staff members have the same interpretation of policy. Involve staff in developing policy. All of these factors are necessary for equity and fairness in the library—it is that simple.

When community members realize that the library does not treat people equitably and fairly, they may get frustrated, find another library, fail to support the library, or even file a lawsuit.

What Is the Big Deal About Policies?

Here are some scenarios that illustrate possible consequences of ineffective or nonexistent library policies. Don't let these happen in your library.

Scenario 1

Even though the library has a Meeting Room Policy that appears to provide fair and equal use of library meeting rooms for community members, meeting room requests and conditions of use are actually decided by the director, based on whether the person requesting the room is a friend of hers or an influential community member. This is a highly personal, subjective, and variable process known only to the director.

Consequences: This library does not provide equitable service because decisions about meeting room use are based on the director's personal preferences. Special favors granted to friends for meeting in the library are not extended equally to the community at large. In a public library, this could be grounds for a lawsuit.

Scenario 2

A man is looking at pornography on a public computer in the library. A staff member notices this and asks him to stop the behavior. This is not the first time this man has been warned about this behavior, and the staff member is not sure what the library's Computer Use Policy says about what to do next. The staff member cannot locate the policy, so she asks the director what the library's policy says she is supposed to do if he refuses to stop. The director responds that the library has no Computer Use Policy and asks the staff member what she thinks is the "right thing" to do.

Consequences: It is impossible to provide fair and equitable treatment in a library with no Computer Use Policy. If a staff member treats the customer the way she "thinks she should" treat him, this library could be in legal hot water.

Scenario 3

The handcrafted shelves holding the art books in your library have collapsed because the weight of the books was just too much for them. Books that were jammed on the shelves every which way tumbled into a massive pile as one shelf after another fell, narrowly missing a woman and her child. Your library has a generic Collection Development Policy, but no Weeding Policy, and your attempts to deselect old and worn out materials from the overcrowded shelves are routinely vetoed by the director based on her personal feelings. Weeding is done in crisis mode, often when shelves collapse.

Consequences: This is dangerous and someone is going to get hurt. The information needs of the community are not being met because the collection is not being developed with a purpose. Broken shelves will need to be replaced.

Scenario 4

A library director speaks freely and without restraint in her public library workplace about her political beliefs, from the national to the local level. She heavily favored one mayoral candidate over another in the last election and made her views known by blurting them all over the library. Some people were offended and spoke out. There is either no Political Activity Policy in this library, or it is not being observed.

Consequences: This creates a one-sided political atmosphere in the library, encouraging those with similar views to speak out against one candidate and making it uncomfortable for those with differing viewpoints. This library may be in violation of state law and this practice works against the basic principles of public libraries.

How Does This Happen?

No library intends to provide unfair and inequitable treatment, discriminate, be unreasonable, cause people physical harm, or break laws. Here are several reasons why libraries might find themselves with ineffective or nonexistent policies:

1. Library policies were not developed for your specific library and community.

2. Library staff members were not involved in developing policy.

3. Library policies are not communicated to staff.

4. Library staff members are not empowered to enforce policies.

5. It is common for library staff to interpret policy based on their personal feelings.

6. Library policies are created following an incident as a reaction to it. They focus on a particular situation that is unlikely to ever happen again.

Policies Created as a Requirement

When a library creates policies only as required by some higher authority, the results are likely to be ineffective. Many librarians use sample policies or templates provided by state libraries or library systems as their own library's policies. It seems so easy to use a ready-made policy, substituting your library's name in all the right places. What librarians who do this fail to realize is that these sample policies and templates are intended to provide a starting point for discussion, or to serve as an outline for developing library-specific policies. Unfortunately, the practice of copying samples and templates has only proliferated with their easy availability on the Internet.

A generic template cannot support your library in accomplishing its unique goals and address the information needs of your particular community. Sample policies are so generic that they have nothing to do with any specific library or community. There is no ownership. There is no thought given to how the policies relate to a library's priorities, plan, or goals and how the policies will support staff in accomplishing the work of the library. These "empty" policies are often meaningless to staff: No one knows what they are, no one enforces them, and they change constantly. These types of policies just don't serve any purpose, and they can be downright dangerous—because they give the illusion that the library has policies, when it doesn't. Here are some warning signs to watch out for:

- Staff members don't know what the library's policies are.

- Staff members have different understandings of what the policies say.

- Staff members do not consistently follow or enforce library policies.

- The library director regularly makes exceptions to library policies for her friends or influential people.

- There are so many exceptions to policy that everyone forgets what the policy says.

- The library director often vetoes staff members when they attempt to enforce library policy.

- Customers go straight to the director for special treatment.

- Customers are treated differently and inequitably.

- Policies change with the wind.

- Staff members aren't informed when policies change.

- Staff members "make up" policy, because policies are irrelevant.

- Staff members are encouraged to do what they think is "right" in matters of policy.

- Volunteers in frontline positions don't know what library policies are, where they can be found, or how to enforce them.

- The library is chaotic.

Policies Every Library Needs

Many states require that public libraries meet minimum policy requirements to qualify as a public library for funding purposes.

Every library must follow the requirements of its local or state government, organization, institution, or school system; however, here are some basic policies every library needs (find some sample policies in Appendix A):

- Personnel
- Circulation
  - Fines and fees
  - Borrowing and lending
  - Access to library records
- Interlibrary loan
- Collection development
  - Selection
  - Weeding
  - Gifts and donations
  - Reconsideration of library material
- Computer use/Internet access
- Behavior
  - Unattended children
  - Cell phone use
- Confidentiality
- Bulletin boards and posting
- Distribution/display of community information materials
- Political activity
- Emergencies
- Exhibits and displays
- Intellectual access
- Meeting room use

- Public use of library equipment
- Community participation
- Volunteers
- Board responsibilities

Tips to Get You Started

To get started selecting and creating policies:

1. Research the policies of similar libraries. Read them and think about what in them applies to your library and what doesn't. Don't copy them.

2. Carefully consider and discuss with staff members what your policies need to say to support you in accomplishing the work of *your* library.

3. Involve staff.

4. Incorporate the foundational ideas of ALA statements such as the Library Bill of Rights, the Freedom to Read, and the Freedom to View Statements (see Appendix C).

5. Investigate ALA's guidelines and positions on issues like Internet filtering, challenged materials, and intellectual freedom.

6. Keep legislation like CIPA and your state statutes in mind when writing library policy. Your policies must comply with federal and state laws.

7. Use your state library's resources (web pages, tutorials, training, consultants, and other resources) to facilitate writing policies.

8. Imagine all possible scenarios that might transpire. The idea is to be prepared in advance.

How to Write a Library Policy

Writing policy is not an easy task, and there are no shortcuts, so it's unsurprising that librarians are tempted to borrow policies from other libraries or use sample policies verbatim. Policies created in a vacuum without careful thought and discussion about how they relate to your library, or those unrelated to your library's goals and your community's information needs, do not work; they are merely smoke and mirrors.

In her book *Creating Policies for Results,* Sandra Nelson says: "Before you can decide whether or not your current policies are effective and comprehensive, you must know what you want to accomplish."[2] If your library does not have a current plan, you don't have to go through the entire planning process before developing policies—but it certainly would help. At the very least, you must determine your library's goals as a starting point (see Chapter 5).

The Policy Development Templates in *Creating Policies for Results* pose a series of questions that will help you develop policies for your library. There is no cutting and pasting here. Careful thought, consideration, and discussion are required to answer the questions and ultimately develop each and every policy; be sure to involve all staff in this process. Here are some similar sample questions to start you thinking:

Questions to Ask When Writing a Customer Service Policy

1. Does a staff member's classification determine the level of customer service they are expected to provide?

2. What types of customer service are provided by each classification?

3. Is there a dress code that staff members are expected to observe?

4. Does the dress code vary based on the classification or duties of the staff member?

5. May staff have food or drink at the public service desks?

6. Under what circumstances, if any, may staff make or receive personal phone calls when they are scheduled on the public service desks?

7. Who is responsible for answering the telephone? How do they address callers? Where do they transfer calls?

8. How should staff balance requests for service from customers who are in the library with those who are calling by phone?

Questions to Ask When Writing a Reference Policy

1. How does the library define reference service?

2. Who is responsible for providing reference service?

3. How are customers made aware of the availability of reference service in the library?

4. Under what circumstances, if any, is a question referred to another library staff member for resolution?

5. Under what circumstances, if any, is a question referred to another library?

6. How do staff members determine to which library to refer a reference question?

7. How is a customer's confidentiality protected during a reference service transaction?

8. How are reference questions handled when there is no reference librarian on duty?

As you can see, asking questions can be a good way to write policies that are specific and meaningful to your library and your community. If you are true to this process, you will end up with useful policies.

Policy Changes

Policies are not set in stone. They can be changed if circumstances change or you find the current policy is not working. Changes in information technology, your community, your resources, and library staff make writing library policies a neverending exercise. Regularly review library policies, revise old policies, and write new ones. When the priorities of your library change, in many cases policies have to be changed to support the library in accomplishing its new goals.

Exercise 11.1

A customer complains to a librarian about another person's inappropriate behavior in the library. What should she do?

_____ Go to her office and rifle through the files, searching for a behavior policy.

_____ Ask the director how to handle it.

_____ Quickly handle the situation based on the library's Appropriate Behavior Policy.

_____ Make something up based on what "feels right" to her.

_____ Call the police.

_____ Tell the person to get over it.

Endnotes

1. Ellen Richardson, "Four Tests for a Legally-Enforceable Library Policy," State of Michigan, www.michigan.gov/hal/0,1607,7-160-17451_18668_18689-54454—,00.html
2. Sandra S. Nelson and June Garcia, *Creating Policies for Results: From Chaos to Clarity* (Chicago: American Library Association, 2003), xv.

Chapter 12

Library Management Essentials

As a library director or manager, you are responsible for over-seeing the efficient and effective day-to-day operation of the library, providing leadership and supervision, and ensuring that the library stays true to its mission, vision, and strategic plan. As a supervisor or department head, you are responsible for the smooth operation of your unit, supervising department employ-ees, and ensuring that your section executes the activities that contribute to the library's mission, vision, and plan.

There is no way to avoid leading when you hold a management position. If you don't want to lead, if you don't think you are up to it, or if you are just not interested in that level of work, you are obligated to stay out of management. There are plenty of people who want management jobs and who have the capability and tal-ent to lead. Sometimes people (not just librarians) get caught up in "climbing the career ladder." Before they know it, they are in a management position—because it seemed like the next thing to do. You may be flattered or honored if you are offered a director position, but don't accept the job without careful consideration. Not everyone is cut out to lead, supervise, direct, or manage, and that's okay. Some librarians can contribute more without the extra pressure and responsibilities that management positions bring. Librarianship is a big profession, with room for librarians at all levels.

If you are a real leader, librarianship welcomes you—especially at this time of immense change. We need strong leaders who can navigate change with ease and help ensure the survival of our libraries and our profession.

What a Library Manager Does

As a library director or manager you must:

- Be fair and unbiased
- Be visible and available
- Communicate clearly and directly
- Conduct yourself in a professional manner
- Create policies
- Delegate responsibilities
- Embrace the talents of your staff
- Follow proper procedures
- Foster partnerships within the community and with other libraries
- Have a clear vision for the library
- Hire, fire, and evaluate staff
- Interact well with diverse people
- Know your customers' information needs
- Lead library staff, volunteers, board members, and Friends of the Library into the future
- Listen
- Maintain relationships on behalf of the library
- Make decisions
- Manage the budget

- Manage time well

- Mentor, coach, motivate, and support staff

- Navigate change

- Organize workflow

- Provide staff with the resources they need to do their jobs

- Pursue funding opportunities to supplement current funding

- Represent the library in the organization and among your peers

- Respect and support staff

- Run effective and efficient meetings

- Solve problems

- Spearhead the creation of a library plan and use it as a guide

- Take initiative

As a manager, you are in a different league. You must rise above the temptation to do favors for your friends and powerful community members. You must put your ego aside and act professionally. This can be difficult if you become director in a library where you were previously a staff member. Effective managers cannot belong to cliques or participate in office gossip; as a leader, it is your charge to bring all sides together to work toward common goals. You must be fair and open to all opinions, weighing positions carefully and objectively before making a decision based on what is best for the library. You cannot act based on hearsay. You must be confident in your decisions and carry through. You may need to explain your reasoning to those with opposing viewpoints. You will need backbone and conviction, and you will have to face problems head-on and immediately, as they happen. You must be direct and act with resolve. To lead effectively, you must stay focused on the library's vision and be grounded in its mission; your daily work will be a product of the library's strategic plan. These tools will equip you to lead, and without them you will be lost.

As the leader, you set the example. Your demeanor sets the tone for the library. What they say about the "trickle down" effect is true. Use your time at work to perform duties that contribute to accomplishing the goals of the library. (There is so much to do in managing a library that you should not find this difficult!) In order to hold other people accountable, you must first hold yourself accountable.

Patti Newell, Assistant Director, Sullivan Free Library, Chittenango, New York

In the beginning, almost 17 years ago, I was a big library user and a friend of the woman who was then the director of our local library. When the decision was made to automate the library, our collection had to be added to the database of our regional library system. Since I had experience working with databases in other jobs, I interviewed for the position and was hired to do this for our library. It took me almost a year working part time to inventory the almost 50,000 items in our collection. During that time, the director and the board members had a chance to see what kind of work I did. When the library needed another part-time aide, I was offered the job—in part, because I could train the staff in the use of the "new" online database.

Seven years later, the library hired a new director, and, when the more senior aide left, the director offered me the Senior Aide position full time. Because of my willingness to take on new projects (such as designing our library's website and becoming a notary public), my dogged tenaciousness when hunting down the answers to reference questions (what do you call the stringy part inside a banana peel?*), and my head for figures, the director asked me to take on more responsibilities as library manager for our two buildings, handling much of the financial and statistical data for the organization.

Eighteen months ago, because of library growth and a new building project, it became apparent that the library needed someone who could make executive decisions when the director was not available. The board offered me the position of Assistant Director because I had proven myself over the years—despite lacking an MLS.

I am currently finishing my BA and expect to start on my MLS next year. When I finish, I will be a "paper-trained" librarian and able to do ... almost exactly what I am doing now. I am pursuing my MLS more as matter of self-satisfaction than because of any career advantage it will give me. I expect I will be with the library where I currently work until I retire.

*I tracked down and emailed a banana grower who consulted a book he referred to as the banana growers "bible" (I do not believe that was the title of the book he referred to); he told me the stringy part of a banana peel is called the "rag."

Personnel

Handling personnel matters is often the most difficult and time-consuming part of a library manger's job. If the library is part of a larger organization such as a municipality, school district, corporation, or association, you must adhere to the personnel policies of the larger organization. In such cases, your personnel or human resources department will assist you with personnel policies and procedures.

Personnel is one area where a manager cannot avoid dealing with issues in the hopes they will go away. In libraries where directors are unable to effectively handle personnel matters, the staff turnover rate is staggering. This turnover rate can be costly in many ways, including lowered staff morale, the time lost in repeatedly training new staff, damaged relationships, and wasted talent.

Hiring Staff

When hiring staff, you must:

- Decide what it is you need—*before* you hire someone. What has to be done? What skills and knowledge are necessary to do the job? Is there an educational requirement for doing what needs to be done? If you post a generic job description, you will not get what you need.

- Ask questions. Using a standard set of questions for every person being interviewed will give you a sense for individual approaches on a similar topic and provide a way to measure applicants' responses against each other. Find out about the applicants during the interview. Remember why you are interviewing. You are attempting to identify the right person for a particular job. Listen. Don't dominate the conversation.

- Contact references. You cannot always tell all there is to know about a person from the interview. It is sometimes very revealing to talk to references.

- Know what days and hours you need the new employee to work. This will usually be the hours that there is no coverage or when there are programs you need them to oversee. Be clear about this from the start. Make sure candidates know they will need to work odd hours or evenings to provide coverage, if necessary, rather than whatever hours may be convenient for them.

- Advocate for librarianship by avoiding the practice of hiring part-time or temporary hourly librarians to avoid paying for benefits like health insurance. You may be saving money, but the low value you place on our profession is damaging.

- Provide thorough and complete new employee training, overseen by a manager. Explain policies and procedures, job expectations, performance evaluation details, library tours, available resources, and databases. Don't delegate this task to a volunteer. It is helpful to have a standardized checklist of all topics to be covered, as this could take more than one session.

Respecting and Supporting Staff

There are many ways to respect and support staff members. Here are a few:

- Designate work areas for staff. Some very small libraries are not able to provide individual workspaces for every staff member; however, an employee must have a place to work. If you are short on space, be creative. Are there tables in public areas where an employee could work? Perhaps he or she could provide reference or another public service as part of their job while working at one of these tables. A staff member needs a place to hang a coat or store a purse to feel respected, welcomed, and connected in the library. When work areas are all reserved for volunteers, you are communicating to staff that they are not as valuable as volunteers. Is this true? Everyone needs to be respected, employees and volunteers alike. Without a place to work, employees will find it difficult to focus, they will be less productive, they will have no sense of belonging, and they will not feel like valued team members.

- Respect employees' work. Refrain from handling the work of employees or interfering with their work. Have enough confidence in them to know that they are doing a good job. If you are concerned about a staff member's perform-ance, talk to the employee about it. Removing items from staff members' desks or doing their work for them when they are absent is not the solution to poor work perform-ance. If you are doing their work because you have fin-ished your own, think again. The work of a library manager is never done.

- Respect the workspaces of staff. Managers are more likely to have offices or separate and larger work areas than the rest of the library staff. If you suddenly need to use a computer, go to your office and use your own computer. No computer emergency requires you to take over a staff member's work area and computer without asking. Employees have the right to a certain degree of personal space at work, and managers need to be cognizant of this.

- Support staff in pursuing continuing education opportu-nities that will help them in their jobs. Manage your resources so that all staff members have an equal oppor-tunity to take classes, workshops, and training. Do not use your entire continuing education budget to send one employee through a degree program, leaving no funds to support continuing education for other staff members.

- Celebrate success. Take the time to congratulate your staff on a job well done. When a project is a success, rec-ognize them for their hard work with a staff breakfast, afternoon tea, or announcement at a public event. It is easy to forget to do this when you are working so hard on a daily basis. Instituting employee of the month programs and recognizing outstanding job performance with reserved parking spaces are other ways to honor and support staff members.

- Provide the resources employees need to do their jobs. This includes equipment, supplies, computers, books, training, and personnel. Resources also include a work area, a computer, software, passwords, contact information, funding, or information about the funds available to them.

Outlining Job Duties and Setting Expectations for Staff

Make sure that employees have clear job duties that they can accomplish. The generic position descriptions used for posting and hiring are not usually specific enough to guide individuals in clarifying their daily jobs. Use the list of job duties you compiled prior to hiring and tailor them to the employee's work style, talents, interests, and abilities.

Identify individual strengths and needs. Is the person goal-oriented? Does the staff member like to work on projects? Is the employee motivated by learning new skills? Many jobs in the library have enough latitude that they can be customized for individuals. Find out an employee's special talents and what he or she is best at doing, likes doing the most, or wants to learn how to do. A new hire is usually looking for new challenges and ways to be productive, and is eager to reach new goals. As a manager, see this as an opportunity for your library. Build these qualities into the job duties. Some people are motivated by feeling a sense of belonging while others are motivated by working independently; each person will require a different approach.

Help people grow in their jobs. Most people want to learn and welcome a challenge. Be open to their new ideas and approaches. Encourage them to address library priorities in innovative ways. Assign staff members to appropriate teams or work groups and develop new talent for the jobs you need done. Whatever you decide, make sure you and the employee have a common understanding about assigned duties, your expectations, and how his or her performance will be measured.

Evaluating Staff

Managers measure the performance of employees and their progress based on established job duties and expectations. This is an ongoing activity, not something that happens only once a year in an annual review. Managers make time for updates and feedback throughout the year and coach employees who are not performing up-to-speed. Do employees understand your expectations? What criteria are you using to evaluate employees? Do employees know how they will be evaluated?

Each employee should have an individualized evaluation form customized to their particular job. (If you are required to use a standardized evaluation form by your institution or organization, you can usually customize at least one section.) Forms must address the specific job duties that you and the employee both understand to be his or her responsibilities. The content of evaluation forms and how you are measuring performance should not be a surprise to employees at the yearly performance appraisal—don't leave them to guess what they are supposed to be doing or to define job duties on their own. Your job as a manager is to make sure job duties and evaluation criteria are understood from the beginning.

It is sometimes helpful to ask employees to complete a self-evaluation prior to their performance appraisal. The evaluation forms you and the employees have completed can prompt discussion about accomplishments, goals reached, improvements needed, planning future goals, training or continuing education, and other job duties an employee would like to explore. After a long year of aiming for high performance, there is nothing more disappointing for an employee than to listen to a manager read off checkboxes grading appearance, promptness, or tidiness—leaving no time to discuss actual job performance, the employee's job satisfaction, or future plans.

Set aside a block of time and reserve a private meeting area for the annual performance evaluation. Open office doors, eavesdropping library customers, and constant interruptions are not conducive to productive performance evaluations. They show the employee that you are not very interested in the whole process. (There is no need to explain to other staff members why you are having a private meeting with an employee.)

Disciplining and Firing Staff

As a manager you are responsible for coaching, disciplining, or firing employees who are not performing up to expectations. This can be one of your most difficult job duties, but act immediately. Don't put off dealing with unsatisfactory performance because it's distasteful. Unsatisfactory performance is unlikely to improve by magic or on its own. In most cases, you will be operating under the personnel policies of your municipality, institution, school district, or organization, which can be very useful in providing guidance about a difficult personnel situation. Personnel policies are usually very clear, outlining exactly what to do throughout the process. Policies differ from library to library; however, here are a few pointers:

- When you are concerned about an employee's performance, talk to him or her about it right away.
- Be direct. If you are giving an employee a verbal warning, tell him or her you are giving a verbal warning and what it is about.
- Make the employee aware of the personnel policy and disciplinary process.

- Tell the employee the specific areas that need improvement.

- Supply the employee with tools to help him or her improve, such as clarification, continuing education, tools to do their job, or step-by-step instructions.

- Clarify expectations and how performance is measured.

- Establish a timeline for improvement and what is expected within a specific time period.

- Explain that if job performance is not improved, you will take further action.

- Follow up with the employee.

- Reevaluate the employee's job performance.

- Take further action if necessary.

If the employee's performance has not improved after the specified number of verbal warnings or within a specified period of time, policy may dictate that you follow up with written warnings, discipline, or firing. Always document your actions and all events associated with employee discipline and firing; you will need this documentation if the employee decides to take legal action. Documentation is a record of actual facts and events, including what was said; it does not involve unloading on paper everything that has bothered you about the employee over the past year (but that you failed to tell them!).

Use common sense, and put yourself in the employee's position. An employee has every right to know that you are dissatisfied with his or her job performance, exactly why you are dissatisfied, and how he or she can improve. Your job as a manager is to communicate this clearly and directly. Start with a verbal warning (not a casual conversation about how work is going in general). Don't issue written documentation as a first step, when an employee has no idea you are concerned with the job performance. This is unlikely to result in improved work performance—and you could end up in a legal mess.

Communication

There are many ways to communicate with staff, volunteers, board members, and Friends groups. You may need to use several communication methods to ensure that you are transmitting information effectively, because people learn and retain information in different ways. Here are some options:

- Email
- Meetings
- Memos
- Newsletters or flyers
- Podcasts
- Videocasts

Communicate in some organized and regular fashion with your staff and volunteers. Staff need information to keep the library running smoothly and to keep your organization going in a direction that accomplishes the library's work. Communication requires deliberate effort—people aren't going to read your mind or pick up what you are thinking by osmosis. People who are good communicators make it look easy, but communicating what you mean, clearly and succinctly, at the appropriate time, is not easy. You need to work at it.

Regardless of the communication method you use, be direct. Say what you mean and mean what you say. Take a moment to gather your thoughts and concentrate on what you have to say or write before you open your mouth or start typing. If you find yourself losing focus, forgetting your point, or becoming distracted, stop and take a moment to gather your thoughts.

Keeping everyone happy is not your priority—managing a functioning library is. Communicate clearly even if you are afraid you will hurt people's feelings or ruffle feathers by instituting a new policy or requiring training. Be decisive, not wishy-washy. If you are chronically unsure about what you mean, everyone and everything you manage will be chronically unsure, including the library itself. Accept that you won't be right all the time. Everyone makes mistakes, and if you make a mistake, you can fix it.

Staff Meetings

Have staff meetings on a regular basis. Staff members need a time and place to communicate and receive new information, provide updates, share new ideas, and voice concerns. Meetings provide a way for everyone to communicate; they are not director's monologues. Share the responsibility for running meetings with staff members. You can rotate this duty, or ask each person to present their own agenda items.

Expect all staff to attend staff meetings, and hold them someplace where you will not be interrupted. Make it clear to frontline staff that, unless it is an emergency, no one is to interrupt the meeting. When you create ground rules for the meeting—and respect them—you show everyone you are serious about the meeting and it is of value to you. Don't divert your attention to chat with a customer who wanders into a staff meeting, leave the room, or answer your phone to chat with family members about what's for dinner. Everyone else will lose interest and understand that the meeting is a meaningless exercise, and communication eventually stops.

Be prompt. When you are 20 minutes late for every meeting, event, or staff lunch, you disrespect everyone who made the effort to be there on time; their reward for arriving promptly is to have to wait for you. Your chronic lateness is a clear message that you do not value their time. Respect staff by respecting their time.

Have an agenda. Create a preliminary agenda of all the things you want to communicate before the meeting. Circulate it to all attendees in advance and ask if they have anything to add. Attaching estimated times for each agenda item can be helpful in moving meetings along; however, don't let these schedules stop necessary discussion. Gather related materials and make copies for attendees before the meeting. It is an unnecessary waste of time and a distraction to run out of a meeting to make copies, leaving everyone waiting.

Stick to the agenda. If you cover everything on the agenda and everyone has had a chance to communicate and participate, end the meeting. If you finish early, don't start looking for additional agenda items to fill the rest of the time. Staff have plenty to do, and they will appreciate the "time bonus" if you end the meeting early. If you forgot something, you can always put it on the next agenda or send an email about it later.

Keep regular staff meetings to one hour. If you occasionally need a two-hour meeting, try having two one-hour meetings instead. If staff meetings regularly go over an hour, maybe you need to meet every week instead of every other week, or appoint a task force to deal with a particular issue that requires more exploration. People tend to stop listening after an hour.

Listening

Active listening skills are essential for managers. When you are having a discussion, acknowledge that you are receptive to what is being said by nodding, staying focused, and keeping your mouth closed except for an occasional "yes" or "I see" to let the person talking know you are with them. Show interest by being attentive and making eye contact. Fiddling with something on the side, diverting your attention, or talking loudly over the person speaking are clear indications that you are not listening. Don't plan your response while the other person is talking. Listen carefully and wait until they are finished before you respond. Try not to make judgments before you have heard everything the speaker has to say. Be open to hearing ideas other than your own.

Barriers to Communication

There are definite barriers to communicating with your staff, customers, and others:

- Background chatter and side conversations
- Interruptions
- Cluttering important messages with too much detail
- Unfocused and pointless talk
- Inability to focus and verbalize clearly
- Wishy-washiness and indecision
- Conflicting, changing, or mixed messages
- Disrespecting others
- Saying "yes" when you mean "no"
- Inability to be direct

Governing Boards

A governing board is the entity responsible for the operation of the library. Libraries have different kinds of governing boards depending on the type of library and organizational structure. School boards govern schools through their principals, who oversee individual school libraries. Special libraries may be responsible to the board that governs the larger corporation, organization, or center they serve. This can be a hospital board of directors, a legal

Diana Lorton, Librarian,
Camino Nuevo Correctional Center,
Albuquerque, New Mexico

Author's Note: Based on my interview with Diana Lorton.

Diana Lorton loves to organize, she has an uncanny ability to see the "big picture," and she can manage diverse teams to reach their goals. She is a problem solver, and can see her way through challenges toward solutions. She is direct, she means what she says, and she is a "no-nonsense" person. A library that hires her to lead a project or reorganize a department, implement a new idea, or motivate staff to embrace change will get results.

As the librarian at the Camino Nuevo Correctional Center (CNCC) in Albuquerque, New Mexico, Diana organizes library materials, supervises inmate assistants, and is responsible for all aspects of day-to-day library operations. She was hired to establish a library in this new facility for women at various stages of being released from the correctional system. Her first task upon arriving on the job was to discard the many old and worn donations and replace them with a fresh, new collection.

Diana takes great pride in the CNCC library. She markets the library by displaying books, highlighting different sections of the collection, and making the library attractive and inviting. She has very few resources and many restrictions, yet always makes the most of what she has. She instills a feeling of ownership, pride, and respect for the library among inmates, inmate assistants, and officers, which has resulted in no lost materials—and an enthusiasm for the library that is unexpected in a prison environment.

As a former secondary school teacher with a bachelor's degree in education, Diana sought a full-time job in a library when her children were grown and headed for college. As a child, she had spent many hours in the Carnegie library in her small midwestern town, and as a mother she regularly brought her children to libraries when they were young.

Because she enjoys people and she has excellent customer service skills, Diana's first library job as a Circulation Desk Assistant in a suburb of Cleveland, Ohio, was a good match. The library was part of the Cleveland Public Library system, so she learned a wide range of circulation tasks applicable to a large library system. When she moved a short time later, she was hired as a library clerk in the Circulation Department of the Siegesmund Engineering Library at Purdue University. There, she found that she was talented at supervising students as well as her own peers. People listened to her when she said something, and she filled a real need in the library.

Diana advanced to Technical Reports/Reference Assistant in the Engineering Library, and was then promoted to Collections Access Operations Director in the Humanities, Social Sciences and Education Library at Purdue. At the time, the library was having challenges efficiently returning books to the shelves and needed someone to help solve this problem. Diana reorganized the operation and rearranged the physical workspace. She supervised a staff of eight full-time employees and 30 student workers, and, as manager of facilities, she was responsible for addressing security issues including inappropriate behaviors. After more than 10 years at Purdue, she retired and moved to New Mexico to be near her family.

Diana enjoys the library environment and her fellow librarians, their knowledge, and their willingness to teach and share information with others. She enjoys learning and she is confident that she has an important contribution to make to our field.

firm's partnership, or a corporation's board of directors, for instance. A board of trustees may have full or partial governing authority over a public library. Academic libraries report to an administrator who is responsible to the board of the institution.

A governing board is responsible for:

- The library's physical and financial well-being
- Determining the budget
- Facility issues, such as roof leaks, building repairs, and air-conditioning installation
- Hiring the director
- Policy decisions
- Planning and setting goals for the library with the director
- Representing the library in the community

Effective board members understand the vision, mission, and library plan and have a working understanding of library law and policy. They comprehend the needs of the community and represent different segments of it. They have working relationships with other people who are involved in the community, school, organization, or institution, and they attend board meetings. They do the work necessary to ensure an effective board, and they have an interest in the success of the library.

Any successful library requires a working partnership between the director and the board. Trust is the key to any board-director relationship. Each must trust that the other is working within acceptable boundaries, that they have each other's best interests in mind, and that they can count on each other in any situation. The board must respect the director for his or her knowledge and skills and the director must respect the board for their contribution to the success of the library. The director and board must also be honest with each other. The board has to be honest with the director about its view of library operations, services, programs, and the library's role in the community. Conversely, the director must be honest with the board about his or her involvement in the community, the current state of library operations, services, and programs, the library's progress in reaching its goals, challenges in meeting the needs of the community, and the condition of the budget. It is a two-way street. The director and board both depend on each other for support, assistance, and cooperation. You need to maintain regular communication through established channels, done in a respectful manner with consideration on both sides. Both the board and the director must accept responsibility for their actions and both must constantly look at themselves to evaluate their performance and progress.

Local Government

In public libraries, the director and board together develop a working relationship with local government. It is beneficial for library board members to be acquainted with members of the local governing boards at the town or county level, and the library director needs to work to establish good relationships with the administrative heads of local government. This relationship is often more important than those with board members—especially if the board is advisory and the library director is a town department head. Good communication, respect, trust, and honesty are essential, as is a working knowledge of the local political scene and how it operates. Often the real work of government is done outside of official meetings, and the more a library director knows about how to *really* get things done, the better for the library.

Friends of the Library

Friends of the Library are nonprofit organizations that support the libraries with which they are affiliated. Minimally, Friends groups have mission statements, bylaws, and a plan, including goals and activities. Strong leaders are needed in Friends' groups to keep things on track and to accomplish goals.

If libraries had enough funding to provide all the services and programs their communities needed, there would be no Friends organizations. Because this is rarely the case, many public libraries rely on Friends to fund special programs and projects, furnish new additions or renovations, or purchase collections. Friends of the Library employ a variety of methods to raise money including book sales, used bookstores, and gift shops.

It is extremely important that there be an understanding between Friends and the library director about how funds will be spent and when they will be directed back to the library. The Friends can play an important role in helping the library accomplish its goals, and the library director must play a strong role in selecting how the Friends will support the library. The library director should prioritize the library's needs by referring to the library's strategic plan and suggesting ways that funds can be used. When they don't understand that the library's priorities are based on the strategic plan, it is not uncommon for Friends groups to spend funds on something the library doesn't need or want. Unless the director informs the Friends that this is an inappropriate use of funds—and why—much-needed funds will be wasted.

The director and the president of the Board of Trustees should be ex-officio members of the Friends. This provides a way for the Friends to gain information about library operations and the priorities stated in the library's plan. To keep a Friends group healthy, the library manager must:

- Make sure that there is constant communication

- Provide Friends groups with fundable projects and programs

- Keep them on track

- Remain an active participant

- Inform local funding sources that funding from Friends, grants, and occasional bond issues does not permit them to reduce the current level of library funding

Budgets

A library manager is responsible for funding the library's plan using available funds. An annual budget, based on anticipated revenues and expenditures, allocates specific dollar amounts for categories such as library services and programs, personnel, materials, marketing, supplies, equipment, travel, and training. Every library manager needs to have a budget and must monitor it regularly using financial reports on revenues and expenditures.

Budget processes vary widely from organization to organization. However, a library manager is often required to first submit a budget request. In your own requests, be realistic by requesting the amount the library *really* needs to accomplish its goals for the year. Since your budget is based on the library's plan, which was developed using input from the community, staff, and library board, it should not be difficult to justify your request and find support. The manager may be allocated an amount by the larger organization or municipality around which he or she must design a detailed budget.

Often, budgets are divided into two main sections: personnel and nonpersonnel. Personnel budgets usually remain constant unless an employee leaves or there are budget cuts. The nonpersonnel budget is where you can put your library's plan to work.

Previous budgets cannot be reproduced to save time, because the library's plan indicates different priorities and activities from year to year. It will take time to develop a realistic budget because there are so many moving targets: Materials and databases go up in cost, and new technologies and new programs are difficult to predict. In most organizations you can reallocate funds, so it is not necessary to be exact in each line item. You do, however, want to stay within your total nonpersonnel budget amount.

When the budget won't cover what you have planned for the year, the manager is responsible for seeking alternative funding. Some alternative funding strategies include the Friends of the Library, grants, partnerships with local businesses, and collaborating with other libraries. Because you already have your plans in place, you should be ready to write proposals, make pitches, and approach funders without delay.

Volunteers

A library volunteer is an unpaid staff member, or any community member who agrees to donate time, talents, and services to the library. Library volunteers are diverse members of the community who share a common interest in helping the library.[1] In many cases, libraries owe their very existence to volunteers. Many libraries have been started, built, and continue to remain open due to the generosity of volunteers. Library volunteers are among their most dedicated workers, and contribute many hours to supporting the provision of library and information services to our communities.

When libraries are started by a group of volunteers who solicit donations to start a collection, there usually comes a time when they will work with the town or village government and their state library to become a sanctioned public library, acquiring funding to hire staff and buy materials. This can be a difficult transition, especially when volunteers find themselves faced with handing over responsibility for running the library to a director. In order for the library to "grow up," volunteers who are accustomed to doing the professional work of catalogers and reference librarians must surrender those responsibilities to paid librarians. It is the responsibility of the director to take charge, to lead, and to make this transition as smooth as possible. When a director fails to take charge, and volunteers continue to run a library after paid staff has been hired, this makes for an unhealthy work environment and impedes progress.

Volunteers may be accustomed to using the library as a social center. Certainly, the library is community meeting place; however, during the transition you may need to orient them about the purpose of the library as an information center.

Managing Volunteers

Someone must be responsible for managing volunteers, and to do so you need a volunteer program mission statement, goals consistent with the library's goals, and a list of volunteer responsibilities. Volunteers can help improve library services by assisting with routine tasks and special projects; they can help patrons use the online catalog and databases, help with providing directional assistance in the library, and assist with professional tasks. Although volunteers are very important to libraries in many ways, remember that they supplement paid staff. If you use volunteers to replace or do the work of paid staff, you lose your best bargaining chip for getting the increased funding you need. No one is going to pay for something they can get for free.[2]

Volunteer Jobs

Here are some examples of appropriate volunteer jobs:

- Shelf reading
- Shelving

- Mending books

- Repairing media

- Picking up and sorting mail

- Teaching patrons about using the Internet or online catalog

- Helping patrons with copy machine

- Sending faxes

- Clearing paper jams

- Bar coding

- Processing new books

- Printing and sending overdue notices

- Story reading

- Decorating windows

- Designing flyers and posters

"Hiring" Volunteers

Create volunteer application forms and job descriptions, complete with lists of required skills or skills assessments. Interview people for volunteer positions and match the candidates' skills to the jobs needed, just as you would for a new hire. Some libraries ask volunteers to sign Volunteer Agreements, which outline rules, job duties, expectations, and guidelines. Recruit though local clubs and organizations, church and synagogue newsletters, volunteer placement agencies, and schools. A sign on the library's front door pleading "DESPERATE FOR VOLUNTEERS" is not the way to attract the best candidates.

The library director or volunteer manager must treat volunteers as part of the organization by providing them with job descriptions, training them to do their jobs, giving them communication and feedback, evaluating their performance, and recognizing them for a job well done. Without volunteer agreements or guidelines for performance, you'll end up with a free-for-all in no time. When one volunteer refuses to do a less-than-desirable part of her job, other volunteers must "take up the slack." They will grumble, begin to think about what they don't want to do, and, before you know it, all your volunteers will only do what they like best. Staff members will be shelving books while volunteers provide reference service. A volunteer coordinator or manager must nip situations like this in the bud. Pretending it is not happening or that it will work out on its own won't make it go away.

Training Volunteers

New volunteers should be trained on the role of the library and its mission, and be made aware of library policies and procedures. Volunteers working in public areas must have additional training on good customer service practices; how to handle upset patrons; library programs, services and hours; what to do in an emergency; electronic databases and how to use them; and using the online public access catalog (OPAC). Volunteers who answer telephones must know about the role of the library; good customer service; telephone etiquette; and when and how to transfer calls. Volunteers doing specialized work such as book repair must be trained in proper techniques, and special instruction may be necessary for volunteers assisting with professional activities such as cataloging and reference work. All volunteers need ongoing training and updates, as libraries and the communities they serve change.

Hold meetings, communicate library news, and provide procedural updates for volunteers on a regular basis. Provide training sessions on library resources and how to use them. Require attendance, self-study, or online tutorials for volunteers providing professional library services.

Keep the volunteer manual updated and make policies and procedures available in their workspaces. Offer them access to local and free continuing education opportunities. Get them together for celebrations and fun occasions and establish a volunteer recognition program for participating in a special project or the most number of hours donated.

Are You a Micromanager?

Take a good, close, and objective look at your management style. Your style matters more than your education, experience, connections, perceived power, or intelligence. A manager's style can make a huge difference, not only in the success of a library, but in an employee's job performance and in their everyday attitude. A micromanager can turn a productive employee into an unhappy camper and create a mega-staff turnover rate.

In his article "Micromanagement Is Mismanagement," Charles R. McConnell defines the micromanager as "the manager who must personally make every decision, take a lead role in the performance of every significant task and, in extreme cases, dictate every small step the workers take."[3] Micromanagers interfere with an employee's ability to do a good job and destroy trust.

Micromanagers rarely ask employees for input, because they don't value their opinions. They believe that they know the correct way to do things and staff members don't. This creates an atmosphere where employees don't feel valued, they are kept in their place, they are not encouraged to contribute, and they are not challenged.

Micromanagers are not able to delegate effectively—or at all. They think they are the only ones capable of doing an important job well, so trust no one else to do it. Some micromanagers delegate only the easy or boring tasks while saving the "significant" or "interesting" jobs for themselves. If a micromanager is brave enough to delegate an important job, he or she will hover and track every move the employee takes, requiring the employee to seek approval on every step. Micromanagers will prohibit the employee from making important decisions and will reject some steps taken by the employee, simply to assert their authority.

Micromanagers suffer by not developing the essential skill of delegation. They are stressed much of the time because they do not trust anyone to do anything. While the micromanager is busy breathing down employees' necks, he or she is wasting time that could be used to develop the library plan, write reports, create policies, or seek funding for building improvements. The micromanager "eventually discovers that work quality diminishes and that turnover increases."[4] Don't let this be you!

Endnotes

1. Preston Driggers and Eileen Dumas, *Managing Library Volunteers: A Practical Toolkit* (Chicago: American Library Association), 2002.
2. Driggers, 2002, 138.
3. Charles R. McConnell, "Micromanagement Is Mismanagement," National Federation of Independent Business, 2006, www.nfib.com/object/IO_31411.html
4. McConnell, 2006.

Chapter 13

Library Marketing

You might think that everyone loves libraries, so marketing them isn't necessary. What's not to like about libraries? Remember, though, communities are constantly changing, and the services and programs provided by libraries are constantly changing to meet their needs. This means, if you want the people you serve to be aware of what you currently have to offer, you must market your library constantly.

Excellent library services, a courteous, knowledgeable, and well-trained staff, and the desire to meet the information needs of your community lie at the heart of any marketing effort. Effective library marketing starts with a clear vision, mission, and well-articulated library plan. If you live and breathe your vision and mission, align yourself with your goals, provide excellent services, and are knowledgeable, you automatically market a positive image for your library every day. Be clear about why your library is important in the community, the value of the services and programs you offer, and the results you are seeking.

Marketing Plan

A marketing plan with specific goals, objectives, and activities will help you stay focused on specific tasks you can accomplish within a defined period of time. It is important to develop a plan to keep you on track, but this does not have to be long and complicated.

Think about these questions as you work on your plan:

- What segments make up your community?

- Who is your target audience and what are the best ways to reach them?

- What products and services do you want your community to learn more about and how to use?

- How can you spread the word about new library programs to the entire population you serve?

- What is unique about your library that you want community members to know?

Your marketing plan should match the goals and objectives of the library's strategic plan. For instance, if a goal in your library's strategic plan is to increase attendance at adult programs among Spanish-speaking community members, your marketing plan should target this audience. Elements of the marketing plan may include:

- Brief overview or executive summary

- Community profile

- Marketing goals and objectives

- Marketing strategy

- Action plan with timeline

- Budget

- Evaluation methods

Branding

Your library's brand is a combination of its name, logo, slogan, names of programs and services, consistent publication design, and symbols you use that create a personality associated with your library in the minds of users. Branding does not have to be elaborate, expensive, or time-consuming, but it is important that your brand remains consistent across all media and reflects the vibrant library you are today. Look at your library's brand. Does it say what you want it to say about your library? Dated drawings of old buildings may have been a charming representation of the library in decades past, but probably do not portray an accurate image of your library today. Slogans like "Books for Everyone" need updating to include the availability of electronic and online resources, programs, and new services. Ask library staff members to submit ideas and designs, include library users in the process, or sponsor a logo contest.

Your Library's Public Image

Staff

The way we present ourselves and provide services to library users is our biggest marketing tool. Everyone working or volunteering in a public service capacity in the library must be informed about what libraries do, the various programs and services offered in your library, and where to refer people for further information. They must know the library's mission, what they are doing there, and how to do it. Post the library's mission and vision statements in a public area, just in case someone forgets or a community member asks.

Frontline staff members working in public areas are responsible for greeting library users, helping them find the information they need, guiding them to the sections or items they need, teaching them to use the databases or online public access catalog (OPAC), circulating materials, and answering reference questions. It is imperative that they like their jobs and do them well. A customer service attitude is essential. One accurate answer—provided in an efficient and friendly manner with an invitation to return soon—

will go miles toward providing positive marketing for your library. Word will spread about the quality of service your library provides, and you will attract more customers.

If frontline staff members don't know the purpose of the library, aren't sure what they are supposed to be doing, or don't have the knowledge to do it, the public image of your library (and librarians in general) will suffer. Many people think that everyone working in a library is a librarian. If the person responsible for answering reference questions responds by saying, "We don't answer questions like that" or "We don't have a reference collection," the user will conclude that librarians in general aren't very helpful or knowledgeable.

Again, you will need to know the databases your library offers and how to use them in order to market these products. Know the content of each database and which is the right choice to fulfill a specific information request. Ask your database provider for marketing materials; vendors are usually happy to supply materials like ready-made posters, brochures, flyers and advertisements, press releases, radio scripts, training materials, and user guides.

If you aren't sure about what you want your library to become in the future, your purpose, or where you are headed, you will project the image that you are unclear and lack direction. In effect, this markets a negative image for your library—and librarianship. A lack of direction will deflate community confidence in the library and in the competence of library staff. Ultimately, you will receive less community support when you need it the most.

Signage and Displays

One way to make your library pleasant and easy-to-use is to have good signage. When entering an unfamiliar library, people must determine its layout. Is it easy to see where the sections are located in your library? Some of the easiest libraries to use have an open space where visitors can stand in a central area and see large signs (often hanging from the ceiling). These signs help map the library by fiction, nonfiction, reference, children, young adult, books on CD, music, public access computers (PACs) and OPACs, etc. A range of Dewey numbers at the end of the nonfiction stacks, a range of letters at the end of fiction stacks, and signs indicating where the books on CD are located make navigating a library pleasant and easy.

You may know where everything in your library is located, but does a newcomer have a hard time finding the fiction section? If people often have to ask where the basic sections are, try improving your signage—help get people to the information they need. Most people want to find what they need on their own, and, when they do, it frees up librarians to do other things. If inadequate signage forces people to ask, you are creating a less than ideal experience for users and creating more work for yourself.

Displaying materials in an attractive way is another easy marketing technique. Librarians often place the bestsellers or new books on a prominent shelf near the entrance to the library. Stacking items attractively or pulling them out of a line to stand with covers facing out breaks up monotony and attracts attention. Information about upcoming programs displayed in corresponding subject areas, low shelving that allows the eye to travel more than 12 inches in any direction, and shelves with available room are all marketing tools you can use every day.

Phone Calls

Are the people answering the phone knowledgeable about library services? Do they know that libraries answer reference questions? If they don't, the outcome can be damaging for the library. When someone answering the telephone becomes perturbed at the ridiculous questions people ask, they counter your library's good marketing strategies.

Exercise 13.1

Librarians must see libraries as destinations of choice. Why would someone come to your library instead of going to a bookstore or another library? Ask yourself these questions about your library as a destination:

1. What does the library look like?

    _____ Dingy _____ Dark _____ Old _____ Full of spider webs

    _____ Bright _____ Views to outside _____ Easy to see across rooms

    _____ Crammed with overcrowded bookshelves _____ Cluttered

2. What does the library smell like?

    _____ Dusty _____ Musty _____ Fishy _____ Clean _____ Dirty

    _____ Fresh _____ Stale _____ Neutral _____ Coffee and doughnuts

3. What does the library sound like?

    _____ Loud _____ Vibrant _____ Silent _____ Social club

    _____ Day care center

4. What do your signs communicate?

    _____ NO this and NO that ___ DO this and DO that

    _____ Negativity _____ Inviting _____ Welcoming

    _____ Policy and instructions

5. What does the library feel like?

    _____ Prohibitive _____ Free and open _____ Secret _____ Exclusive

    _____ Fair _____ Oppressive _____ Diverse _____ Comfortable

    _____ Easy going

6. Librarians in the library:

    _____ Shush _____ Talk in normal voices _____ Try to catch you doing something wrong _____ Don't know much about databases _____ Scowl _____ Are friendly _____ Are helpful

7. Do the toilets back up every other day?

8. Is your library like an oven in the summer because the cooling system never works?

9. Is it usually easy to find a place to park?

10. Can you find a librarian when you need one?

11. Is it easy to find information?

Is the message on the library's answering machine clear, succinct, and useful? Are people getting the information they need without having to push too many buttons, listen to too many menus, or wait too long? Or, do they have to listen to a long, drawn-out, rambling, unplanned, outdated, and aimless speech that gives very little useful information? It is amazing what a sensible and succinct automated telephone message will do to promote your library.

Imagine that on the other end of every call is a benefactor searching for a deserving library where she can donate her millions, and that her decision depends on the service she receives in that one call. Or simpler yet, just imagine that your library is customer service oriented.

Communicating to the People You Serve

Newsletters

You can communicate what is going on at your library by publishing a print newsletter or sending an electronic newsletter via email. A newsletter can be a very simple one-page document, created with a word processing program. Even better, if someone on your staff has the skills to use InDesign, QuarkXpress, Publisher, or PageMaker, you can produce a more professional looking publication. Prominently display your branding elements, and make sure the newsletter is attractive, easy to read, and projects a positive image of your library. Keep articles short and to the point. Write articles with your entire community in mind, and distribute newsletters to people who aren't regular library users or members of the Friends group.

If you don't have a budget to mail newsletters, place them in public places with the other free publications. Your local copy shop may be willing to partner with you on this venture by donating copy costs if you include a "thank you" to them in the newsletter.

Also, convenient online products allow you to easily create and send attractive email newsletters. Some offer free trials and low monthly subscription rates, such as iContact (www.icontact.com) and Constant Contact (www.constantcontact.com/index.jsp).

Articles and Columns

Write a regular column in your local newsletter or nearby city newspaper about library activities and services. A nearby library runs a weekly column in the regional section of my city newspaper called "Library Corner," where community members can read about new library services, programs, activities, staff member profiles, and progress on branch library renovations. A recent column announced the addition of two new online databases, explained their content and how to access them from home, and even provided step-by-step instructions on how to construct searches. The article outlined everything readers needed to know about getting started using these databases, and offered a contact name for those needing extra help. I'm sure many new library users were attracted to the library through this column, and others learned something new about how to use databases.

Another nearby library is covered less frequently, but when it is, the content includes topics like the history of the library, the large number of volunteers, library staff and their pets, or circulation statistics. These articles provide a venue for library staff and volunteers to make themselves and their building more visible, but do not inform the community about library services, resources, or new databases. Visitors and tourists may be prompted to go to the charming library building, but community members with information needs are ignored. Most people in the community served by this library don't even know that the library offers online databases.

Products

The following products can help you market your library to your community:

- Annual reports

- Bookmarks

- Bibliographies

- Brochures

- Mailing lists of community groups and business leaders

- Marketing materials from database vendors

Getting Out of the Library

Spreading the word about your library and the services you offer is essential. You can have the best library in the world, but if the only people who know what you offer are your regular library customers, you have some work to do. Position yourself in the community by emerging from the four walls of the library to serve on organizational or municipal committees and task forces, speak at club and association meetings, set up a booth at the local farmer's market or craft fair, or create a satellite branch in the shopping mall.

Offer to speak to local clubs and groups about library services of interest. Sometimes targeting the interests of small groups can be an easier task than marketing to an entire corporation or organization. Talk to groups of retired people on online periodicals for older persons, classes on computer use, and email instruction. Address a group in your organization or corporation about electronic resources in the library and your availability to perform customized searches for them.

Events and Themes

You can use many events to promote your library throughout the year. Find some ideas at the Chase's Annual Events website (www.mhprofessional.com/?page=/mhp/categories/chases/content/special_months.html). Hold events and activities around a particular subject throughout a given month to attract community members who may be interested in that topic but never thought to come to the library to learn about it. Remember to hold programs for people of all ages in your community—children, teens, adults, senior citizens—and those from all income levels, ethnicities, backgrounds, races, and creeds.

For example, March is International Listening Awareness Month. You might observe a listening theme and promote listening skills at your library. The International Listening Association (ILA) provides prepared public service announcements at its website (www.listen.org/pages/march_psas.html) that you can use to help publicize your listening events. You might link to ILA's free Listening Self-Assessment Test from the library's website. You could prepare bibliographies of library materials on the topic of listening, and you could present programs on listening skills for people of all ages.

You can use monthly themes to generate ideas for serving a segment of the population that you would like to reach. July is National Wheelchair Beautification Month. Imagine the activities you could create around this theme while involving people in wheelchairs, their friends, and families! September is Healthy Aging Month. Maybe you are aware that there are many elderly people in your community, but you are seeing fewer and fewer of them in the library every year. During September you might spotlight healthy aging by having presentations, classes, or workshops on topics such as nutrition, bone health, or memory exercises. You could present an outreach program at the local nursing home. The Healthy Aging Campaign (www.healthyaging.net) offers a printable online brochure, resources including workshop kits, and tips on healthy aging that you can use to design programs for older adults.

Seven Things You Can Do Now to Market Your Library

1. Do a signage audit.
2. Offer a variety of programming for different ages and interests.
3. Speak to a club.
4. Make the collection attractive.
5. Involve your customers.
6. Use one social software tool for your library.
7. Write an article or column about a new library service.

Staying Connected to the Larger Organization

Stay involved with the larger organization: your municipality, corporation, association, institution, school, or hospital. Sometimes librarians are not included in organizational meetings where strategic planning, goals, activities, and policies are decided, so it is important to stay in close communication with your boss or the person you report to higher in the organization. If a library is left behind when it comes to the mission and direction of the larger organization, there will come a day when it becomes impossible for the librarian to justify the relevance of the library to the organization, jeopardizing its very existence. Just because you know how important libraries are, don't assume that everyone else thinks the same way. Stay in close contact with the leaders of your organization and in close alignment with the path of the organization. Volunteer to serve on committees and task forces. Participate and collaborate with others in your organization and show them the value of the library. Be absolutely certain that your boss values the library, represents the library well in the organization, and will advocate for the library when it comes to positioning in the organization. If this person will be speaking on behalf of the library in organizational meetings, it is imperative that you are on the same wavelength. This takes constant communication and effort on your part; they probably have a lot to do in addition to overseeing the library. Make yourself visible. Let them know what you are doing and where you are headed.

Social Software

Use blogs, podcasts, videos, wikis, and RSS feeds to market your library. Many social software tools encourage participation and interactivity. The advantage of these tools is that users can choose what information they want delivered to them and where to contribute, thus providing specific kinds of information or ways to participate based on their needs. (See more on these tools in Part III.)

Chapter 14

Removing Barriers

Many librarians are reluctant to take the next steps necessary to increase or enhance services and programs in their libraries. They are focused on keeping things the way they are or are convinced that their circumstances prevent them from making changes or trying new ideas. Often their reasons for not moving ahead or trying something new are perceived rather than real.

Barrier 1: Your Library Is Disadvantaged

It can become a habit to say or think, "Our library is disadvantaged. We have a small budget, too little space, and not enough staff. There is no tax base, and legislators are too busy with other priorities to be concerned about our little library." If your library is struggling with a small budget, too little space, and not enough staff, you are not alone. But, librarians who repeat this mantra eventually come to believe it's true—and also manage to convince others. These librarians have accepted their dim circumstances as "the way things are," and have given up hope that anything will ever change, because events are out of their hands. When someone suggests a new idea, program, or way to provide services, they look at that person as if he or she is from another planet. What are they thinking?

When you don't have enough funds or staff to do your work, it can be discouraging. But when you recite the phrases "not enough space," "small budget," and "short-staffed" enough times, you effectively place these barriers in your own way. The more you repeat these obstacles, the more real they become to you. The more you tell others about them, the clearer their perception of your library becomes. Over the years, your library's identity becomes equated with smallness, poverty, inadequate staffing, and as a place that is not innovative, creative, or leading edge. Eventually, no one will bother to suggest new ideas, other libraries will keep their distance, and potential partners will fail to approach you when they recall you can't do anything new. You have created your own reality.

Exercise 14.1

What obstacles are in your way?

Check any that apply to you:

_____ Your library is disadvantaged, and for this reason any new ideas are not possible.

_____ Things are fine just the way they are.

_____ Technology can't improve on the programs and services your library offers.

_____ You know all there is to know about being a librarian.

_____ You know all about your community and their information needs without asking them.

_____ Collaborating or partnering with other libraries is not an option, because your library is "different."

Barrier 2: Things Are Fine Just the Way They Are

Another common obstacle blocking librarians from moving their libraries forward is a false confidence that things are fine just the way they are. They have become comfortable over the years doing things the same way, and resist taking risks. They surround themselves with people who support them in keeping things the same because they, too, want things to stay the same. The library is stuck in the last century while the rest of the world races ahead.

In these libraries you will find card catalogs and tractor-fed printers chugging out catalog cards. When you suggest a new idea, program, or way to provide services, staff will immediately launch into a litany of the virtues of doing things the way they've always been done, listing everything that could go wrong with the new idea. They are well practiced at keeping new ideas at bay.

There was a time when librarians could get away with this, but those times are long gone. Technology has catapulted libraries into the future, and we must take a leadership position. Librarians cannot afford to stand still for a nanosecond if libraries are going to survive. Librarians who refuse to take risks or maximize the use of technology to serve their customers are sinking the ship.

Barrier 3: You Know All There Is to Know About Librarianship

Some accidental librarians have jumped through all the hoops required by their states to practice librarianship or to be a library director. They have passed certification tests, submitted the required documentation, attended classes and workshops, and joined library associations. Now, many of them think that they know all about librarianship—because in their minds, jumping through the hoops is the same as having an MLS and certifies them forever.

These librarians aren't interested in new ideas or what other librarians are doing because they have everything all figured out. One day these librarians will find themselves on their own without collaborations or partnerships with other libraries or librarians. This is a recipe for failure.

Barrier 4: You Know All There Is to Know About Your Community

When you think that you know all about your community—without asking community members—you will end up serving only the people you know about. The others will go to nearby libraries because you don't know about them or their information needs, thus, they aren't being served. You may confirm that you are doing a good job by pointing to the results of a customer satisfaction survey distributed to the people you serve. Those results are useful in justifying serving the same satisfied people and continuing to ignore the people you aren't serving. As your community changes, though, your world becomes smaller and smaller.

Barrier 5: Your Library Is Different

Sometimes when a library is built from the ground up by community volunteers, they think their library is different from all the rest. To some degree this can be healthy, because it creates ownership for people who have contributed a huge amount of time and effort. They should be proud that they built a library from nothing, as this is no small task. However, when this perception that their library is "different" causes a separation between their library and other libraries, other librarians, partnerships, collaborations, grants, and other alternative funding, or when it leads to reluctance to participate in accepted library principles and practice, the results can be devastating. No library or librarian can afford to isolate themselves today. Our connections are more important than ever.

Removing Barriers

All of the barriers discussed are founded in fear and lack of confidence, so the first step in removing them is to get brave and take risks. Rather than focusing on everything that could go wrong, think about what could go right. Accept that you don't know everything—no one does! Risks can be scary, but they can also be fun. Even when the results are less than successful, you will usually learn something new or meet some interesting people. Often failures lead to future successes. Start small.

Martha Liebert, Retired Director, Martha Liebert Public Library, Bernalillo, New Mexico

Author's Note: Based on my interview with Marta Liebert.

Martha Liebert was the driving force behind the public library in Bernalillo, New Mexico, from its inception in the 1960s until her retirement in 1989. In 1965, she and several other mothers recognized the need for a local library that offered story hours for their young children, so they joined forces and made it happen. They went door-to-door in the community seeking donations from residents and received duplicate items from neighboring libraries. In 1966, the library was incorporated, and the town provided $500 to purchase books and a typewriter. A local timber company funded materials for the shelves, which were built and installed by carpenters from the public schools and painted by members of the Veterans of Foreign Wars. Originally occupying a room in the Bernalillo Town Hall, the library was relocated several times over the years before it eventually moved into its own building in 2006.

Martha's strong leadership, outstanding dedication, and personal commitment were largely responsible for the growth and development of a vital community library and gathering place. The library's core offerings included a renowned Southwest collection, a comprehensive circulating book collection, popular children's programming, and varied adult programs. Under her directorship, story hours, arts and crafts activities, recreation, and games were daily events. Families and children from Bernalillo and nearby towns, pueblos, and schools flocked to music and dance performances, story telling, photo exhibits, quilt shows, summer reading programs, puppet shows, traveling zoo programs, and humanities programs of all kinds. Library staff members held classes and group sessions for adults in painting, art, foreign languages, quilting, and English as a Second Language. A grant from the New Mexico Humanities Council in the 1970s supported a project to collect and organize historical photographs from Sandoval County, New Mexico.

Central to the library's mission was Martha's belief that education is a tool you can use to move forward in life. Martha is gifted with the ability to welcome, communicate with, and assist people of all ages, backgrounds, abilities, educational levels, and socioeconomic status, and she believes in educational opportunities for all. Her goal was to help people in the community discover that education is important and to encourage them to take advantage of the library to learn. To this day, Martha is stopped by people in the community who want to tell her how instrumental the library was in their early development. Since her retirement, Martha says she misses people the most.

In 1986, Martha was awarded the Community Achievement Award by the New Mexico Library Association for her role in establishing and sustaining library service in Bernalillo. She continues to be a true inspiration for librarians and others in her community and throughout New Mexico.

Seeing Opportunities

Believe it or not, many librarians in small, underfunded, and understaffed libraries have been able to see beyond the barrier of "being disadvantaged" by focusing on the library's opportunities rather than on its challenges. Librarians in circumstances similar to yours have built new buildings, attracted alternate funding, implemented emerging technology, and hired additional staff for new and innovative library services and programs. Some ways to do this include:

- Focusing on the library's vision
- Looking for opportunities
- Taking risks
- Using the talents of staff
- Using limited funds creatively
- Partnering
- Collaborating
- Using expertise in your community
- Working smartly
- Taking advantage of the resources available
- Thinking positively
- Using your strengths

Attracting Funding

Refrain from spreading the word about how poor your library is. When you make sure everyone knows you don't have enough money to try new ideas or innovative technology, buy more new library materials, hire staff, or repair the building, you help make it so. When your library has been poor for 50 years, it will likely remain poor for the next 50 years—unless you do something different.

Start by engaging in thoughts and activities that attract funding. You can attract funding by having a vision, mission, and library plan, knowing your priorities, getting out of the library, pitching your ideas, collaborating, trying new approaches, being creative with your funding, and using the expertise of community members when they offer.

Funding is always a library issue. You aren't alone. The difference between libraries that attract funding and those that don't usually lies in the attitude and approach of the library director or manager. Librarians who actively seek funding eventually find success. Librarians who do not actively seek funding will not find success. It's as simple as that.

As libraries begin to attract funding, they gain momentum and confidence. This can motivate them to tackle bigger fish: to approach legislators about sponsoring capital outlay bills for new buildings or building repair, or to write proposals for federal grants, for instance. They use their current funding to leverage new funding. They form mutually beneficial relationships with their governments so that they are not "on their own" when there is a building maintenance crisis. Business leaders notice the library's progress and offer to collaborate or partner on a project, contribute expertise, or donate a piece of land.

Be smart with your words. Librarians who declare publicly to funders, in newspapers, at meetings, and throughout the community, that volunteers successfully do the work of professional librarians—free of charge!—cannot expect that anyone is going to provide funds to hire paid librarians. Why would they, when untrained people can do the work of librarians for free? Your job is to attract funding, not repel it.

Valuing Librarianship

Asserting that anyone can do the job of librarians, or that passing a certification test is the same as an MLS, not only keeps you from being adequately funded but it devalues librarianship. If you don't value librarianship, no one around you will, either. When you assume that MLS librarians and others with expertise have nothing to offer, you are turning away a group of people who may be able to contribute significantly. No library can afford to reject offers of assistance from people with expertise. If you think you already know all there is to know about librarianship and operating your library, you are blocking the way for anyone to contribute.

Learning Continuously

Librarians who think they know all there is to know about librarianship are also unlikely to learn more, and continuous learning in our field today is imperative. There is always something to learn about librarianship, even for librarians with the most advanced degrees, extensive experience, and expertise. Librarianship is a dynamic and changing profession that supplies you with new things to learn by the minute, and learning is one of the most exciting aspects of librarianship.

Trying a New Mantra

You might find you can turn things around by changing your mantra. Positive mantras aren't reserved for librarians in large libraries with lots of money and plenty of staff; anyone can try them. If you insist on repeating misperceptions or untruths to yourself, eventually they will become self-fulfilling, but the converse is also true.

Don't repeat phrases like:

> "We are just a small library."
> "We don't have enough money and we never will."
> "We don't have enough space."
> "We are short-staffed."
> "We've always done it that way."

Instead, try working on something new and refreshing:

"We are open to opportunities that come our way."

"We are open to ideas for alternative funding."

"We welcome assistance from people with expertise."

"Let's talk about how to make this happen."

"The possibilities for using technology in the library are exciting. Let's learn more."

"There is always room for new ideas."

"Small libraries have big possibilities."

"Our library's vision is _____, and we plan to get there."

Part III

Technology and the Library

Chapter 15

Public Access Computers

Vital libraries offer public access computers (PACs), which members of the community they serve can use to access the Internet, search databases, and use basic computer applications. When we think about PACs we usually think of public, school, and university or college libraries, but PACs are part of every library. Even the smallest, most specialized libraries have at least one computer for library users to access information via the Internet. The use of PACs varies depending on the kind of library. For instance, in university libraries, PACs may be limited to use for scholarly research and educational purposes, while in special libraries, they may be intended for use in addressing information needs in a particular subject area.

According to a study conducted by the American Library Association (ALA) and Florida State University's Information Use Management and Policy Institute in 2007, 99.1 percent of public libraries in the U.S. offer free public access to the Internet.[1] The Internet has become an essential information resource with links to a multitude of reference resources, such as other library catalogs; federal, state and local laws, legislation, and documents; news; public opinion sites; and databases on a wide range of topics. PACs in public libraries provide community members who do not have computers at home the opportunity to access the world of information. The emergence of computers in public libraries has served to reduce the digital divide, helping to equalize opportunities to access information across all socioeconomic levels.

In fact, according to the Libraries Connect Communities: Public Library Funding & Technology Access Study, 73 percent of the nation's public libraries are the only source of free public access computing in their communities. The main purposes for PAC use in public libraries are:

1. Students seeking educational web resources

2. Job seekers sending resumes and applications

3. People wanting to learn computer- and Internet-searching skills.[2]

Other common reasons people use PACs in public libraries include email, searching library databases, gaming, social networking, and using basic computer functions such as word processing, presentations, and spreadsheets.

Although libraries clearly supply a necessary service by providing PACs, this has put a big strain on them. The increasing numbers of people using library PACs, combined with the escalating costs of technology, limited space, added demands on staff, and outdated infrastructures, have created a big challenge for libraries of all kinds. Library budgets have remained essentially flat in recent years while the costs of providing free public access computing services have increased. It is interesting to note that, as we are incorporating Library 2.0 technologies, which require more bandwidth and more computer power, more than 58 percent of libraries have no plans to add new computers in 2008, and 76 percent report a lack of space that limits their ability to add more computers in their facilities.[3]

If you are experiencing the challenges that come with the increased usage of public computers, including demands for faster speeds and improved computer power, you are not alone. How you navigate your way in the coming years will vary depending on your library's mission, the needs of the community you serve, and your library's plan. None of us, though, can ignore that PACs are essential for fulfilling the role of libraries as information centers; there is no choice but to continue to incorporate them in our future.

What Makes a Computer a PAC?

PACs are computers for public use. Most libraries keep PACs in a separate area or room, or they are configured in a central location near the reference desk or circulation desk where library staff is available to assist customers in their use. PACs are not to be confused with OPACs (online public access catalogs), as they provide different functions. OPAC computers in libraries are dedicated to searching the library or library system's catalog and performing customer account functions, such as renewing materials, placing holds, or updating customer records. On the other hand, PACs are used for other public computing functions, such as accessing the Internet, searching databases, downloading documents, gaming, social networking, printing, emailing, and word processing.

In many libraries, the PACs are often all in use, requiring users to make advance reservations, sign in, or wait in line. Most libraries need to establish time limits for using PACs, otherwise many people would stay on these computers for hours even while lines formed behind them.

A well-functioning library has separate computers available for people to search the online catalog. You can't require people who want to look something up in the online catalog to stand in line for their turn on a PAC or ask them to reserve a computer in advance and then sign in. People who want to search the online catalog are usually looking for a specific item in the library—a book by a certain author, the title of a particular CD, or an instructional DVD on a certain subject. They want to find an OPAC computer easily and quickly perform their search so they can retrieve the items they are seeking, place a hold on an item at a different branch, update their patron record, or renew materials online. Whatever the task, chances are they want to get on and off the OPAC computer quickly.

To provide both PAC and OPAC services effectively and efficiently, even the smallest libraries need at least two public computers: a PAC and an OPAC computer.

Software for PACs

Microsoft Vista, Internet Explorer, Adobe Acrobat Reader, and Microsoft Office Suite are the typical software choices for PACs. Some libraries use open source software (OSS), which is software that is developed and improved by its own community of programmers. OSS is usually free and can be copied and shared with anyone; the source code is openly shared, there is no restriction on its use, and no person or company holds exclusive rights to the software. OSS choices appropriate for libraries include:

- Ubuntu (www.ubuntu.com) – A Linux-based operating system that contains a web browser, presentation, document, and spreadsheet software, and instant messaging

- Firefox (www.mozilla.com/firefox) – A relatively fast and intuitive web browser

- OpenOffice.org (www.openoffice.org) – A multiplatform productivity suite that includes a word processor, spreadsheet, presentation manager, and drawing program

- NeoOffice (www.neooffice.org) – A full-featured set of office applications based on OpenOffice.org, for Macs

Security, Maintenance, and Management

Secure your PACs so that the public cannot (inadvertently or intentionally) harm or disable them. You don't want anyone to damage programs, install unwanted software, introduce viruses, or get into your administrative settings. Without protections, you will constantly be battling computer problems. If you don't have a technically savvy staff, paying outside technical support personnel to restore and repair damaged computers can get very costly, very quickly. Industry estimates indicate that anywhere from 7 to 20 percent of all IT support calls are spyware-related. Viruses, worms, and Trojans cost global companies (including libraries around the nation) between $169 billion and $204 billion in 2004, according to digital risk management firm mi2g.[4]

Use security measures to prevent this type of damage and to protect your PACs and your sanity, while saving money. It is much easier to secure computers from malware (see the sidebar on page 243) up front than to fight the uncontrolled onslaught of problems caused by unprotected computers. Libraries that don't properly secure and maintain their PACs waste incredible amounts of staff time and money—ironically, this happens most commonly in libraries with no staff time to spare and little to spend.

Here are some common hints that you could use more security measures on your library PACs. Do any of these sound familiar?

- One of your library's PACs keeps opening a politically charged popup window over and over. You cannot close these windows fast enough to make them disappear. The only remedy is to restart the computer. This happens several times a day.

- Many of your PACs display a message that says the antivirus software is out of date.

- The desktop scene on one of the last PACs in the computer room—the one hardest to monitor—has been changed to a rap video scene. The next day it shows a hard metal rock band, and on the following day a risqué "girls gone wild" scene. What does tomorrow hold? You are always surprised.

- Your ISP (Internet Service Provider) contacted you recently about spam being sent from a library computer. You were warned that the library's Internet service would be suspended if this happens again. You can't tell from the computer sign-in sheets who the culprit was. Possibly this was done via the wireless network from outside the library, but you are unsure about how to track it down.

Security Tips

Although there is no way to guarantee PACs' immunity to threats, here are some suggestions to help secure them:

1. Keep your operating system, antivirus software, anti-spyware, and anti-malware up to date. Enable the automatic updates for these programs, as many threats are immediate and no time delays are safe.

2. Set your antivirus software, anti-spyware, and anti-malware to automatically scan your computer on a regular basis.

3. Restrict access to the administrative levels of your PACs to prevent anyone from damaging your hardware or software. You can lock patrons out to varying degrees using operating system security features, so remember not to restrict access so much that users cannot accomplish what they need to do. Use different passwords for different age groups or computer areas, allowing computers in the children's area to access only children's programs, for instance.

4. Use disk protection software that restores a computer to its original state after every user session or at the end of every day.

5. Change default usernames and passwords, set security levels in the operating system and programs to "high," block popup windows, and beware of macros.

6. Monitor the PAC area by physically examining computers and peripherals, and by scanning computers for problems.

7. Walk around the PAC area and observe.

8. Image the hard drive.

What Is Malware and What Can You Do About It?

Malware (or malicious software) is any computer program designed to harm or compromise your computers, such as computer viruses, worms, Trojans, adware, and spyware. Anti-malware is software that protects your computers from malware by finding, preventing, and removing it. Antivirus software, anti-spyware, anti-adware, and anti-Trojan software are all examples of anti-malware.

Following are some tools you can use to help keep your computers clear of this type of malicious software.

Antivirus
- AVG Anti-Virus (www.grisoft.com)
- ESET NOD32 Antivirus (www.eset.com)
- Kaspersky Anti-Virus (usa.kaspersky.com)
- McAfee Virus Scan (www.mcafee.com/us)
- Norton Antivirus (www.symantec.com)
- Trend Micro Antivirus (us.trendmicro.com)
- ZoneAlarm Antivirus (www.zonealarm.com)

Anti-Spyware
- AVG Anti-Spyware (www.grisoft.com)

- CounterSpy (www.sunbelt-software.com)

- Spy Sweeper (www.webroot.com)

- Spyware Doctor (www.pctools.com)

Anti-Malware

- CyberDefender (www.cyberdefender.com)

- Kaspersky Internet Security (usa.kaspersky.com)

- McAfee Total Protection (www.mcafee.com/us)

- Norton 360 (www.symantec.com)

- Panda Internet Security (www.pandasecurity.com/usa)

Disk Protection

- CenturionGuard (www.centuriontech.com)

- Clean Slate (www.fortresgrand.com)

- Deep Freeze (www.faronics.com)

- SteadyState (www.microsoft.com/windows/products/winfamily/sharedaccess)

Maintenance Tips

Here are some important maintenance tips for PACs:

1. Regularly update programs like Adobe Acrobat Reader and office suites on all library computers.

2. Make an exact copy of one hard drive and copy it to the other computers. This will make original setup easy, and serve as a backup and recovery tool as well. (This only works for computers with the same manufacturer, model, and specifications.)

3. Visually inspect computers and "test drive" them regularly looking for damage, unauthorized changes, mal-
   functions, or inefficient operation.

Management Tips

If you have worked with PACs, you know all too well about the
pitfalls. Many computer management tools will help you do your
job more easily, save you money, and help provide improved
library services—all at the same time. Libraries with small budgets
tend to neglect purchasing PAC management tools due to the cost,
but unfortunately, they probably lose money in the long run by not
managing their PACs. Here are a few ideas to consider:

1. Charge for printing. Print management software displays
   a page count and total cost with multiple payment
   options on the screen. Users can pay using smart cards,
   so cash boxes and cashiers aren't necessary. The amount
   of waste in a library where there is no monitoring or
   enforced charge for printing is astounding; reams of
   paper can be found in the recycle bins each week. When
   there is no incentive for people to be careful about what
   and how much they print, many people will print with
   wild abandon, only to decide that (1) they don't want
   what they printed after all, or (2) it is going to cost more
   than they wanted to pay. They throw away their print job
   with no consequences. When waste like this is acceptable, you are teaching people that money is no object in
   your library. Do you have a bottomless budget when it
   comes to paper, ink cartridges, and printers?

2. Reservation/time management software is more efficient
   and fair than manual sign-in sheets and relying on the
   memory of library staff. When public computer use is
   going up, reservation and time management software can
   lessen the burden on library staff, freeing them from
   monitoring how long people are on computers and

referring back to handwritten manual logs that are impossible to read. People record inaccurate start times—and sometimes don't record them at all. When their hour is up, they will insist that they wrote the wrong time on the log—you know how it goes. Why not eliminate this headache from your list of things to do?

3. Disk protection software refreshes public computers to their original settings between sessions or at the end of the day, saving library workers the time it takes to clean up messes or explain away offensive materials inadvertently left behind by previous users.

The "Look" and Location of PACs

To minimize demands on library staff, PACs should look and function as simply and as similarly as possible. When library users sit down to use a PAC, they shouldn't be confused or need to ask for assistance to find and start a program. These computers must be easy to use, have standard programs loaded, and be able to print easily and download information from the Internet without constant challenges. You can make it easier on staff and users alike if multiple PACs all "look" the same. This means that they all have the same programs, the desktop views are the same, they all have the same set of desktop icons, and they act like each other. This way, a user familiar with using one library PAC can choose any library PAC and feel familiar and comfortable, knowing the functions they can perform with ease and confidence.

This sounds easy, but, of course, it takes lots of effort and staff time up front. Balance this out with the significant time and effort you will save on providing constant computer assistance, troubleshooting ongoing and repeating computer problems, and soothing frustrated customers. Most importantly, staff's stress level will be greatly reduced. In libraries where every PAC looks and acts differently, staff members spend an inordinate amount of time helping patrons and solving technical problems—soon frustrated patrons are the only kind they have.

Unfortunately, this happens all too often in small libraries with insufficient staff who lack the time or expertise to support the public computer environment they have created for themselves. Sounds like a monster with a mind of its own, doesn't it? Well, it can be. Staff members in libraries like this are always running after computer problems. Instead, why not position your library ahead of the curve by solving these problems before they happen?

Let's say that your library has 10 independently running PACs of all ages, capabilities, brands, and configurations:

- Some have Adobe Acrobat Reader.

- Some have PowerPoint.

- Some have Excel.

- One has Access.

- There are several different versions of Word.

- Only two have ports for USB drives.

- Some have CD/DVD drives.

- There are 10 different desktop themes, views, and sets of icons.

Information about each machine is not posted or otherwise made available to computer users, and it is too much for library staff to memorize all the facts about each machine. Day in and day out, patrons discover at the final stages of completing a task that their computer of choice isn't equipped to do the job. Unwanted pop-up windows randomly appear on all PACs, occasionally disabling some, and one computer chronically crashes, stalls, and displays error messages. Computer mice stick and need cleaning. Computers are infected, and personal information is insecure.

Libraries with PAC situations like these are unable to meet the information needs of the people they serve, and are less than shining examples of libraries as information centers. Staff members are frazzled, and annoyed patrons are constantly asking for assistance. Running after situations like this is futile. The only answer is to stop, take a look, make a plan, and take action. Position yourself ahead of the problem.

Something else to consider when you are planning a space for PACs is the location. Consider the following when picking that all important location:

- Can customers easily get to the computers?
- Can customers easily get out of the computer area in case of fire or an emergency?
- Are the printers located conveniently for the people using computers?
- Is there enough space around each computer for people to comfortably work?
- Are the computer workstation areas private?
- Is there library staff based nearby for quick assistance?
- Is there a separate computer or area for children? Teens and young adults? Adults?

Selecting PACs

The PACs you select will be determined by the needs of the people you serve, your budget, and your staff's technology competencies. Here are some steps to use as a guide:

1. Decide how you will be using PACs to help meet your customers' information needs as identified in your community needs assessment and strategic plan.

2. Know what the computers will be used for, i.e., word processing, Internet, games, social networking, children's educational games, database searching.

3. Talk to other librarians about their successes and recommendations.

4. Ask the technology contact at your state library agency for guidance.

5. Develop a list of the minimum specifications required to perform the tasks you have identified.

6. Read reviews.

7. Investigate group purchasing opportunities and nonprofit buying power through your municipality, state library, consortium, corporation, or regional library system.

8. Compare prices.

9. Plan on a four-year hardware replacement cycle.

What About Thin Clients?

An alternative to using networked or stand-alone computers as PACs is to use thin clients, which run multiple workstations from one CPU. Thin clients save space, are easier to secure, easier to manage, all look the same, cost less, and require less library staff time to troubleshoot and maintain.

Thin client applications and data are all stored on one server; the thin clients themselves are empty boxes connected to the server. The thin clients do not process anything and do not need internal memory. They run at the speed of the server and come equipped with USB ports that will support CD/DVD drives, flash drives, and other peripherals. Programs are loaded onto and operate from the server rather than from each individual computer. This means that you only need to deal with one machine—the server—and all thin clients will "look" alike. Only the server needs to be secured, not every workstation. Updates need to be downloaded to only the server, not to every workstation.

Thin clients are eco-friendly. According to studies by the Fraunhaufer Institute, thin clients consume up to 50 percent less electricity and reduce CO_2 emissions. They weigh only one third as much as a PC, taking up between 11 and 20 percent of the space—thus ship more cost-effectively, too.[5] "There is no magic formula or answer to whether your library should or should not use thin clients. Before taking the plunge, be sure to educate yourself and technology team members about the relative merits about PCs and thin clients."[6] Things to think about when considering thin clients include:

- What are the up-front costs?
- What do you need to purchase and what will the vendor provide?
- Is there a subscription fee?
- Is there a contract? What is the term of the contract?
- What will the vendor do and what are your responsibilities?
- How is the vendor's technical support?
- What do other libraries that use thin clients recommend and say about their experiences?

What PAC Support Staff Must Know

To succeed at providing public access computing, the library must have staff designated to support this service. All frontline staff must either know how to assist people using technology or be able to find someone who can. Computer support staff must know the standard PAC configurations, so if they see anything amiss they can report it. Anyone who provides PAC support must know the library's computer use policies and have the authority to enforce them. They must know how to use the basic software on the library's PACs and how to troubleshoot common problems. Patrons often ask for assistance with using email, resolving broken links, recovering lost print jobs, and downloading documents in various formats, and staff must be prepared to handle these requests. Computer support personnel must be regularly updated about new technologies in the library and how to use them, informed of library resources available using PACs, and encouraged to add to their knowledge through continuing education.

What PAC Users Need to Know

Educate the people using PACs in your library about safe computer use. A flyer, initial on-screen message, or short training session can inform users about viruses, spyware, online predators, and protecting their private information. If your library prefers to minimize security measures to make computer use easier for the public, make sure that your patrons know they are responsible for taking safety precautions. If they assume the library's computers are secure and the library has taken responsibility for protecting them, they may find out the hard way that this is not the case.

In libraries without computer management software that refreshes computers between sessions, computer users need to know that if they do not properly log out of their email account or banking records, the next person on the computer can easily go right into their accounts. Cookies, caches, and browser and search histories tell the next user quite a lot about the previous user's interests, habits, usernames, passwords, and Internet travels. Let PAC users know what to watch out for in email attachments, instant messaging, and chat rooms and warn them about the use of credit card and debit account numbers on public computers.

Internet Connectivity

Libraries need reliable broadband high-speed Internet connections. Dial-up lines can't handle the heavy graphics, social networking, and gaming sites in use today. Slow speed annoys people focused on finding information to meet an immediate need and prohibits users from capturing common files in a reasonable amount of time. If DSL or cable is unavailable at your library's location, look into satellite connectivity. Contact local ISPs for library rates, partner with local businesses, or collaborate with schools to make this affordable.

Set up wireless access in your library. Public access computing also means providing Internet access to people using their own computers in the library, and wireless networking is fairly easy and low cost to implement. Purchase a wireless router, connect it to the incoming wiring, and place it where there is a good signal—in as many locations as possible throughout the library. Separate security measures apply to wireless connectivity, too. Do you want people outside the building to be able to access the library's wireless network?

Technology Planning and PACs

Technology planning is strategic planning for library technology, which includes PACs. The process is an outgrowth of the library's strategic plan, but focuses on how technology will help the library meet the information needs of your community. To create a technology plan, first review your community information needs from your needs assessment. Then, focus on PACs, asking these questions:

- Which information needs can be addressed using PACs?

- How will you use PACs to address these needs?

- What are the hardware specifications, software, locations, capabilities, peripherals, etc., necessary to meet the specific identified needs?

- Are you effectively using PACs to maximize delivery of services?

- How can you improve your use of PACs to improve services?

Create this portion of your technology plan based on the needs you are going to address using library PACs in a specified period of time. Define your goals, objectives, action plans, and evaluation methods, just as you did for your strategic plan (see Chapter 5). Where do you want to be in that time and what technology will it take to get there? What will it cost? Who will do the work? What is the expected lifespan of the technology? What are the ongoing costs?

Computer Use Policies

It is essential to have a computer use policy in place. Post it in the PAC area or make it available for library users to read, inform computer users about the policy before they use the computers, and ensure that all people working in the library know what the policy is and who is responsible for enforcing it. In the case of blatant computer misconduct, you do not want to have to wonder what to do. Library volunteers in charge of the PAC area should not resort to applying their personal biases because they do not know the library's computer use policy. Everyone must be clear about what constitutes acceptable use of library computers, and there should be no question about how to proceed when the policy is being violated.

Endnotes

1. American Library Association, and Information Institute, College of Information, Florida State University, "Libraries Connect Communities: Public Library Funding & Technology Access Study 2006–2007," in *ALA Research Series* (Chicago: American Library Association, 2007), 5.
2. American Library Association, 3.
3. American Library Association, 4.
4. Monique Sendze, "The Battle to Secure Our Public Access Computers: It's Hard to Fight Enemies You Can't See, So We've Set up Perimeters to Keep Them Out," *Computers in Libraries* 26:1 (2006): 10–16.
5. "Thin Clients Saving Energy," Technology News Daily, March 15, 2007, www.technologynewsdaily.com/node/63352007
6. Kimberly Bolan and Robert Cullin, *Technology Made Simple: An Improvement Guide for Small and Medium Libraries* (Chicago, IL: American Library Association, 2007), 40.

Chapter 16

Automated Catalogs

Long, long ago libraries housed large cabinets consisting of many small drawers filled with cards representing the materials in the library. These were called card catalogs. Aside from browsing up and down the aisles or picking the librarian's brain, manually searching through the card catalog was the only way for someone to find an item in a library's collection. In those days, librarians were concerned about properly formatting catalog cards, inserting the correct punctuation marks in the right places, indenting the right number of spaces, skipping the right number of lines in certain places, and filing the cards correctly in the drawers according to the "filing rules." Multiple cards were generated for a single item, with added entries, tracings, and subject headings typed as headings to create as many access points as possible. Multiple access points made finding materials easier and accommodated as many ways as possible that a library user might approach the card catalog. Some libraries had separate author, title, and subject card catalogs, whereas smaller libraries may have elected to interfile all the cards in one big card catalog.

Thankfully, by now, most libraries have automated their catalogs, and their card catalogs have been given away or sold as antiques on eBay. Automated catalogs are now decades old, and there are systems designed for all sizes of library collections and budgets. These catalogs are web-based and customizable, with most bugs having been worked out and prices that are affordable. If you walk into a library today and see a big card catalog filled with cards, what would you think?

1. You are in a time warp.

2. The library staff is resistant to change.

3. This is a museum piece meant to elicit amazement and stimulate conversation.

4. This can't really be a library.

5. They are keeping the card catalog so the volunteers have work to do, such as print and file cards.

Ironically, the most extreme cases of card catalog separation anxiety occur in small libraries that are severely strapped for space and money. If your library is hanging on to the card catalog for dear life, refusing to let this "harbinger of childhood memories" slip into the past, let this be an intervention. Take a deep breath, find yourself a quiet corner, read this chapter, and do something!

To Automate or Not to Automate

Do you still have a card catalog in your library? If so, ask yourself why. If the reason is anything other than "to provide effective access to library materials," it is time to free up some space by moving that big piece of furniture out. If your answer is that you maintain a card catalog to provide access to materials, it is time to consider automation software. As you are thinking, here are some more questions to ponder:

- If you have rejected the idea of automating, why?

- Have you investigated automation products lately?

- How much money do you spend generating cards?

- How much time is spent filing cards?

- Could the time used to print and file cards be used in another, more useful, way?

- Are people using the card catalog to find information?

- Do you still instruct library users on how to use the card catalog?

- Do you maintain the card catalog? Does it accurately reflect what is in the collection?

Here are some reasons to automate:

- Searching the catalog will be easier.

- Users will be able to search the library catalog from outside the library.

- You will be able to provide better information services.

- It will be easier to edit and update bibliographic information.

- You will create more space in the library.

- Your library's image will improve.

Integrated Library Systems

As catalogs migrated to a digital format over the last few decades, a generation of products called integrated library systems (ILS) were developed. These modular systems provide broad functionality—including cataloging, serials control, acquisitions, and circulation modules, an online catalog, and user services such as placing holds, renewing materials, and viewing personal accounts—within a common database infrastructure. An integrated online catalog depends upon a bibliographic database and works interdependently with circulation and cataloging modules. As soon as the catalog record for an item is entered into the database, it is reflected in the online catalog. When a library user checks out an item, the online catalog indicates that the item is on loan and when it is due. Expectations of an online catalog include the location, call number, and circulation status of every item. ILSs also include patron modules, which tie material records to customer records, allowing customers to sign into their own accounts, view items they have on loan, view overdue items, renew items, and place materials on hold.

Initially, core modules were not designed to operate independently or across vendors, so libraries purchased all their ILS functionality from a single vendor. The interdependency of these modules, based on an underlying database structure, gave vendors the ability to capture a library's business for extended periods of time. Libraries were not free to shop around for the best in individual modules from different vendors, and, because of the cost and proprietary nature of integrated systems, neither did libraries freely change vendors.

Open Source ILSs

Although the great majority of library automation software is proprietary, some viable open source ILSs have emerged in recent years. One open source ILS (and one of the most ambitious statewide library automation efforts), Evergreen, was developed by the Georgia Public Library Service for use by the Georgia Library PINES program, a consortium of 270 public libraries. Evergreen (open-ils.org) is now available for other libraries to use, and Equinox Software provides commercial support and assistance to libraries interested in implementing Evergreen. Koha (koha.org), originally developed for a consortium of libraries in New Zealand, is the first full-featured open source ILS. LibLime (liblime.com) provides support services for Koha and other library open source software. LearningAccess ILS (www.learningaccess.org/tools/ils. php) specializes in library automation for rural and underserved communities, with good support. Learning Access has developed a turnkey version of the system, aVISTA, which runs on the Apple Mac Mini.

The Future of ILSs

With the emergence of separate products to manage electronic content, a more flexible ILS model is being developed. While the core ILS modules remain tied to single vendors, it is now possible to add unique and customized components from other vendors. The term "dis-integrated" has been used to describe this environment. The disadvantage of dis-integration is the cost to libraries in staff time to integrate the separate elements so they work well together.

The emergence of web services, or machine-to-machine interoperable applications, has given libraries the opportunity to enhance the customer experience. By using application programming interfaces, or APIs, you can provide dynamic content on your library's online public access catalog (OPAC), such as a list of "other books you might like," an image of the book or CD cover, interactive maps to library branches, or RSS feeds of new materials recently added to the collection. Librarians can use tools like web services to meet the expectations of today's sophisticated users.

The ability to search books and electronic content from one interface has become essential. Today's users are unlikely to have the patience to go to different interfaces within a library's website to separately search books, multimedia materials, periodicals, articles, and individual databases. Unfortunately, this is still the case with most library web catalogs. Customers are likely to find this aspect of library catalogs inconvenient and somewhat archaic, given their search experiences on the larger web. It is important for us to keep the customer's needs in mind when talking with vendors and selecting online catalog products and to require vendors to make our needs and our customers' needs a priority.

Selecting Automation Software

If you are looking for automation software, familiarize yourself with the products that are available and their features by doing some preliminary research. These resources are invaluable:

- Every April, *Library Journal* publishes "Automation Marketplace," which includes the latest trends in automation products, profiles of vendors, product details, and contact information.[1]

- *Computers in Libraries* publishes an ILS update annually, which provides a snapshot of ILS products and their features.[2]

- Pamela Cibbarelli's *Directory of Library Automation Software, Systems and Services* is an annual directory containing a wealth of information on library automation systems and vendors.[3]

- Marshall Breeding's Library Technology Guides (www.librarytechnology.org/index.pl?SID=20080124926269531) keep up with developments in the library automation field.

- Perceptions 2007: An International Survey of Library Automation (www.librarytechnology.org/perceptions2007.pl) provides some very useful information.

Decide What Features You Want and Need

First, decide what you want and need in your automation software. What features must you have? What features would be nice to have? What features don't you need? What features don't you want? Start with the big feature choices and make a list of them.

For instance, do you want client-server software or a software as a service (SaaS) solution? The client-server model is when the library purchases the software, installs it on the library's server, and keeps all data on the library's server. The SaaS model is when the vendor hosts the software on hardware housed and maintained by the vendor, all of the data is stored on the vendor's server, and only the software interface is installed on the library's computer. You lease the software and the service, usually for an annual subscription and maintenance fee.

An increasing number of ILS sales to small libraries involves SaaS implementations.[4] This is an affordable solution for libraries with limited budgets; however, if you decide on this option, be very clear with the SaaS provider about ownership of the data, your rights to it, migrating it, and the cost of technical support. This can end up being a very costly option if you can't get your hands on your own data and the vendor charges you heavily for certain kinds of technical support. When the vendor holds the data, are you at its mercy if things go down? Who does the backups, and what is being backed up? Will the vendor restore your data if necessary, or will you need to pay thousands of dollars to do this?

Will you need to purchase hardware to support the software and house the data? Do you want an ILS or just a catalog? Do you want your catalog accessible via the web so community members can search it from home? Is the platform Mac or PC? Does it have an application program interface (API) that allows you to use other software applications within the catalog? Do you need data conversion services?

Make sure library staff speaks the same language as the vendor's technical support staff. Small libraries in SaaS relationships with foreign vendors whose staff speaks limited English are over the barrel; any language barrier can create unnecessary communication breakdowns at the worst possible times. Do you want the vendor to be fluent in English?

Uninterrupted technical support is vital. Ensure that you will have support whenever you need it. If there is only one person in the technical support division, what happens when they go on vacation? What is the cost for ongoing technical support, if not included in the base price, and what does it cover? Do you have to pay for initial and refresher trainings? Where will you be flying the trainer from and to? Where will your staff have to travel to? Airfare to and from foreign countries is getting more expensive by the day. Does the vendor provide updates and develop new features? If the system remains the same, with no enhanced search capabilities or fresh looks, the library falls behind.

Talk to your colleagues in similar sized libraries. What products are they using? What is their biggest challenge? What would they change? Would they choose the same system today? Ask your state library agency. Talk to vendors at conferences and ask questions. Try the product out in person. Ask for demo disks. Take field trips to other libraries to see the products in action. Read reviews of automation vendors and systems.

Is the vendor viable? Research the company's financial information in online databases such as Hoover's and Gale Business and Company Resource Center. Check references of at least three libraries currently using the product. Ask a standard list of questions of each vendor, just as if you were interviewing someone for a position. Ask how quickly its technical support responds. Call technical support with a question, which will tell you something about how you will be treated should you purchase the product.

Using the print resources and your list of desired features, make a preliminary list of potential products and vendors. Think of the big picture, what is best for the library, your community, and library staff—not what suits you personally. You are responsible for selecting the product that will serve the needs of your users and allow your staff to maintain it.

Here are some final words of wisdom from Roy Tennant: "Guard your data with your life. Vendors come and go but our data remains. Before you sign a contract know how to extract and migrate your data. It's the only thing you really own. Selecting a vendor is as much about deciding whom you wish to work with on a regular basis as it is about selecting a specific technology solution. Choose your vendors carefully."[5]

Narrowing Your Vendor List, the RFP, and Your Selection

Contact vendors on your list and ask them about product development and new or unique features in their products. This will update you on what may be in development, give you a sense for the level of the vendor's customer service, and (hopefully) put you in contact with a real person in the company.

Ask about pricing and request some preliminary quotes so you can get a sense for the features and products in your range. Products are usually priced based on single-user or multiple-user fee structures. Multiple-user costs sometimes allow unlimited users and sometimes a limited number of simultaneous users. Determine how you think your system will be used in advance of requesting quotes; this will make a difference. Find out if all modules are included or if you are required to buy these separately. Can you buy only the cataloging and circulation modules, if those are the only ones you want? Can you add more modules at a later date? Does the web-based OPAC come with the system, or do you have to buy it separately?

Is the software easy to install, or will you need to hire outside support to install it? If there is a demo, try it out. What reports do you want to generate? What do you have to make the software do to generate that report? The simplest of results can be amazingly difficult to generate on some systems.

All systems are different, so the challenge lies in comparing apples, oranges, peaches, bananas, and grapes. The only sensible way to navigate through this maze is to decide on the features you want first, then sort through the vendors that offer them. Organize this information by creating a spreadsheet of your requirements and comparing them with vendor capabilities. Narrow your choices to around six vendors. The big factors will be client-server vs. SaaS, price, and platform.

If you are required to issue a request for proposal (RFP) by your municipality, university, or school, use the spreadsheet listing your requirements as a guide. Even if you are not required to issue an RFP, consider going through this process; it is a good way to clarify your needs and narrow down vendors based on what you want. You will have the opportunity to arrange for demos and presentations by the top contenders, which will help you make an educated choice about your final selection and negotiate a contract.

Selecting a User-Friendly OPAC

Ultimately, the OPAC you select must serve the customer—whether that means librarians or the people we serve. Can users find what they want easily and efficiently using your OPAC? The first screen that appears when a visitor selects "Library Catalog" on a library's home page can vary depending on the catalog (see Figures 16.1 though 16.4).

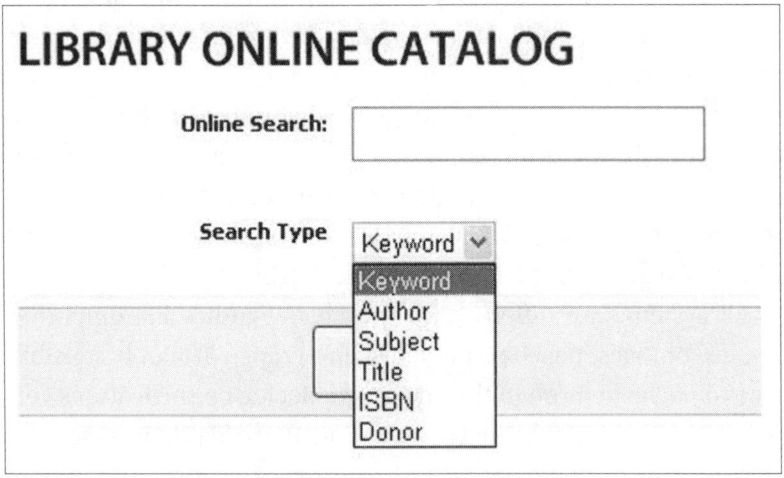

LIBRARY ONLINE CATALOG

Online Search:

Search Type   Keyword ▾

Keyword
Author
Subject
Title
ISBN
Donor

Figure 16.1 Search via a dropdown menu

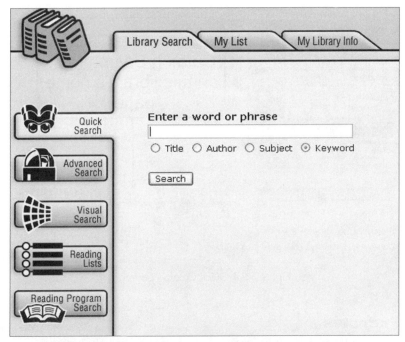

Figure 16.2 Search using radio buttons (note the Visual Search, Reading Lists Search, and Reading Program Search options

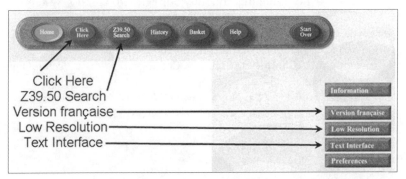

Figure 16.3 Choices that could be included before searching begins

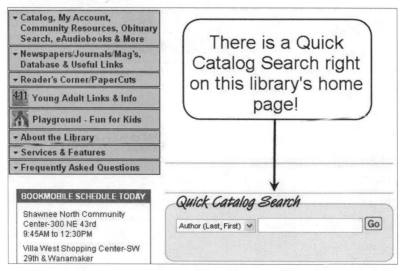

Figure 16.4 Quick Catalog Search

Endnotes

1. Marshall Breeding, "An Industry Redefined: Private Equity Moves into the ILS, and Open Source Support Emerges (Automation Marketplace 2007)," *Library Journal* 132:6 (2007): 36–46.

2. Richard Wayne, "Helping You Buy: Integrated Library Systems," *Computers in Libraries* 26:9 (2006): 23–31.

3. Pamela Cibbarelli, *Directory of Library Automation Software, Systems, and Services* (Medford, NJ: Information Today), 2006.

4. "Introduction (Chapter 1) (Library Catalogs)," *Library Technology Reports* 43:4 (2007): 5–14.

5. Roy Tennant, "Facing the Not Knowing," *Library Journal* January 15, 2007, www.libraryjournal.com/article/CA6403655.htm

Chapter 17

Online Reference Tools

The Internet and other new technologies have introduced innovative ways for librarians to provide reference service. Our ability
to access readily available online content helps us immensely in
our role as information retrievers and disseminators. New technologies give us the opportunity to meet information needs in our
communities outside the library building, providing reference
service to people wherever they are, at any hour of the day.

Online Reference Resources

Reference resources on the web have been a boon for libraries,
especially those that cannot afford to purchase all the latest reference tools. Even the smallest of libraries with the leanest budgets
have been able to provide Internet access and computers, thanks
to government and private funding for this purpose over the last
decade. Online reference resources have greatly expanded our
ability to provide reference service in all types of libraries.

We now have so many more resources at our fingertips than we
ever imagined possible. Small underfunded libraries weren't previously able to purchase an adequate reference collection, and the
high cost of reference books prohibits many libraries from owning
the best printed resources recommended for a core collection.
Today we can access many reference sources online free of charge.
If you develop your reference collection with these sites in mind,
you can maximize your budget for reference materials. You are
missing out on an enormous reference resource if you fail to tap

into the Internet's potential at your library—and Googling every reference question doesn't count.

Your Library's Ready Reference Web Page

Online, you can get free access to almanacs, biographical dictionaries, currency converters, census data, dictionaries, atlases, news, quotations, telephone directories, ZIP code directories, and more. Many libraries create a web page with links to local and popular reference websites (see Figure 17.1) , which serve as a great, ready reference tool for librarians as well as a great resource for library customers wherever they may be—in the library, at home, or at work.

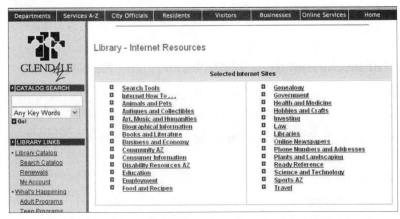

Figure 17.1 Selected Internet Resources from the Glendale (AZ) Public Library

Look at these other sites that list free online reference tools to get a start on selecting appropriate resources for your own library's reference web page:

- Bartleby.com Reference (www.bartleby.com/reference)

- Best Free Reference Web Sites 2007 ALA/RUSA (www.ala.org/ala/rusa/rusaourassoc/rusasections/mars/marspubs/marsbestref2007.cfm)

- Internet Public Library Reference Center
  (www.ipl.org.ar/ref)

- Librarians' Internet Index (www.lii.org)

- Ready Reference Web Sites from Michigan State
  University Libraries (www.lib.msu.edu/sowards/
  home/home2.htm)

- Refdesk.com (www.refdesk.com/essentl.html)

- Selected Ready Reference Resources from the New York
  State Library (www.nysl.nysed.gov/reference/
  readyref. htm)

Link to your reference page from your library's home page. Set
some time aside initially to collect and compile the links that best
meet the needs of your customers, organize them for easy access,
and compose the page.

Start by bookmarking your favorite online reference tools on
Delicious (del.icio.us). Del.icio.us is a social bookmarking tool that
allows you to store your bookmarks online and access them from
anywhere. By storing these bookmarks on del.icio.us you will free
yourself up to (1) capture good reference sites whenever you come
across them, wherever you may be, and (2) access these sites
whenever you need them, wherever you may be. For instance, you
can work on this project in your office, and later access the bookmarks from the reference desk or a handheld device.

Once you have a solid collection of reference web resources,
create a simple web page to make them available through your
library's site. Don't forget to add important links to your local government, school district, academic institution, or parent company,
as well as timely links to resources like federal tax forms during tax
season. Customize your site to your library, making links to the
library calendar, library news, and staff directory.

Update the page regularly, checking for broken links, and
adding any new resources you have discovered. If users routinely

see error messages when using your reference page, they will quickly abandon your site. Once you lose someone, they are unlikely to return, because there are so many other choices for finding information on the web.

On your page note the date it was last updated or checked for broken links, a significant piece of information when it comes to evaluating reference sites. A reference site that was last updated in 2005 is probably not going to be very useful. Make notes about and search for new reference resources as a part of your job. Subscribe to reference email discussion lists and reference blogs for leads to new tools.

Electronic Reference Tools

Your library or library system may subscribe to electronic databases that provide additional valuable reference resources to your library customers. If you don't know what electronic databases are available to you, contact your state library or regional library system to double check. Many libraries do not take advantage of the electronic databases that are funded by state libraries and library systems and provided to member libraries (free of charge or for a nominal fee). This is a tremendous, yet underutilized, resource. If you are in a small library with a budget to match, there is no excuse for (1) being unaware of the electronic databases available to you, (2) neglecting to use them in doing your work, or (3) hiding them from library customers.

Take some time to look carefully at these databases. What do they contain? Sometimes we assume databases only access periodical articles; many librarians don't know that they may hold reference materials and popular magazines as well as scholarly journal articles. Find out what databases are available, and learn what is in them and how to search them. If you don't know you have access to a resource, you are not going to use it. As a librarian, you are responsible for retrieving and disseminating information to meet the needs of your users, so you have to be proactive in finding out what is available to you. Your lean reference collection may be less exasperating when you know about the databases that are only a click away.

For example, popular electronic databases available free to public libraries throughout New Mexico include Business Rankings Annual, Encyclopedia of Associations, International Directory of Company Histories, Who's Who Among African Americans, and Contemporary Authors. Many small libraries— which are unlikely to have these volumes on their reference shelves—will find these resources very handy. The need to refer people to other libraries is decreased when we have such rich online resources readily available.

Knowledgeable Reference Staff

Another vital element to providing reference through online and electronic resources is educating reference staff about these resources. Those responsible for providing reference service must:

1. Know the library has access to online and electronic databases

2. Know what they are and about their content

3. Know how to use them

Reference staff should never be in the dark about the existence of these tools and how to use them; they are essential to quality reference service.

Hold periodic training sessions and updates for reference staff on online and electronic resources. These resources change and are updated, and there are always new resources emerging. Different databases utilize different search strategies, and it is necessary to understand them all. Take advantage of training provided by electronic database vendors and use the marketing and informational materials they produce for librarians and customers alike.

Provide reference staff with information about periodical holdings that include full-text online versions. These could be printed lists, listed on a library web page or in the OPAC. This will make it easier to answer questions about periodicals holdings. Make a list of full-text reference books available through electronic databases as a reminder of additional resources or as a training tool.

How Has the Internet Changed Reference Service?

Suddenly, you can provide reference service from anywhere. Once you experience how liberating this is and the effect it can have, you will wonder what took you so long. Your library's reference resources web page allows anyone to access the library's online reference collection, at any time, from anywhere. Adding a link to the library's electronic databases will add to its impact.

Before you get too excited, remember that you can't find everything on the Internet—increased access to online resources and electronic databases does not mean you don't need a reference collection in the library. Some print reference resources are essential for providing well-rounded and complete reference service. However, adding online ready reference resources to your collection gives you more possibilities, allows you to provide ready reference service to your online customers, and provides a more efficient way to answer some reference questions.

You no longer need to passively sit at the reference desk—or be close to the reference book collection—waiting to provide reference service. Some reference librarians even "roam" the library, actively seeking business. We are no longer limited to the books in our library's reference collection, so we no longer feel anchored to a reference desk.

Providing Online Reference Service

For a long time we have answered reference questions in person and by phone, but now we can answer them by email, web forms, chat, instant messaging (IM), and texting (short messaging service or SMS). This makes reference service much more customer service–oriented. We are reaching out to our customers and letting people contact us in multiple ways. Customers can now request information in the way that is easiest and most convenient for them.

Check with your state, county, or regional system about cooperative online reference services that may already be in place. Some systems are funding virtual reference initiatives with LSTA funds, and you don't want to miss out on this opportunity. You can purchase a proprietary system; however, any library of any size can provide reference by email, live chat, web forms, and IM (Figures 17.2 through 17.5).

E-mail us a question

What is your e-mail address?
(required)

Which Oregon library do you want to answer your question?
Any library in Oregon will do

What is your zip code?
(required)

What level of information do you need?
Select one

How can we help you?
(required)

Ask

Figure 17.2 Email reference request from Oregon State Library

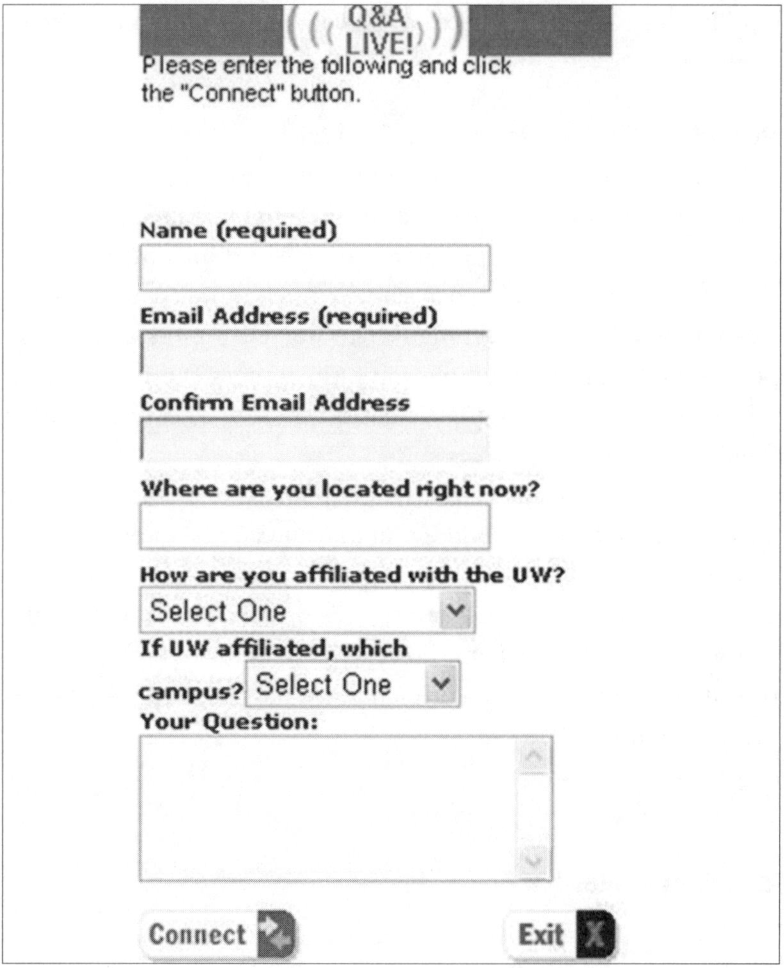

Figure 17.3 Live reference chat from University of Washington Libraries

To find out about other libraries offering online reference services, view their sites and visit LibSuccess.org (www.libsuccess.org/index.php?title=Online_Reference). You can offer IM reference service using the major chat clients: AOL's Instant Messenger (AIM; www.aim.com), Yahoo! Messenger (www.yahoomessenger.com), Windows Live Messenger or MSN Messenger (im.live.com), and Google Talk (www.google.com/talk). Use a multiservice IM client

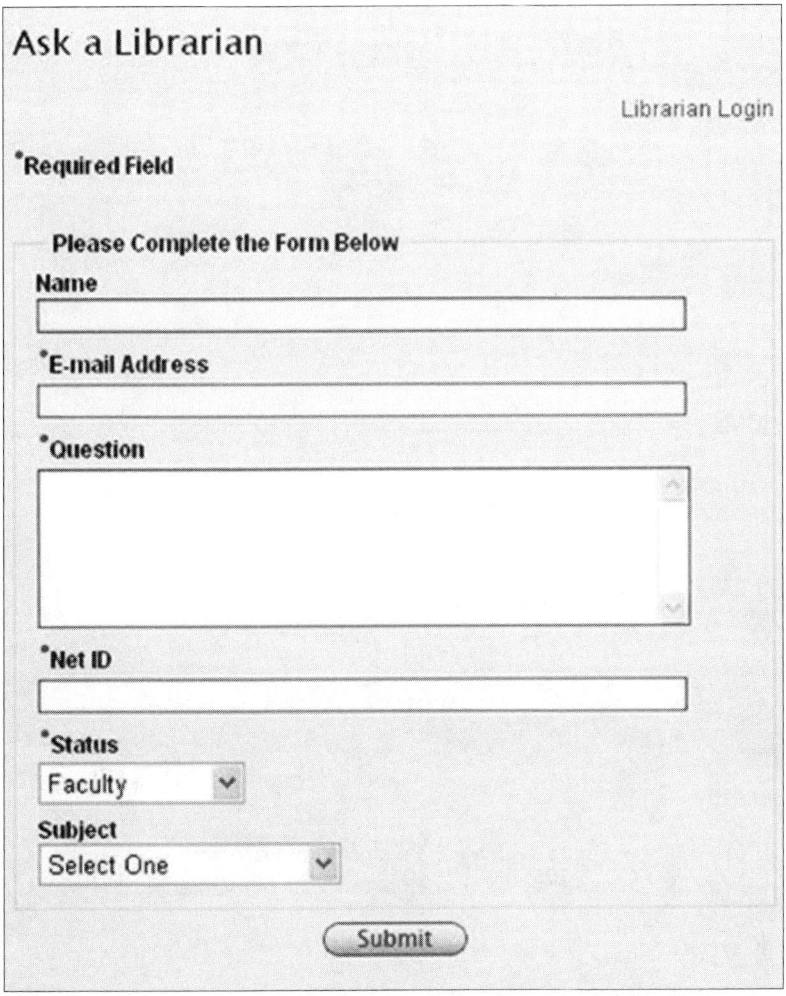

Figure 17.4 Web form for reference requests

like the web-based Meebo (www.meebo.com) to pull instant messages from several chat clients into a single interface. Other multiservice IM applications like Pidgin (www.pidgin.im) and Trillian
(www.trillian.cc) provide similar functionality but require you to
download and install software on your computer. The advantage of

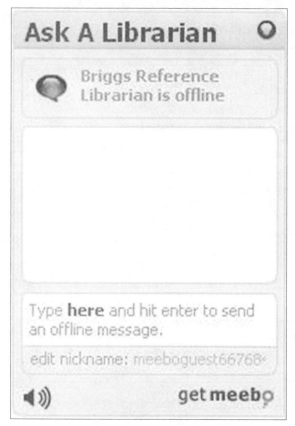

Figure 17.5 Meebo widget for IM reference
from Briggs Library at the University of Minnesota

a web-based application is that you can sign into your multiservice IM account from any computer (see Figure 17.5).

Now that IM has become commonplace, mobile text messaging has become the latest way of communicating, especially among younger people. A few libraries offer SMS reference service. This involves texting a short query to a unique library number. Google SMS provides this service for quick information like ZIP codes, flight status, weather, and stock quotes.

Here are some things to think about as you plan your online reference service:

- Hours of operation
- Placing a reference widget on your library's website
- Training reference staff
- Promoting online reference services

Chapter 18

Library 2.0

For centuries we have thought about libraries as buildings where people come to find the knowledge they are seeking. Librarians were known as "guardians of knowledge." They were based in the library, and served customers inside the building by helping them find information in books and other printed materials. Since the Internet enables people to access vast amounts of information wherever they are, with just a few keystrokes, these concepts of library and librarian are becoming outdated.

Library 2.0 introduces a new paradigm, which expands our view of the library beyond its four walls, our view of library service beyond providing information in the library building, and our view of library customers to expand the concept of participation. Librarians, who have long used the tools available to them to meet the information needs of everyone in their communities, were 2.0 pioneers—long before it was the rage. Before all the technological tools of the last few decades, the first 2.0 tools allowed librarians to reach out to people who couldn't come to the library building or use traditional printed materials with services such as bookmobiles, homebound services, and services for the blind and physically disabled.

Think about new technology as a tool to help librarians in doing the work of the library—and all the possibilities that suggests. Library 2.0 has energized our profession and eliminated some of the barriers to our thinking about providing services outside the library building. Ideas about what Library 2.0 means abound, including differing and opposing definitions and viewpoints.

The debate about the meaning of Library 2.0 will continue to change and evolve as new technology and tools emerge, and the information-seeking behavior of the people we serve evolves. Library 2.0 has different implications for different libraries and different community needs; no one definition or application will suit all libraries. You can't wait for the dust to settle on this issue before you take action, though. Librarians must consider what Library 2.0 means for them, for their libraries, and for their communities, so they can participate in this exciting movement and use it to accomplish their work.

What Is Library 2.0?

Library 2.0 means using the tools available to you to provide enhanced library services to library customers, reach out to potential users where they are, and create interactive and comfortable library services and programs. Some of these tools may involve technology, but technology isn't required to participate. Library 2.0 is:

- Serving your customers where they are
- Outreach to your entire population
- Attracting customers who don't use your library
- Inviting participation
- Providing good customer service
- Creating attractive and easy-to-use library services for all
- Changing to meet the information needs of everyone you serve
- Partnering with other libraries to enhance library services
- Enhancing the library experience by using the latest methods available

- Nothing new to librarians who already understand and employ these concepts

Following are some definitions of Library 2.0 from a few librarians in the midst of the discussion.

Sarah Houghton-Jan gives this definition:

> Library 2.0 simply means making your library's space (virtual and physical) more interactive, collaborative, and driven by community needs.

She suggests starting with blogs, gaming nights for teens, and collaborative photo sites, for example. The basic drive is to get people back into the library by making the library relevant to what they want in their daily lives, to make the library a destination and not an afterthought.[1]

According to Michael Casey:

> Library 2.0 is all about library users—keeping those we have while actively seeking those who do not currently use our services. It's about embracing those ideas and technologies that can assist libraries in delivering services to these groups, and it's about participation—involving users in service creation and evaluation. Library 2.0 is an operating model that allows libraries to respond rapidly to market needs. This does not mean that we abandon our current users or our mission. It is a philosophy of rapid change, flexible organizational structures, new Web 2.0 tools and user participation that will put the library in a much stronger position, ready to efficiently and effectively meet the needs of a larger user population.[2]

Michael Stephens says:

The principles of Library 2.0 seek to put users in touch with information and entertainment wherever they may be, breaking down the barriers of space, time and outdated policy. It is a user-centered paradigm focusing on knowledge, experience, collaboration, the creation of new content and encouraging the heart.[3]

What Does Library 2.0 Mean for You?

As you know, librarians are responsible for meeting the information needs of everyone in the community they serve. If you only serve the people who come into the library, or if you are basing your Library 2.0 efforts on the needs of regular library users, you must start by assessing the information needs of your entire community (see Chapter 4). Create a plan for your library (see Chapter 5), and then use 2.0 tools to help you reach your library's goals.

If you are already serving your entire community and using your library plan as a guide, begin to think about how you might improve services and programs or attract new customers by using new technology and other Library 2.0 tools available to you. Ask yourself what information needs your library can meet using a Library 2.0 approach. How can you provide better customer service, make the library's website easier to use, or promote the use of online databases to people outside the library? How can you make the library experience (both in the building and on the web) more pleasant for everyone? How can you attract new library users and encourage their participation?

Library 2.0 focuses librarians on meeting the information needs of changing populations. With the emergence of the Internet and online information tools such as Google, Ask.com, Amazon, MapQuest, and Wikipedia, many people now bypass libraries when they need information. They equate libraries with books and consider them to be slow, antiquated, unappealing, and irrelevant, preferring the faster, increasingly familiar, and easier to use online environment. Savvy Internet users have little patience for searching the library's online catalog and databases. Many of them are unlikely to stick around library websites long enough to discover the rich resources libraries have to offer. A recent report from the Pew Internet and American Life Project revealed that only 13 percent of people in the U.S. go to a public library as a source of information when they need to address problems; 58 percent said they use the Internet.[4] This gives librarians some important information about where most people go for information. Library 2.0 tools can help libraries create a presence on the Internet that attracts people who are looking for information.

What Can You Do to 2.0 Your Library?

Here are some things you can do to introduce 2.0 into your library:

1. Educate yourself about Library 2.0

2. Understand how Library 2.0 can benefit your library and the people you serve

3. Pick a few Library 2.0 ideas that will help your library reach an identified goal

4. Implement these ideas

5. Reevaluate their effectiveness in helping to reach the goal

6. Readjust and refine

Educating Yourself

Before you can implement Library 2.0 technology you must learn what is available and what these tools do. Check out the suggested materials in the Recommended Reading list at the end of the book, subscribe to Library 2.0 blogs, investigate what other libraries are doing, participate, experiment, go to conferences like Internet Librarian (www.infotoday.com/il2008), and learn about the technology tools as they emerge. Here are some places to start:

- Investigate resources on the Library 2.0 Reading List (www.squidoo.com/library20)

- Take the 23 Things tutorial at School Library Learning 2.0 (schoollibrarylearning2.blogspot.com/2007/02/23-things_27.html)

- Look around Five Weeks to a Social Library (www.social libraries.com/course)

- Find Time for Emerging Technologies (unconferencewa library.pbwiki.com/Finding%20time%20for%20emerging %20tech)

- Read Learning 2.0 (plcmcl2-things.blogspot.com)

- Join the Library 2.0 group on Ning (library20.ning.com)

- Attend the SirsiDynix Institute: The 2.0 Meme—Web 2.0, Library 2.0, Librarian 2.0 (www.sirsidynixinstitute.com/ seminar_page.php?sid=56)

- Read some Library 2.0 blogs:

  - Blyberg.net (www.blyberg.net)

  - Information Wants to be Free (meredith.wolfwater.com/wordpress)

  - LibraryCrunch (www.librarycrunch.com)

  - David Lee King (www.davidleeking.com)

  - iLibrarian (oedb.org/blogs/ilibrarian)

  - Tame the Web (tametheweb.com)

  - The Shifted Librarian (theshiftedlibrarian.com)

- Librarian in Black (librarianinblack.typepad.com)

- Walking Paper (www.walkingpaper.org)

Choosing the Tools that Support Your Library's Plan

Which 2.0 tools can you use to provide better services and programs? Look at your library's plan and identify how these tools can enhance services or help accomplish specific goals and objectives. For instance, if your library plans to increase awareness about new library acquisitions, posting and updating this information on the library's web page and creating an RSS feed might be appropriate Library 2.0 methods for reaching this goal. A wiki could be the right tool if your library wants to invite community members to participate in discussions about library resources, programs, and services. Don't create an RSS feed or a wiki just because they are cool or hot. What customer needs are you meeting? What is it you are trying to accomplish? What service are you providing? Is it in the library's plan? What is the best tool for the job? How are you going to market it? Who is responsible for site monitoring or updating? How will you measure its success?

Library 2.0 Technology Tools

Some technology tools your library might use include blogs, social networking sites, wikis, social bookmarking tools, instant messaging (IM), videocasting, podcasting, screencasting, RSS feeds, and gaming.

Blogs

Blogs are online journals consisting of entries about whatever interests the author. Readers can add comments, so there may be a dialogue associated with any entry. Libraries can use blogs as newsletters, a communication tool for library staff, or online book clubs. Librarians host blogs on a variety of topics related to libraries and librarianship, a good place to find out what is going on in our field. A list of library blogs and blogs by librarians can be found at Library Weblogs (www.libdex.com/weblogs.html).

Microblogs

Twitter is a communication tool that allows you to convey short messages (or a microblog) of up to 140 characters to your circle of friends via the Twitter website. Some libraries use Twitter to post new acquisitions or publish bulletin type messages. Twitter messages can be accessed through IM clients and mobile phones. Some examples of libraries on Twitter are:

- Cleveland Public Library (twitter.com/Cleveland_PL)

- Lunar and Planetary Institute Library (twitter.com/LPI_Library)

- Casa Grande Library (twitter.com/cglibrary)

Social Networking

MySpace (www.myspace.com) is the largest social networking site used by libraries to create profiles. Each profile includes a blog, calendar, bulletin, and music sharing capabilities. Here are some examples of libraries on MySpace:

- Brooklyn College Library (www.myspace.com/brooklyn collegelibrary)

- Denver Public Library Teens (www.myspace.com/denver_evolver)

- Hobbs Public Library (www.myspace.com/booksrcool)

- Ball State University Libraries (www.myspace.com/brackenlibrary)

- Barnard Zine Library (www.myspace.com/barnardzine library)

- Libraries on MySpace (groups.myspace.com/myspace libraries)

Facebook (www.facebook.com) is the social networking site favored by college students; individual librarians and libraries can join. Here are some examples of libraries on Facebook:

- Mills Library at McMaster University (www.facebook.com/profile.php?id=7233086835)
- Regina Public Library (www.facebook.com/pages/Regina-SK/Regina-Public-Library-/7519206045?ref=s)

Flickr (www.flickr.com) is an online photo-sharing site that strives to give access to photos in as many ways as it can. You can view photos on the Flickr website, in RSS feeds, by email, or by posting to blogs. Here are a few library Flicker accounts:

- Lester Public Library (www.flickr.com/photos/lester publiclibrary/collections/72157602264429004)
- North Carolina State University Libraries Special Collections Research Center (www.flickr.com/photos/ncsu_scrc)
- Library of Congress 1930s–1940s Color Photos (www.flickr.com/photos/library_of_congress/sets/ 72157603671370361)
- Newton Free Library (www.flickr.com/photos/newton freelibrary)

Wikis

Wikis are web-based tools for creating, collecting, and organizing resources and documents for teams, projects, or personal use. Library-related wiki examples include:

- Doucette Library of Teaching Resources Wiki (wiki. ucalgary.ca/page/Doucette)

- Ohio University Libraries Biz Wiki (www.library.ohiou.edu/subjects/bizwiki)

- Oregon Library Instruction Wiki (instructionwiki.org)

Social Bookmarking

Social bookmarking combines the knowledge of the masses with the concepts of cataloging, letting you use tags or keywords of your own to describe your bookmarks. Commonly shared tags link you to other people who are interested in that topic, who want to know more about that topic, or have bookmarked an item on that topic. Examples of social bookmarking tools include:

- Delicious (del.icio.us)

- Furl (www.furl.net)

Instant Messaging

Instant messaging (IM) is a great way to connect online with library users and answer reference questions when and where they need the service (see Chapter 17). Lesley Williams, Director of Reference Services at the Evanston (IL) Public Library, says, "We feel that there is a possibility that we're losing younger patrons, that they're not necessarily thinking of using the library as a resource. If you don't have a way of communicating with them through Internet Messaging (IM), you really seem irrelevant."[5]

Using IM at Evanston Public is one way of increasing the library's relevance and visibility among teens in the community. Teens use IM and cell phone texting to communicate. Talking on the telephone, sending emails, and talking to a librarian in person are not the way they prefer to interact. The objective is to connect with users who might not use the library if it weren't for IM.

Libraries need to be accessible and approachable for everyone in the community.

Videocasting

Librarians can use videocasting in many ways to connect with their customers. Here are a few examples that include library instruction, library tours, tutorials, book reviews, and marketing:

- Fairfax (VA) Public Library Self-Service Checkout Instruction (www.youtube.com/watch?v=iYwta1lCp8 Y&feature=related)

- Greater Victoria Public Library News (www.youtube. com/watch?v=J9MqhqIZRIM)

- Brown University Library Video Tutorial (www.brown.edu/Facilities/University_Library/ tutorials/gateway_videos.html)

- UC San Diego Biomedical Library Tour (video.google. com/videoplay?docid=5161576846247354338)

- Seattle Public Library Virtual Tour (www.spl.org/ videos/VirtualTour5-10-2007/VirtualTour5-10-2007.html)

- Delray Beach Public Library "I Love My Library" (www.youtube.com/watch?v=FcNIsWExKEw)

- The One Minute Critic (oneminutecritic.wordpress.com)

Other uses for library videocasts include oral histories and "meet the staff" videos.

Podcasting

Podcasts offer libraries a way to speak directly to the people they serve, providing news, book reviews, interviews, or any content that can be conveyed using an audio recording. They serve as an alternative way to provide information to people who learn by listening rather than reading. Because podcasts can be downloaded to iPods and other MP3 players, people can listen to them while exercising, during their commute, or whenever convenient for them. Customers can subscribe to the library's podcasts through an RSS feed, receiving all updates and news as they are broadcast.

Screencasting

Screencasting is another 2.0 tool you can use for people who prefer to see content as it is explained. Libraries often use screencasts to provide instruction on using databases and other library resources. In screencasting, a visual recording is made of the computer screen (including mouse and cursor movements), with an accompanying audio recording. For instance, as the narrator performs a database search, the screencast shows every step that is taken and includes audio explaining every move. Screencasts are very useful for handling short, routine instruction requests.

RSS Feeds

RSS feeds are a great way to keep up with blogs, websites, radio shows, and news alerts. Libraries who put RSS feeds on their websites or blogs offer users the opportunity to receive alerts whenever new material is posted. This takes the burden off the user to regularly check the site for new information, as it is conveniently delivered to them in their reader. RSS feeds are a good way for libraries to use technology to disseminate information. (See Chapter 9 for more on creating and reading RSS feeds.)

Gaming

In an effort to attract teens, many libraries are providing services to gamers. Games can be played on personal computers, game consoles, or handheld devices. They can be played by an individual against the computer or by several users against one another. "Gaming can be educational in spite of all the negative attention. Gaming itself is a learning medium, in that the gamer must learn how to play to win a game."[6] Users acquire new skills, exercise problem-solving skills, develop eye-hand coordination, and even exercise while gaming.

Library 2.0 Nontechnology Tools

Delivering information to users where they are in the way they prefer to receive it can also include nontechnological methods, for example:

- User friendly signage

- Knowledgeable staff

- Bookmobile service

- Outreach to the homebound

- Roving reference librarians

Planning, Promoting, and Educating

Embrace the basic concept of how Library 2.0 can benefit your library by helping to meet the information needs of the people you serve. Start by learning as much as you can about what is available to you, commit yourself to participating, and stay up-to-date.

Endnotes

1. Sarah Houghton-Jan, "Library 2.0 Discussion," Librarian-in-Black, December 19, 2005, librarianinblack.typepad.com/librarianinblack/2005/12/library_20_disc.html
2. Michael Casey, "Library 2.0 Reading List," Squidoo, www.squidoo.com/library20
3. Michael Stephens, "Library 2.0 Reading List," Squidoo, www.squidoo.com/library20
4. Leigh Estabrook, Evans Witt, and Lee Rainie, "Information Searches That Solve Problems: How People Use the Internet, Libraries, and

Government Agencies When They Need Help," in *Pew Internet & American Life Project* (Washington, DC: Pew Research Center, 2007), v.

5. Robert Channick, "Libraries Using IMs to Attract Young Clients," *Chicago Tribune*, September 13, 2007.

6. Meredith Farkas, *Social Software in Libraries* (Medford, NJ: Information Today, Inc., 2007), 217.

Part IV

Career
Development

Chapter 19

Getting Connected and Finding Support

One of the best ways to learn about librarianship, stay updated in our field, find out how to do new tasks and jobs, or find help in troubleshooting a problem is to connect with other librarians. Networking with colleagues to discuss common concerns or to find and lend support is essential if we want to learn and grow in our profession. Librarians are naturals at connecting, networking, helping, and supporting others. We enjoy finding and sharing information, and helping others find the information they need. We have a common belief in lifelong learning and the power of information to improve the lives of others, and we want information to be free and available to all. It is not in our nature to withhold information; as a profession we are very generous about sharing our knowledge with others. This will work to your advantage as you reach out for assistance and support.

Start by joining local organizations, associations, and work groups. Look in your own library, library system, consortium, state library association, or state library agency for opportunities to network and become involved. Attend a meeting or class, or volunteer to be on a committee or task force concerning a topic of interest.

Your Own Library

Look around your own workplace. If you work with MLS librarians, make an effort to connect with them. Other librarians are the best place to begin, because not only can they support you in your work, but they can also help you connect with a network of librarians. They will introduce you to other librarians who can help with specific problems, suggest you as an association committee member, or explain some basic theory and practice. Experienced librarians can be your best allies, mentors, and guides.

State and Regional Library Associations

Wherever you live, there is a state or regional library association for you to join. The mission of most library associations is to encourage, promote, and support the profession of librarianship and the welfare of libraries through continuing education, leadership, networking, and advocacy. Anyone interested in libraries and librarianship is usually welcome to join, and membership fees are affordable; many associations offer memberships on a sliding scale based on income. State library associations hold conferences and workshops where you can learn new skills and meet librarians from all kinds of libraries throughout your state or region. They offer opportunities for serving on committees and task forces, where you will learn more about the profession and have a chance to participate in advancing libraries and librarianship. Local library associations will keep you current on library issues and legislation in your state or region, and many have websites, blogs, and email lists you can join.

Regional library associations, such as Border Regional (www.brla.info), Mountain Plains (www.mpla.us), New England (www.nelib.org), Pacific Northwest (www.pnla.org), and Southeastern (sela.jsu.edu), offer additional opportunities for librarians to network and connect with other librarians in a wider geographic range. American Library Association (ALA) maintains a list of state and regional associations and contacts (www.ala.org/ala/ourassociation/chapters/stateandregional/stateregional.htm), where you can find a link to your state or regional library association's website. Contact them, find out about what they do, join, and participate.

Library Systems and Consortia

If your library is part of a library system or consortium, look for opportunities to connect with supportive librarians within your own system or group. Get out of your daily work environment and look for opportunities to join committees, work groups, or task forces where you can meet like-minded colleagues.

Online Communities

The Internet offers other ways to find support and learn what is going on in our field. The advantage to online communities is that you can visit when it is convenient for you. You can also head straight for a particular topic to find people who are working on the same issues, people who have experience with something you want to know more about, or websites with the answers you need. Although at times this may be a quicker solution, you will miss the personal contact and face-to-face networking opportunities offered by participating in classes, meetings, and committee work. Start by visiting online communities that are geared toward librarians, libraries, and nonprofits, for example:

- LISjobs.com Message Boards (lisjobs.com/forum) –
  Designed primarily for librarians and information professionals who are looking for jobs or career advice. There
  are forums on topics such as Professional Development
  and Participation, Work/Life Balance, Jumpstart Your
  Career, Management and Moving Up, Professional
  Success, and Education.

- WebJunction (www.webjunction.org) – A cooperative of library staff sharing and using online resources that help them to identify and understand appropriate technologies and apply them in their work. WebJunction is intended for people who work in all kinds of libraries and other organizations that support public access to information technology. The website is rich in content, offering courses for a minimal fee (some free for partner states), free webinars, topical and regional discussion boards, and resources on patron services, management, and technology.

- TechSoup (www.techsoup.org) – Offers nonprofits, including libraries, a one-stop resource for their technology needs by providing free information, resources, news and articles, discussion forums, and support. In addition to online information and resources, the site offers a product philanthropy service where nonprofits can access donated and discounted technology products and software provided by corporate and nonprofit technology partners.

Electronic Discussion Groups

A good deal of communication and discussion of specific or regional topics occurs on electronic discussion groups. Check your state library association, regional library system, consortium, state library agency, or other local library groups and chapters for electronic discussion groups to join. These are invaluable in staying aware of local meetings, events, and opportunities for networking and finding support. Here are some national discussion groups that may pique your interest:

- ACQNET-L (serials.infomotions.com/acqnet) – Acquisitions and collection development

- AUTOCAT (www.cwu.edu/~dcc/Autocat-ToC-2007.html) – Cataloging and authority control

- BUSLIB-L (list1.ucc.nau.edu/archives/buslib-l.html) – Business librarians

- CHMINF-L (www.indiana.edu/~cheminfo/network.html) – Chemical information sources

- COMLIB-L (listserv.uiuc.edu/archives/comlib-l.html) – Communications librarians

- DLDG-L (listserv.indiana.edu/cgi-bin/wa-iub.exe?A0 =DLDG-L) – Dance librarians

- ExLibris (palimpsest.stanford.edu/byform/mailing-lists/exlibris) – Rare books, manuscripts, and special collections

- GOVDOC-L (govdoc-l.org) – Government information and the Federal Depository Library program

- Law-Lib (home.olemiss.edu/%7Enoe/llfaq.html) – Law librarians

- LIBADMIN-L (listserv.williams.edu/archives/lib admin-l.html) – Library administrators

- LIBJOBS (www.ifla.org/II/lists/libjobs.htm) – Employment service list for librarians

- LIBLICENSE-L (www.library.yale.edu/~llicense/mailing-list.shtml) – Electronic content licensing for academic and research libraries

- LIBREF-L (www.library.kent.edu/page/10391) – Reference librarianship

- LM_NET (www.eduref.org/lm_net) – School library media specialists

- MAPS-L (www.listserv.uga.edu/archives/maps-l.html) – Maps, air photo, and geospatial systems forum

- MEDLIB-L (www.mlanet.org/discussion/medlibl.html) – Medical librarians

- MLA-L (listserv.indiana.edu/cgi-bin/wa-iub.exe?A0= MLA-L) – Music Library Association mailing list

- NEWLIB-L (www.lahacal.org/newlib) – Discussion list for new librarians

- NGC4Lib (dewey.library.nd.edu/mailing-lists/ngc4lib) – Next generation catalogs for libraries

- oss4lib (oss4lib.org/mailing-list) – Open source systems for libraries

- PACS-L (epress.lib.uh.edu/pacsl/pacsl.html) – Public access computer systems

- PIJIP-COPYRIGHT (roster.wcl.american.edu/cgi-bin/wa.exe?A0=PIJIP-COPYRIGHT&X=5D71B 90996102E1081&Y=mpalmedo@wcl.american.edu) – Program on information justice and intellectual property copyright listserv

- PRISON-LIB (lists.topica.com/lists/PRISON-LIB/?cid=2065) – Prison and jail librarians interest group

- PROJECT WOMBAT (www.project-wombat.org/one_list_three_ways.shtml) – Difficult reference questions

- PUBLIB (lists.webjunction.org/publib) – Public librarianship and public libraries

- PUBYAC (www.pubyac.org) – Children and young adult services in public libraries

- SERIALST (www.uvm.edu/~bmaclenn/serialst.html) – Serials in libraries discussion forum

- SYSLIB-L (listserv.buffalo.edu/cgi-bin/wa?A0=syslib-l) – Systems librarianship

- TAGAD-L (lists.topica.com/lists/tagad-l) – Teen advisory groups in pubic libraries

- Web4Lib (lists.webjunction.org/web4lib) – Library-based World Wide Web managers

- XML4Lib (lists.webjunction.org/xml4lib) – XML and its use in, by, and for libraries and library users

- YALSA (www.ala.org/ala/yalsa/electronicresourcesb/ websitesmailing.cfm#discussion) – Young adult library services discussion lists

You can find links to ALA open discussion groups, forums, and interest groups at www.ala.org/ala/ourassociation/discussion groups/listaladiscussion.htm, and links to ALA electronic discussion lists at lists.ala.org/wws.

Blogs

There are many librarian-written blogs on topics surrounding libraries and librarianship, each with a differing focus, view, and angle. Some include information about a blogger's personal life, some focus on their professional activities and accomplishments, and others offer opinions on library issues and trends, technology, library conference sessions, and library news. Blogs can be very educational and helpful in keeping up-to-date on quickly changing topics and getting insight into different points of view on issues in our field.

Many blogs encourage comments, so electronic discussions on specific topics often take place in the comments section following a blog posting. If you find some blogs you particularly like and visit often, subscribe to their RSS feeds, and updates will be delivered to your blog reader all in one place. Here are some librarian blogs to get you started. Follow the links in them to other blogs that look interesting to you—and have fun:

- Free Range Librarian (freerangelibrarian.com) – K.G. Schneider's blog on librarianship, writing, and everything else, since 2003

- iLibrarian (oedb.org/blogs/ilibrarian) – News and resources on Library 2.0 and the information revolution, by Ellyssa Kroski

- Information Wants to be Free (meredith.wolfwater. com/wordpress) – Meredith Farkas, a librarian, writer, and tech geek, reflects on the profession and the tools we use to serve our patrons

- Librarian.net (www.librarian.net) – Putting the rarin' back in librarian since 1999, by Jessamyn West

- LibrarianInBlack.net (librarianinblack.typepad.com) – Resources and discussions for "tech-librarians-by-default," by Sarah Houghton-Jan

- LISNews.org (lisnews.org) – Librarian and information science news

- Libraryman (www.libraryman.com/blog) – Libraries, community, technology, and PEZ, by Michael Porter

- OPL Plus (opls.blogspot.com) – Judith Siess's blog for librarians in all smaller libraries

- The Shifted Librarian (www.theshiftedlibrarian.com) – Shifting libraries at the speed of byte, by Jenny Levine

- Stephen's Lighthouse (stephenslighthouse.sirsi.com) – Stuff of interest to Stephen Abram that may be of interest to other library folk

- Tame the Web (tametheweb.com) – Libraries, technology, and people, by Michael Stephens

- Walt at Random (walt.lishost.org) – Library voice of the radical middle, by Walt Crawford

- What I Learned Today (www.web2learning.net) – Web 2.0 and programming tips, by Nicole Engard

National Library Associations

National library associations can connect you with librarians working in libraries similar to yours. In a specialized library, it can be difficult to make connections on a local level with librarians who understand your specific topic-related questions and concerns. Although it can be costly to join a national library association, it can be well worth it for the connections and specialized support you will receive.

Evelyn Pockrass, Librarian, Indianapolis (IN) Hebrew Congregation

Little did I imagine when I volunteered to help set up a teen section for a revitalized synagogue library in 1988 that I would become the librarian—and still be there many years later. Although I had previously volunteered in school libraries, as a professional social worker I had no training in how to operate any library, let alone a congregational library.

When my congregation's professional librarian resigned in January 1990, the rabbi encouraged me to apply for the job. After I was hired I scoured the public library for every book I could find about librarianship. Our congregational library had numerous pamphlets and guidebooks that enabled me to organize the library, and the Church and Synagogue Library Association (CSLA) guides were exceptionally helpful.

It was always important to me to have as much professional guidance as possible.

Our library joined the local chapter of CSLA, we were already members of the Association of Jewish Libraries, and later joined INCOLSA (Indiana Cooperative Library Services Authority). Membership in CSLA has provided me with unique experiences in interfaith relations. I became active locally as well as nationally, serving as president from 2005–2006. Through this experience I have made librarian friends of many denominations throughout North America.

Interestingly, I learned quickly that many professional librarians are overwhelmed by the work in a congregational library! Most are specialists, and in a church or synagogue library, the librarian and/or the library committee does everything. Activities performed by church and synagogue librarians include selecting, processing, cataloging, covering books, shelving, computerizing, weeding, programming, writing publicity, creating bulletin boards, leading book club sessions, being a source for reference questions, seeking and training volunteers, developing and working with a budget, writing reports, finding books for the educators and clergy, and managing book fairs.

I enjoy every moment of my job. The greatest feeling is when I can assist someone in finding a book of interest, particularly a volume that might not be readily available in another library. It is gratifying to hear congregants and visitors say how much they love our library. It is as though being a librarian should have been my vocation originally, but I am glad that I found it later in life, as it has become a work of meaningful devotion. When I enter our congregational library, I always feel I have the best seat in the house!

Here are some national library associations to investigate:

- American Association of Law Libraries (AALL; www.aall net.org)

- American Indian Library Association (AILA; www.ailanet.org)

- American Library Association (ALA; www.ala.org)

  - Allied Professional Association (ALA-APA; ala-apa.org)

  - American Association of School Librarians (AASL; www.ala.org/aasl)

  - Association for Library Collections and Technical Services (ALCTS; www.ala.org/ALCTS)

  - Association for Library Service to Children (ALSC; www.ala.org/ALSC)

  - Association of College and Research Libraries (ACRL; www.ala.org/acrl)

  - Association of Specialized and Cooperative Library Agencies (ASCLA; www.ala.org/ascla)

  - Library Administration and Management Association (LAMA; www.ala.org/lama)

  - Library and Information Technology Association (LITA; www.ala.org/lita)

  - Public Library Association (PLA; www.pla.org)

  - Reference and User Services Association (RUSA; www.ala.org/rusa)

  - Young Adult Library Services Association (YALSA; www.ala.org/yalsa)

- American Theological Library Association (ATLA; www.atla.com)

- Art Libraries Society of North America (ARLIS; www.arlisna.org)

- Catholic Library Association (CLA; www.cathla.org)

- Chinese American Librarians Association (CALA; www.cala-web.org)

- Church and Synagogue Library Association (CSLA; www.cslainfo.org)

- Evangelical Church Library Association (ECLA; www.eclalibraries.org)

- Medical Library Association (MLA; www.mlanet.org)

- Music Library Association (MLA; www.musiclibrary assoc.org)

- National Church Library Association (NCLA; www.lclahq.org)

- Patent and Trademark Depository Library Association (PTDLA; www.ptdla.org)

- Special Libraries Association (SLA; www.sla.org)

- Theatre Library Association (TLA; tla.library.unt.edu)

Publications

There are many journals, newsletters, bulletins, and magazines written for librarians. Some provide content in print only, some are online only, and some offer both options. Often a publication will offer an abbreviated online version, requiring a paid subscription to access the full version. In these publications, you will find like-minded librarians facing similar problems, solutions to your dilemmas, library news, librarian profiles, how-to-do-it articles, opinions, survey results, book reviews, and more. If your library cannot purchase a subscription to a publication that interests you, check with your state library or nearest large library system about ILL options and see if the full text is included in your subscription databases or posted online. Here are a few publications for librarians that may interest you:

- AILA (American Indian Library Association) Newsletter (www.ailanet.org/publications)
- American Libraries (www.ala.org/ala/alonline)
- American Society for Information Science and Technology (ASIS&T) Bulletin (www.asis.org/Bulletin)
- Ariadne (www.ariadne.ac.uk)
- Bates InfoTip (www.batesinfo.com/tip.html)
- The Cyberskeptic's Guide to Internet Research (info today.stores.yahoo.net/cybsguidtoin.html)
- Booklist (www.booklistonline.com)
- Charleston Advisor (www.charlestonco.com)
- CHOICE (www.ala.org/ala/acrl/acrlpubs/choice/home.cfm)
- Cites & Insights (citesandinsights.info)
- Computers in Libraries (www.infotoday.com/cilmag)
- Current Cites (lists.webjunction.org/currentcites)
- D-Lib Magazine (www.dlib.org)
- EContent (www.ecmag.net)
- E-JASL: The Electronic Journal of Academic and Special Librarianship (southernlibrarianship.icaap.org)
- EJEL: Electronic Journal of e-Learning (www.ejel.org)
- Information Outlook (www.sla.org/io)
- Information Technology and Libraries (www.lita.org/ala/lita/litapublications/ital/ital information.cfm)

- Internet Resources Newsletter
  (www.hw.ac.uk/libWWW/irn)

- Journal of the Medical Library Association (www.pub
  medcentral.nih.gov/tocrender.fcgi?iid=150885)

- Library Journal (www.libraryjournal.com)

- Library Philosophy and Practice
  (www.webpages.uidaho.edu/~mbolin/lpp.htm)

- Library Technology Reports (www.techsource.ala.org/ltr)

- Library Worklife (ala-apa.org/newsletter/current.html)

- LISNews (www.lisnews.org)

- MLS: Marketing Library Services
  (www.infotoday.com/MLS)

- Multimedia & Internet @ Schools (www.mmischools.com)

- Search Engine Journal (www.searchenginejournal.com)

- Searcher (www.infotoday.com/searcher)

- Smart Libraries Newsletter (www.techsource.ala.org/sln)

- Teacher Librarian (www.teacherlibrarian.com)

- Video Librarian (www.videolibrarian.com)

Also look for bulletins and newsletters from your state library
association, state library agency, local chapters of special library
associations, regional systems, and consortia; these are often sent
as a membership benefit.

Chapter 20

Librarian Certification

Public Librarian Certification

According to *Public Library Standards: A Review of Standards and Guidelines from the 50 States of the U.S. for the Colorado, Mississippi and Hawaii State Libraries*, 24 states mandate certification or educational training requirements to practice public librarianship.[1] State laws usually govern public librarian or public library director certification, although requirements vary widely from state to state. Some states *require* certification for librarians working in public libraries, and others offer *voluntary* certification.

Some states require an MLS to become a certified public librarian, whereas some states do not even require an undergraduate degree to be certified as a public library director. New Jersey requires a Professional Librarian license (an MLS is required) for employment as a professional librarian in any library serving a population of 10,000 or more that is supported by public funds. Virginia has a similar certification requirement for librarians working in public libraries in municipalities of 5,000 or more.

Some states mandate certification for all levels of library staff, and some states certify only librarians or library directors. Many states require that public library directors in libraries serving populations over a certain number have a master's degree from an ALA-accredited institution. Arizona and Texas have certification requirements only for the head librarians of county libraries. Indiana has five levels of certification for library directors, and Louisiana has two. New Mexico doesn't certify public librarians, but certifies public library directors in libraries serving communities with populations between 3,000 and 10,000 by requiring nine credit hours of library science courses and passing a written test; there is no postsecondary certificate or degree requirement for certification in New Mexico. Vermont certification is designed for public library directors with no formal training and requires the completion of 150 credits for a "Certificate of Public Librarianship."

For a public library to receive state funding, some states require certification on some level. To become certified, some require proof of library courses completed, and copies of degrees and diplomas, where others just require completing an application or passing an exam. Some charge a fee and some are free. Some states require recertification or renewal based on continuing education credits, while others don't require recertification or continuing education activities at all.

There are also wide discrepancies in the level of knowledge in library science required from state to state for certification as a librarian or library director. For example, one state might say that a daylong study class and reviewing an eight-page instruction manual is adequate preparation for passing a test to be certified as a library director. Yet, another state might say you must have an MLS to practice public librarianship at any level.

As you can see, not only is there no national standard for certifying or licensing public librarians, the different states' requirements are all over the place. No two states require the same standards, guidelines, or basic level of knowledge to be a librarian.

Michele Haytko, Branch Manager, Perkiomen Valley Library, Montgomery County-Norristown Public Library, Schwenksville, Pennsylvania

I do not have a master's degree. I am currently working on my undergraduate degree. I am 27 years old and have been working in libraries for 11 years. I began my career as a page, in a small branch library—the library I grew up in. I went to college for a year and got married, but couldn't afford to continue college, so I went to work 30 hours a week as a cataloger in a small library. I was promoted to collection development and acquisitions, which I simply adored. I needed a full-time position, so I left and went to a government library, where I started as a Ready Reference Specialist before being promoted to the Lead Marketer and the Head of the Legal Library.

In search of a position closer to home and a better paycheck, I left the library world and spent 14 months in the corporate world managing library accounts and doing collection development for libraries who couldn't afford to have a collection developer on staff. I missed being in a library, and I disliked the idea of selling things that libraries didn't need or couldn't afford. I took a huge cut in pay and accepted a position as an Assistant to the Electronic Resources Librarian. In February 2007, I was promoted to Branch Librarian and I am so excited to take this adventure!

I have completed the non-professional library program sanctioned by the Commonwealth Library (Pennsylvania) and have taken courses in Reference, Collection Development, Cataloging, and Library Management. At the completion of these studies in December 2006, my final grade point average for all courses was a 4.0. While pursuing my undergraduate degree part-time, I also serve as a staff writer for a local yoga magazine.

As a librarian without a master's degree I've always felt as if I had to try harder to make people see me and not the piece of paper I don't have. It's been hard, but I know I am competent. A degree will not change who I am or what I can do— it will only make me better.

Library Practitioner Certificate Program

This certificate, offered by the Western Council of State Libraries, is for library directors or managers without masters' degrees in library and information science. It requires a librarian to have a GED or high school diploma, have library experience, complete 162 contact hours in different competency areas, and renew his or her certification every three years based on continuing education credits. The Council—made up of 22 state library agencies west of the Mississippi—first defined library practitioner competencies and then developed the certificate program to address those competencies. This effort begins to establish some standardization for certifying librarians without MLS degrees across states; however, at this time, the Library Practitioner Certificate Program does not replace individual state certification requirements.

School Librarian Certification

School librarians, school library media specialists, and teacher-librarians have yet another set of professional degree requirements. They can pursue a master's degree from an ALA-accredited library school or a master's degree in education with a specialty in school library media from an educational institution accredited by the National Council for Accreditation of Teacher Education (NCATE). Many public schools require their librarians and library media specialists to be certified as teachers in addition to having some coursework in library science. Some states require school librarians to have an MLS with a specialization in library media, while in others a master's degree in education with a specialty in school library media or educational media is required.

The reality is that not all schools require school librarians to be certified or qualified. As budgets are cut and schools look for ways to save money, some schools are replacing school librarians with paraprofessionals or educational aides. School systems are increasingly requiring librarians to oversee multiple school libraries, eliminating some positions altogether.

Academic and Special Librarian Certification

There is no certification to practice academic or special librarianship.

Certified Public Library Administrator

ALA's Certified Public Library Administrator program is a voluntary post-MLS certification program for public librarians with MLS degrees and three years or more of supervisory experience.

Endnotes

1. Christine Hamilton-Pennell, "Public Library Standards: A Review of Standards and Guidelines from the 50 States of the U.S. For the Colorado, Mississippi and Hawaii State Libraries," 2003, 13, www.cosla.org/research/Public_Library_Standards_July03.doc

Chapter 21

Continuing Education, Distance Education, and Degree Programs

It is essential that all library workers continue to keep up with new advances and developments in our field. Ours is not a static profession. Since technology is such an important part of doing our work, the landscape of librarianship as it relates to technology is shifting and changing almost daily. All aspects of the field are evolving: information acquisition, collection, organization, retrieval, and dissemination. The ways in which we market libraries, manage information, provide services, make information available to customers, and create new ways to reach underserved populations are all in a state of flux.

To make educated decisions in your work, you must learn about your options by taking classes and workshops, online courses and tutorials, reading blogs and listening to podcasts, attending conferences, and networking with other librarians. This is the time to get out there and learn about what is going on in other libraries. If you have limited time or money, there are many free online opportunities. If you investigate the options, you will find a learning opportunity that will work for you. The following sections give you some places to start.

Colleges, Universities, and Postsecondary Institutions

Educational institutions that grant library science degrees and certificate programs offer regular credit courses, noncredit courses, and courses for continuing education credit. General continuing education divisions in other colleges, universities, and postsecondary institutions may offer classes in searching the Internet, computer networking, web page design, word processing, and customer service techniques—all of which can be useful for librarians. (See Appendix B for LIS education resources.)

Felicia Cheney, Director, Edgartown (MA) Free Public Library

I graduated with a degree in economics from the University of Chicago in 1985. I did many things for many years, eventually establishing a small tax prep business. I took a part-time position at our local library for my off tax season work. Well, I love our library and I loved working with the public, but I did get tired of only doing the checking in and checking out. So, I eventually resigned.

About a year later, I bolted away one morning and proclaimed to my husband that I would be the next director of the Edgartown Public Library. Well, the short story is, 8 months later I became the director and I've been running ever since. I started library school at Clarion (online) in January 2006.

Library Associations

National, regional, special, and state library associations offer continuing education opportunities as a benefit of membership.

American Library Association

The American Library Association (ALA) Continuing Education Clearinghouse (www.ala.org/apps/contedu/SearchMain.cfm) is a searchable database of current continuing education opportunities offered by ALA, its divisions, and other units.

Special Libraries Association

The Special Libraries Association (SLA) Click University (www.clickuniversity.com) offers classes, workshops, certificates, and live online sessions for members. Local SLA chapters regularly present continuing education classes and workshops for members and non-members. Check your SLA chapter's website or newsletter.

State and Regional Library Associations

Educational opportunities on the state and regional association level often include mini-conferences, leadership conferences, or ongoing workshops. Visit your state or regional library association's website or read its newsletter.

Other Associations

Look around your local area for groups or local chapters of national organizations that focus on marketing, technology, writing, web development, fundraising, speaking, and business networking. It is amazing what these "non-library" groups offer that you can apply in your work as a librarian. Examples include the Association of Fundraising Professionals (www.afpnet.org) and the American Marketing Association (www.marketingpower.com).

Conferences

Conferences are ideal places to take classes, meet other librarians, and network. You can attend conferences held by national library associations, state or regional library conferences, or conferences on technology, for instance. Look at preliminary programs and make wise choices. There are many great conferences where you can spend a solid three to four days of learning. The website Library Related Conferences (homepage.usask.ca/~mad 204/CONF.HTM) lists conferences worldwide of interest to librarians.

National Conferences

ALA conferences are full of diverse continuing education opportunities for librarians and library workers from all kinds of libraries. The SLA annual conference offers many learning opportunities designed with special librarians in mind. Specialized training opportunities can be found at the national conferences of associations such as the Art Libraries Society of North America, Music Library Association, and American Indian Library Association. For links to ALA Affiliates, go to www.ala.org/ala/ourassociation/othergroups/affiliates/affiliateslisting.htm.

State and Regional Conferences

State library associations and regional library associations hold conferences that offer continuing education sessions and preconference sessions for librarians of all kinds. ALA maintains a conference calendar that includes state conferences (www.ala.org/ala/ourassociation/chapters/planningcalendar/planningcalendar.htm).

Technology Conferences

Information Today, Inc. presents the Computers in Libraries conference, Internet Librarian conference, and Internet@Schools West conference (www.infotoday.com/conferences.shtml), where librarians have their choice of many sessions on technology topics. Local technology conferences can be a wonderful opportunity to get outside your comfort zone, mix with the techies in your area, and learn about some of the newest developments in technology. You will meet local vendors, make valuable contacts, and learn new ways to help you do your work.

State Library Continuing Education Departments

Continuing education divisions at your state library agency provide continuing education opportunities for librarians in your state. Although they do focus on providing training for public librarians, some classes and workshops can be appropriate for librarians from all kinds of libraries. Check your state library agency's website for the continuing education link.

Library Membership Organizations and Cooperatives

Various library membership organizations, groups, and cooperatives provide continuing education as one of their services. Some states have multiple regional networks, and some networks encompass several states. See if your library belongs to a regional network and take advantage of the educational services it offers. Here are some of the larger regional library networks:

- Amigos (www.amigos.org) – Members are libraries primarily in the Southwestern U.S.

- Bibliographical Center Research (BCR; www.bcr.org/training) – This multistate library cooperative serving libraries in 42 states, Guam, and Canada delivers training and technical assistance in the use of information services.

- National Network of Libraries of Medicine (www.nlm. nih.gov/network.html) – This network provides continuing education classes on medical and consumer health related topics regionally.

- NELINET (www.nelinet.net/edserv/index.htm) – This is a cooperative of academic, public, and special libraries in New England.

- Nylink (nylink.org/education) – All kinds of libraries and cultural organizations throughout New York State and surrounding areas belong to this membership organization.

- PALINET (www.palinet.org/education_program.aspx) – This organization provides an extensive education program for member libraries primarily in Delaware, Maryland, New Jersey, Pennsylvania, and West Virginia.

- SOLINET (www.solinet.net) – This organization serves libraries in the Southeastern U.S.

Free Web-Based Training and Tutorials

Lack of funds is no longer an issue when it comes to continuing education. Here are some free online tutorials and training opportunities that will keep you busy:

- Association for Library Services to Children online tutorials (wikis.ala.org/alsc/index.php/Online_tutorials)

- Basic Tutorial on Searching the Web, University of South Carolina Beaufort Library (www.sc.edu/beaufort/library/pages/bones/bones.shtml)

- Blended Librarian Online Learning Community (blendedlibrarian.org)

- Collection Development Training, Arizona State Library (www.lib.az.us/cdt)

- Copyright Crash Course, University of Texas (www.lib.utsystem.edu/copyright)

- Copyright Primer, University of Maryland (www-apps.umuc.edu/primer)

- Free Friday Forums from BCR (www.bcr.org/training)

- Idaho's Alternative Basic Library Education (ABLE) Program (libraries.idaho.gov/able)

- Idaho's Supplemental Alternative Basic Library Education (SABLE) Program (libraries.idaho.gov/sable)

- Infopeople (infopeople.org/training/webcasts/list)

- Internet Tutorials (www.internettutorials.net)

- Introduction to MARC Tagging, OCLC (www.oclc.org/support/training/connexion/marc)

- Librarianship, Texas State Library and Archives Commission (www.tsl.state.tx.us/ld/tutorials/professionalism/lib.html)

- Library 2.0 at Ning free library-related elearning sites (library20.ning.com)

- Marketing the Library, Ohio Library Council (www.olc.org/marketing)

- MORE: Minnesota Opportunities for Reference Excellence (www.arrowhead.lib.mn.us/more/contents.htm)

- National Library of Medicine Distance Education Resources (www.nlm.nih.gov/bsd/dist_edu.html)

- Needs Assessment Tutorial, University of Arizona Library (digital.library.arizona.edu/nadm/tutorial)

- Online Privacy Tutorial, ALA (ala.org/ala/washoff/oitp/emailtutorials/privacya/privacy.cfm)

- PubMed Online Training (www.nlm.nih.gov/bsd/disted/pubmed.html#qt)

- Online Programming for All Libraries (OPAL; www.opal-online.org/progslis.htm)

- Professionalism, Texas State Library and Archives Commission (www.tsl.state.tx.us/ld/tutorials/ professionalism/prof.html)

- Reference Excellence on the Web, Ohio Library Council (www.olc.org/ore)

- Simple Book Repair Manual, Dartmouth College Library (www.dartmouth.edu/··preserve/repair/repairindex.htm)

- SirsiDynix Institute (www.sirsidynixinstitute.com)

- WebJunction Courses (www.webjunction.org/do/ Navigation?category=372)

- WebJunction Learning Webinars (webjunction.org/ do/Navigation?category=15543)

- WebJunction Rural Webinars (webjunction.org/do/ Navigation;jsessionid=719D88480CF01905D2C862E9AA3 D6B0B?category=13496)

As you can see, there are plenty of learning opportunities available for librarians. Make a continuing education plan for yourself based on the skills or topics you need to know to accomplish the work of your library. Is there something in your library's plan that you are not sure how to implement? Do you think there might be a new technology that would benefit your library but you don't know enough about it? Could you use a little help in sharpening your management techniques? Continuing education is the way to find out. Remember, as librarians we are on the leading edge, we are inquisitive, we are innovative, and we are continuous lifelong learners!

Appendix A

Sample Library Policies

Sample Weeding Policy

Overview

Weeding the Library collection is as essential to the health of the Library as adding new titles. Systematic weeding is an integral part of book selection. Each item earns its place in the Library based on quality, reliability, current usefulness, and appearance, and must contribute to the reliability, reputation, and attractiveness of the Library.

Responsibilities

Final authority for this policy rests with the Library's Board of Trustees, while the responsibility for implementing this policy lies with the Library Director. The Library Director may delegate weeding duties to specific staff members, but the recommendations of staff members are subject to review by the Director. Weeding must be done without bias by individual librarians, whose personal preferences and interests are not to dominate their work. Attention to the needs and interests of the community is essential, and librarians will strive to include materials in the collection that reflect all sides of controversial questions. Basic works of significant historical or literary value should be kept indefinitely. Current bibliographies are consulted prior to withdrawal.

Weeding Criteria

Every item requires individual consideration, each being judged from the standpoint of its relevance to the Library's mission and vision, its value to the community, and its relationship to the rest of the collection. Materials are candidates for weeding if they are:

- Factually inaccurate

- Worn or damaged beyond repair

- Superseded by a new edition or more suitable materials on a subject

- Of no literary or scientific merit

- Not being used

- Irrelevant to the needs or interests of the community

- Duplicate titles no longer in demand

- Materials of limited appeal that are available through interlibrary loan

Guidelines

Author's Note: Every community is different, so guidelines will vary. Take the time to create weeding guidelines that will develop your collection to suit your community. Indicators such as these, arranged by general classification number, will be very useful for weeding purposes.

000 General: Withdraw encyclopedias older than 5 years, and almanacs and computer guides older than 2 years. Materials on Library science and journalism may be kept longer than 5 years, depending on their condition and relevance.

100 Philosophy and Psychology: Collection should contain popular topics in psychology. Withdraw items more than 10 years old and items that have not circulated in 5 years.

200 Religion: The collection should have at least one up-to-date item on each religion represented in the community and those

prominent in current world affairs. Withdraw items more than 10 years old and items that have not circulated in 5 years.

300 Social Sciences: Materials on government and economics should be replaced regularly with new editions and withdrawn if they are more than 10 years old. Withdraw materials on finance, employment, college guides, and educational testing if they are more than 3 years old. Materials on customs, etiquette, and folklore may be kept longer than 10 years, depending on their condition and relevance. Withdraw any materials in this section that have not circulated in 3 years.

400 Linguistics and Language: Retain only dictionaries and materials on grammar for languages being studied or spoken in the community. Withdraw items more than 10 years old and items that have not circulated in 5 years.

500 Pure Sciences: Retain materials on mathematics, general biology, natural history, and botany for 10 years, but withdraw materials on the other sciences as new research supersedes older ideas. Withdraw items more than 10 years old and items that have not circulated in 5 years.

600 Applied Sciences and Technology: Materials on technology older than 5 years should be withdrawn. Retain repair manuals for older cars and appliances as long as there is a need for them in the community. Keep materials on collectibles such as clocks, guns, and toys as well as cookbooks longer than 10 years, depending on use and relevance. Withdraw materials on medicine (except anatomy and physiology) older than 5 years. Withdraw items more than 7 years old and items that have not circulated in 3 years.

700 Arts and Recreation: Retain materials in art and music until they are worn and unattractive. Materials on crafts and sports may be retained indefinitely if they contain basic technique, are well illustrated, and have circulated within 3 years. Withdraw photography materials if they are more than 7 years old and address

outdated technique and equipment. Withdraw materials that have not circulated in 3 years.

800 Literature: Keep basic materials, especially literary criticism. Discard works of minor writers no longer read or discussed in literary histories or read in area schools, unless there is an established demand in the community. Keep literary histories unless they are superseded by materials of better quality.

900 History and Geography: Materials on history can be kept generally for 15 years if they have circulated 3 times. The main factors to consider include demand, accuracy, and fairness of interpretation. Weed personal narratives and war memoirs in favor of broader war histories. Retain local history materials. Weed materials containing dated viewpoints. Materials on travel become dated in 4 years, however personal narratives of travel can be kept for 10 years, especially if they are of high literary or historical value. All local material and accounts of local people are kept. Biographies may be weeded as demand for them ceases unless the person treated is of permanent interest or importance. Biographies of outstanding literary value are kept until worn.

Adult Fiction: Discard works no longer popular, especially second and third copies or old best sellers. Retain works of durable demand or high literary merit.

Children's and Young Adult Fiction: Discard topical fiction on dated subjects, abridged or simplified classics, and duplicate copies of series books no longer popular.

Children's and Young Adult Nonfiction: Use similar criteria as for the adult collection, paying attention to accuracy and relevance.

Periodicals: Due to space restrictions, magazines are generally kept no more than 2 years, and newspapers are kept generally no more than 1 month. Exceptions to this practice include periodicals in the fields of genealogy, local history, social commentary, and finance.

Local Documents: These documents cover issues with widely varying life spans in local interest and impact. Because the Library is not a permanent archive of local documents, these materials may be withdrawn based on use, currency, local relevance, the available space, format of materials, and the availability of the information at another location. The Library will not return these documents to the agency of origin upon withdrawing.

Audio-Visuals: Worn, damaged, rarely used, and faddish are the general criteria taken into consideration when weeding audio-visual items. Weed formats that are no longer used such as vinyl records, 8-track tapes, and beta video recordings.

Frequency

Weeding is not a major project undertaken once every several years, when there is no longer room to shelve materials or when shelves break due to overcrowding. The collection as a whole is reviewed systematically and on an ongoing basis, keeping in mind the general selection criteria and the terms in this policy. The following chart serves as a very broad guideline for the frequency with which each section should be reviewed.

Dewey Range	Weeding Frequency in Years
000	3
100	4
200	5
300	3
400	5
500	2
600	2
700	3
800	5
900	4
BIOGRAPHY	2
FICTION	2
A-V	2

Disposal

Most materials weeded from the Library are sold through the Friends of the Library book sales. Some materials are donated to other libraries, schools, daycare providers, nursing homes, social service providers, jail libraries, and/or third-world countries. Materials that are not suitable for selling or donating are offered free of charge to Library users.

Sample Computer Use Policy

To use a Library computer you must have a valid Library card.

You are solely responsible for what you access on Library computers. The Library does not warrant or assume any legal liability or responsibility for the accuracy, completeness, or usefulness of documents and information accessed on the Internet using Library computers.

Parents and legal guardians are responsible for a minor's conduct on Library computers.

There is no guarantee of privacy on Library computers.

Library staff is available to assist with simple computer-related questions but are unavailable to provide complex technical support.

The Library does not offer email accounts.

Accessing pornographic or obscene materials is prohibited on Library computers. If you are found accessing these types of materials, you will be informed that you are accessing inappropriate materials and told to log off of the computer. Staff will monitor your computer use and if you are found accessing pornographic or obscene materials again, you will be told to log off of the computer and leave the computer area. Your Library card and name will be noted and a block will be placed on your card until you meet with the Library Director. The Library Director will clarify the Library's policy on accessing pornographic and obscene materials with you,

you will be asked to sign a statement that you understand and agree to comply with this policy, and upon doing so your card will be unblocked and computer privileges restored. A note will remain on your record and if you are found accessing pornographic or obscene materials on Library computers again, the Library will consider taking legal action, including criminal prosecution.

Customers must comply with applicable copyright laws and licensing agreements while using Library computers.

All existing laws and city policies apply to conduct when accessing the Internet on Library computers.

Damage or unauthorized access to the Library's computers, databases, network, hardware, or software settings is prohibited.

The Library and the city shall not be liable for any damages or costs of any type arising out of or in any way connected with use of the Library's computers.

Failure to comply with this policy may result in loss of computer or Library privileges in addition to any appropriate legal action, including criminal prosecution.

Sample Political Activity Policy

The Library serves as an information resource for the entire community and seeks to make information available to all area residents on a wide variety of political issues and candidates. However, in order to avoid the appearance of an endorsement by the Library of any candidate for office or issue appearing on the ballot, the following policy with respect to political activity on Library premises has been adopted.

1. The Library will provide space for campaign literature or position papers from any and all candidates or issues.

2. No candidacy or issue petitions will be circulated or posted at the Library.

3. Public presentations by candidates for office or supporters of ballot issues may use the Library's meeting room if they are sponsored by a nonpartisan organization and all candidates or sides of an issue are invited to participate.

4. Public presentations by individual candidates or supporters/opponents of a ballot issue may not be held on Library property.

5. The Library may not be used as a campaign headquarters or meeting site for campaign committees.

6. Library staff members have an obligation to maintain the political neutrality of the Library, and will refrain from any campaign activities while on Library property.

Sample Donations Policy

The Library uses the following guidelines when accepting donations.

Money

Monetary donations can be designated for the purchase of Library materials; however, the donor may not specify the specific titles or items to be purchased. Monetary donations may be made for other specific purposes when the project has been approved by the Library board. Monetary donations can be made in memory of or in honor of an individual, and the Library will place book plates in books indicating the name of the person honored or memorialized when requested by the donor. Donors will receive a receipt for monetary donations.

Materials

The Library accepts donations of materials with the understanding that the Library does not guarantee that the materials will be added to the collection. Some materials may be added to the collection or used to replace worn copies already in the collection; however, some materials may be sold by the Friends of the Library, donated to other organizations, or given away to Library users free of charge. In a few cases, materials are discarded. Book plates are not placed in donated books added to the collection. Although Library staff cannot determine the value of donated materials for tax purposes, the donor may request a receipt stating the number of items donated; the donor may determine the value.

The Library does not accept the following items or materials:

- Magazines, including *National Geographic Magazine*
- Newspapers
- Readers Digest Condensed Books
- Encyclopedia sets more than 5 years old
- Textbooks
- Moldy, damp, mouse-infested, or insect-infested materials
- Smelly materials
- Torn, ripped, yellowed or falling apart materials
- Materials made in violation of copyright laws
- Artwork, equipment, and furniture

Sample Library Meeting Room Use Policy

Meeting rooms are available to people in the community served by the Library on an equitable basis, regardless of the beliefs or affiliations of individuals or groups requesting their use. Library-related activities such as discussion groups, slide or film programs, study groups, or lectures sponsored or given by the Library take priority; however, community groups are invited to reserve meeting rooms for educational, recreational, and civic purposes provided that they do not interfere with Library services or programs.

1. There are two Library meeting rooms. The large meeting room measures 45' by 30' with a maximum capacity of 125 people; the smaller meeting room measures 20' by 15' and may be used by groups of up to 12.

2. Reservations for use of the meeting rooms must be made in advance, and one person in the group must agree to take responsibility for assuring that these guidelines are followed.

3. Reservations are made by completing an application form and submitting it to the Assistant Librarian. Reservations for meeting rooms are not assured unless an application form is signed and submitted and the group's representative has been notified that the meeting room has been reserved for their group.

4. Verbal or written cancellation of a meeting room reservation is required in advance. Failure to notify the Library of a cancellation may result in the denial of any future requests by the sponsoring organization.

5. Use of the meeting room must not interfere with the operation of the Library. People attending meetings held in the Library meeting rooms are to park on the street or in the municipal lots that are available near the Library.

6. Meeting rooms are available only during hours when the Library is open.

7. Keys to the meeting rooms will not be given to any group.

8. No admission fee may be charged to attend a meeting held in a Library meeting room.

9.   All meetings must be open to the public. Private parties or meetings by invitation only are not permitted.

10.   No smoking or alcoholic beverages are allowed in the building or near the main entrance outside.

11.   Groups holding meetings must assume responsibility for any loss or damage to Library property. Rooms are to be left in the same condition they were found. Nothing may be hung on or taped to the walls of the meeting rooms.

12.   The Library is not responsible for materials, supplies, or equipment owned by the group.

13.   Light refreshments may be served in the meeting space; however, there are no kitchen facilities available. Groups serving refreshments must leave the meeting rooms clean and empty all trash.

14.   The Library reserves the right to refuse the use of the Library meeting rooms or cancel a reservation when the Library Board determines that this is in the best interest of the Library and/or Town.

15.   The Library meeting rooms will not be available for use on holidays, when the Library is otherwise scheduled to be closed, or in the event of closure due to an emergency or inclement weather.

16.   Use of the meeting rooms does not constitute an endorsement of the group by the Library.

Appendix B

LIS Education Resources

Associate Degree and Certificate Programs in Library Technology

The types of associate degree or certificate granted by the following schools vary by institution. The AAS (Associate in Applied Science Degree), AA (Associate in Arts Degree), and AS (Associate in Science Degree) are commonly granted in the library technology field. Degrees and certificates (C) are in Library Information Technology, Library Media Technology, and Library Technology.

Arizona
>   Mesa Community College – AAS, C
>   Northland Pioneer College – AAS, C

California
>   Citrus College – AA, C
>   City College of San Francisco – AA, C
>   College of the Canyons – AA, C
>   College of the Sequoias – C
>   Cuesta College – AS, C
>   Diablo Valley College – AS, C
>   Fresno City College – AS, C
>   Hartnell College – AA, C
>   Imperial Valley College – AS, C
>   Palomar College – AA, C
>   Pasadena City College – AS, C
>   Sacramento City College – AS, C
>   San Bernardino Valley College – AA, C
>   Santa Ana College – AA, C

Colorado

> Pueblo Community College – AAS, C

Connecticut

> Capital Community College – AS, C
>
> Three Rivers Community College – C

Georgia

> Georgia Perimeter College – AAS

Idaho

> College of Southern Idaho – AA

Illinois

> College of DuPage – AAS, C
>
> College of Lake County – AAS, C
>
> Illinois Central College – AAS
>
> Joliet Junior College – C
>
> Wilbur Wright College – AAS, C

Indiana

> Ivy Tech Community College – AS

Kansas

> Emporia State University – C

Kentucky

> Bluegrass Community & Technical College – AAS, C

Maine

> University of Maine at Augusta – AS, C

Michigan

> Oakland Community College – AAS, C

Minnesota

> Minneapolis Community and Technical College – AS, C

Nebraska

> Nebraska Community Colleges

New Mexico

> Clovis Community College – AAS
>
> NMSU–Dona Ana Community College – AAS, C
>
> Northern New Mexico Community College – AAS, C

North Carolina
>   Central Carolina Community College – AAS, C

Ohio
>   Belmont Technical College – AAS

Oklahoma
>   Rose State College – AA, C

Oregon
>   Portland Community College – AGS (Associate of General Studies), C

Pennsylvania
>   Northampton Community College – C

Texas
>   Palo Alto College – AS

Washington
>   Highline Community College – AAS
>   Spokane Falls Community College – AAS, C

Information on these programs comes from *The College Blue Book: Occupational Education*, 35th ed. (2008, New York: Macmillan Information) and the list of U.S. Library Technician Programs (colt.ucr.edu/ltprograms.html).

Bachelor's Degree Programs in Library and Information Science

If you are ready to concentrate on library and information science in your undergraduate studies, these institutions offer bachelor's degrees.

California
>   University of California, Los Angeles

Connecticut
>   Southern Connecticut State University

District of Columbia

University of the District of Columbia

Kentucky

Murray State University

Maine

University of Maine at Augusta

Minnesota

Bethel University

St. Cloud State University

Mississippi

University of Southern Mississippi

Montana

University of Great Falls

Nebraska

Chadron State College

University of Nebraska at Omaha

New York

St. John's College

North Carolina

Appalachian State University

Ohio

Ohio University–Eastern

Oklahoma

Northeastern State University

University of Oklahoma

Pennsylvania

Clarion University of Pennsylvania

Kutztown University of Pennsylvania

Texas

University of Houston

University of North Texas

Virginia
>   Longwood University
>   Concord University

West Virginia
>   Mountain State University

Information on these programs comes from *The College Blue Book. Degrees Offered by College and Subject*, 35th ed. (2008, New York: Macmillan Information).

ALA Accredited Master's Degree Programs in Library and Information Science

If you want to pursue a master's degree in library and information studies, it is important to find a program that is accredited by the American Library Association (ALA). Many employers require an ALA-accredited master's degree for librarian positions. The master's degree in the library field is frequently referred to as the MLS; however, ALA-accredited programs also offer Master of Arts, Master of Librarianship, Master of Library and Information Studies, and Master of Science degrees.

There is considerable diversity among programs; therefore it is necessary to investigate each program for specific information. Look at program websites, program catalogs, class descriptions, and the mission, vision, goals, and objectives of each program to decide which is a good match for you. If you want to specialize in a specific area of librarianship, such as rural, health sciences, children or young adult, databases, or archives, make sure that the school you choose offers the specialization or provides courses in your area of interest.

Many ALA-accredited programs provide distance-learning opportunities for students through a variety of delivery methods. In some cases students can complete an entire program remotely and in other instances by attending some on-campus courses. A regional residency may be required.

United States

Alabama

University of Alabama

Arizona

University of Arizona

California

San Jose State University

University of California, Los Angeles

Colorado

University of Denver

Connecticut

Southern Connecticut State University

District of Columbia

Catholic University of America

Florida

Florida State University

University of South Florida

Georgia

Valdosta State University

Hawaii

University of Hawaii

Illinois

Dominican University

University of Illinois–Urbana-Champaign

Indiana

Indiana University

Iowa

University of Iowa

Kansas

Emporia State University

Kentucky
>   University of Kentucky

Louisiana
>   Louisiana State University

Maryland
>   University of Maryland

Massachusetts
>   Simmons College

Michigan
>   University of Michigan
>   Wayne State University

Mississippi
>   University of Southern Mississippi

Missouri
>   University of Missouri

New Jersey
>   Rutgers, The State University of New Jersey

New York
>   University at Albany, State University of New York
>   University at Buffalo, State University of New York
>   Long Island University
>   Pratt Institute
>   Queens College
>   St. John's University
>   Syracuse University

North Carolina
>   North Carolina Central University
>   University of North Carolina at Chapel Hill
>   University of North Carolina at Greensboro

Ohio
>   Kent State University

Oklahoma
>   University of Oklahoma

Pennsylvania
    Clarion University of Pennsylvania
    Drexel University
    University of Pittsburgh
Puerto Rico
    University of Puerto Rico
Rhode Island
    University of Rhode Island
South Carolina
    University of South Carolina
Tennessee
    University of Tennessee
Texas
    University of North Texas
    University of Texas at Austin
    Texas Woman's University
Washington
    University of Washington
Wisconsin
    University of Wisconsin–Madison
    University of Wisconsin–Milwaukee

Canada
Alberta
    University of Alberta
British Columbia
    University of British Columbia
Nova Scotia
    Dalhousie University
Ontario
    University of Toronto
    University of Western Ontario

Quebec
> McGill University
> Universite de Montreal

Information on these programs comes from *Library & Information Studies Directory of Institutions Offering Accredited Programs: 2007–2008* (2007, American Library Association) and *Library & Information Studies Directory of Institutions Offering Accredited Master's Programs: 2007–2008* (Chicago: American Library Association, www.ala.org/ala/accreditation/lisdirb/lis_ dir_ 2007-2008_re.pdf).

Appendix C

Library Issues and Legislation

Library Bill of Rights (ALA)

Author's Note: Remind yourself about these rights by reading them periodically. Spend time being honest with yourself about the degree to which you abide by them. Over the years you may find that you have developed some habits that don't align with what this document says—even in a small way. This is the time to correct your course. Try substituting the word "librarian" for the word "libraries," because librarians are responsible for upholding these rights.

I. Books and other library resources should be provided for the interest, information, and enlightenment of all people of the community the library serves. Materials should not be excluded because of the origin, background, or views of those contributing to their creation.

II. Libraries should provide materials and information presenting all points of view on current and historical issues. Materials should not be proscribed or removed because of partisan or doctrinal disapproval.

III. Libraries should challenge censorship in the fulfillment of their responsibility to provide information and enlightenment.

IV. Libraries should cooperate with all persons and groups concerned with resisting abridgment of free expression and free access to ideas.

V. A person's right to use a library should not be denied or abridged because of origin, age, background, or views.

VI. Libraries which make exhibit spaces and meeting rooms available to the public they serve should make such facilities available on an equitable basis, regardless of the beliefs or affiliations of individuals or groups requesting their use.

Reprinted with permission from the American Library Association (ALA) (www.ala.org/ala/oif/statementspols/statementsif/library billrights.cfm).

Freedom to Read Statement (ALA)

The freedom to read is essential to our democracy. It is continuously under attack. Private groups and public authorities in various parts of the country are working to remove or limit access to reading materials, to censor content in schools, to label "controversial" views, to distribute lists of "objectionable" books or authors, and to purge libraries. These actions apparently rise from a view that our national tradition of free expression is no longer valid; that censorship and suppression are needed to counter threats to safety or national security, as well as to avoid the subversion of politics and the corruption of morals. We, as individuals devoted to reading and as librarians and publishers responsible

for disseminating ideas, wish to assert the public interest in the preservation of the freedom to read.

Most attempts at suppression rest on a denial of the
fundamental premise of democracy: that the ordinary
individual, by exercising critical judgment, will select
the good and reject the bad. We trust Americans to recognize propaganda and misinformation, and to make
their own decisions about what they read and believe.
We do not believe they are prepared to sacrifice their
heritage of a free press in order to be "protected" against
what others think may be bad for them. We believe they
still favor free enterprise in ideas and expression.

These efforts at suppression are related to a larger
pattern of pressures being brought against education,
the press, art and images, films, broadcast media, and
the Internet. The problem is not only one of actual censorship. The shadow of fear cast by these pressures
leads, we suspect, to an even larger voluntary curtail-
ment of expression by those who seek to avoid controversy or unwelcome scrutiny by government officials.

Such pressure toward conformity is perhaps natural
to a time of accelerated change. And yet suppression is
never more dangerous than in such a time of social ten-
sion. Freedom has given the United States the elasticity
to endure strain. Freedom keeps open the path of novel
and creative solutions, and enables change to come by
choice. Every silencing of a heresy, every enforcement
of an orthodoxy, diminishes the toughness and
resilience of our society and leaves it the less able to
deal with controversy and difference.

Now as always in our history, reading is among our
greatest freedoms. The freedom to read and write is
almost the only means for making generally available

ideas or manners of expression that can initially command only a small audience. The written word is the natural medium for the new idea and the untried voice from which come the original contributions to social growth. It is essential to the extended discussion that serious thought requires, and to the accumulation of knowledge and ideas into organized collections.

We believe that free communication is essential to the preservation of a free society and a creative culture. We believe that these pressures toward conformity present the danger of limiting the range and variety of inquiry and expression on which our democracy and our culture depend. We believe that every American community must jealously guard the freedom to publish and to circulate, in order to preserve its own freedom to read. We believe that publishers and librarians have a profound responsibility to give validity to that freedom to read by making it possible for the readers to choose freely from a variety of offerings.

The freedom to read is guaranteed by the Constitution. Those with faith in free people will stand firm on these constitutional guarantees of essential rights and will exercise the responsibilities that accompany these rights.

We therefore affirm these propositions:

1. *It is in the public interest for publishers and librarians to make available the widest diversity of views and expressions, including those that are unorthodox, unpopular, or considered dangerous by the majority.*

    Creative thought is by definition new, and what is new is different. The bearer of every new thought is a rebel until that idea is refined and tested. Totalitarian systems attempt to maintain themselves in power by the ruthless suppression of any concept that challenges the established orthodoxy. The power of a democratic system to adapt to change is vastly strengthened by the freedom of its citizens to choose widely from among conflicting opinions offered freely to them. To stifle every nonconformist idea at birth would mark the end of the democratic process. Furthermore, only through the constant activity of weighing and selecting can the democratic mind attain the strength demanded by times like these. We need to know not only what we believe but why we believe it.

2. *Publishers, librarians, and booksellers do not need to endorse every idea or presentation they make available. It would conflict with the public interest for them to establish their own political, moral, or aesthetic views as a standard for determining what should be published or circulated.*

Publishers and librarians serve the educational process by helping to make available knowledge and ideas required for the growth of the mind and the increase of learning. They do not foster education by imposing as mentors the patterns of their own thought. The people should have the freedom to read and consider a broader range of ideas than those that may be held by any single librarian or publisher or government or church. It is wrong that what one can read should be confined to what another thinks proper.

3. *It is contrary to the public interest for publishers or librarians to bar access to writings on the basis of the personal history or political affiliations of the author.*

    No art or literature can flourish if it is to be measured by the political views or private lives of its creators. No society of free people can flourish that draws up lists of writers to whom it will not listen, whatever they may have to say.

4. *There is no place in our society for efforts to coerce the taste of others, to confine adults to the reading matter deemed suitable for adolescents, or to inhibit the efforts of writers to achieve artistic expression.*

    To some, much of modern expression is shocking. But is not much of life itself shocking? We cut off literature at the source if we prevent writers from dealing with the stuff of life. Parents and teachers have a responsibility to prepare the young to meet the diversity of experiences in life to which they will be exposed, as they have a responsibility to help them learn to think critically for themselves. These are affirmative responsibilities, not to be discharged simply by preventing them from reading works for which they are not yet prepared. In these matters values differ, and values cannot be legislated; nor can machinery be devised that will suit the demands of one group without limiting the freedom of others.

5. *It is not in the public interest to force a reader to accept the prejudgment of a label characterizing any expression or its author as subversive or dangerous.*

    The ideal of labeling presupposes the existence of individuals or groups with wisdom to determine by authority what is good or bad for others. It presupposes that individuals must be directed in making up their minds about the ideas they examine. But Americans do not need others to do their thinking for them.

6. *It is the responsibility of publishers and librarians, as guardians of the people's freedom to read, to contest encroachments upon that freedom by individuals or groups seeking to impose their own standards or tastes upon the community at large; and by the government whenever it seeks to reduce or deny public access to public information.*

    It is inevitable in the give and take of the democratic process that the political, the moral, or the aesthetic concepts of an individual or group will occasionally collide with those of another individual or group. In a free society individuals are free to determine for themselves what they wish to read, and each group is free to determine what it will recommend to its freely associated members. But no group has the right to take the law into its own hands, and to impose its own concept of politics or morality upon other members of a democratic society. Freedom is no freedom if it is accorded only to the accepted and the inoffensive. Further, democratic societies are more safe, free, and creative when the free flow of public information is not restricted by governmental prerogative or self-censorship.

7. *It is the responsibility of publishers and librarians to give full meaning to the freedom to read by providing books that enrich the quality and diversity of thought and expression. By the exercise of this*

affirmative responsibility, they can demonstrate that the answer to a "bad" book is a good one, the answer to a "bad" idea is a good one.

The freedom to read is of little consequence when the reader cannot obtain matter fit for that reader's purpose. What is needed is not only the absence of restraint, but the positive provision of opportunity for the people to read the best that has been thought and said. Books are the major channel by which the intellectual inheritance is handed down, and the principal means of its testing and growth. The defense of the freedom to read requires of all publishers and librarians the utmost of their faculties, and deserves of all Americans the fullest of their support.

We state these propositions neither lightly nor as easy generalizations. We here stake out a lofty claim for the value of the written word. We do so because we believe that it is possessed of enormous variety and usefulness, worthy of cherishing and keeping free. We realize that the application of these propositions may mean the dissemination of ideas and manners of expression that are repugnant to many persons. We do not state these propositions in the comfortable belief that what people read is unimportant. We believe rather that what people read is deeply important; that ideas can be dangerous; but that the suppression of ideas is fatal to a democratic society. Freedom itself is a dangerous way of life, but it is ours.

Reprinted with permission from the American Library Association (ALA) (www.ala.org/ala/oif/statementspols/ftrstatement/freedom readstatement.cfm).

Freedom to View Statement (ALA)

The FREEDOM TO VIEW, along with the freedom to speak, to hear, and to read, is protected by the First Amendment to the Constitution of the United States. In a free society, there is no place for censorship of any medium of expression. Therefore these principles are affirmed:

1. To provide the broadest access to film, video, and other audiovisual materials because they are a means for the communication of ideas. Liberty of circulation is essential to insure the constitutional guarantee of freedom of expression.

2. To protect the confidentiality of all individuals and institutions using film, video, and other audiovisual materials.

3. To provide film, video, and other audiovisual materials which represent a diversity of views and expression. Selection of a work does not constitute or imply agreement with or approval of the content.

4. To provide a diversity of viewpoints without the constraint of labeling or prejudging film, video, or other audiovisual materials on the basis of the moral, religious, or political beliefs of the producer or filmmaker or on the basis of controversial content.

5. To contest vigorously, by all lawful means, every encroachment upon the public's freedom to view.

Reprinted with permission from the American Library Association (ALA) (www.ala.org/ala/oif/statementspols/ftvstatement/freedom viewstatement.cfm).

Code of Ethics of the American Library Association

As members of the American Library Association, we recognize the importance of codifying and making known to the profession and to the general public the ethical principles that guide the work of librarians, other professionals providing information services, library trustees and library staffs.

Ethical dilemmas occur when values are in conflict. The American Library Association Code of Ethics states the values to which we are committed, and embodies the ethical responsibilities of the profession in this changing information environment.

We significantly influence or control the selection, organization, preservation, and dissemination of information. In a political system grounded in an informed citizenry, we are members of a profession explicitly committed to intellectual freedom and the freedom of access to information. We have a special obligation to ensure the free flow of information and ideas to present and future generations.

The principles of this Code are expressed in broad statements to guide ethical decision making. These statements provide a framework; they cannot and do not dictate conduct to cover particular situations.

I.   We provide the highest level of service to all library users through appropriate and usefully organized resources; equitable service policies; equitable access; and accurate, unbiased, and courteous responses to all requests.

II. We uphold the principles of intellectual freedom and resist all efforts to censor library resources.

III. We protect each library user's right to privacy and confidentiality with respect to information sought or received and resources consulted, borrowed, acquired or transmitted.

IV. We respect intellectual property rights and advocate balance between the interests of information users and rights holders.

V. We treat co-workers and other colleagues with respect, fairness, and good faith, and advocate conditions of employment that safeguard the rights and welfare of all employees of our institutions.

VI. We do not advance private interests at the expense of library users, colleagues, or our employing institutions.

VII. We distinguish between our personal convictions and professional duties and do not allow our personal beliefs to interfere with fair representation of the aims of our institutions or the provision of access to their information resources.

VIII. We strive for excellence in the profession by maintaining and enhancing our own knowledge and skills, by encouraging the professional development of co-workers, and by fostering the aspirations of potential members of the profession.

Reprinted with permission from the American Library Association (ALA) (www.ala.org/ala/oif/statementspols/codeofethics/code ethics.cfm).

Copyright Law of the United States

Librarians must know about the Copyright Law of the United States because much of our work is affected by it. Copyright law protects the creator of a work from the reproduction, performance, display, or other use of their work without permission or compensation by restricting how the public can use information, creative works, and knowledge. Librarians are concerned with equal access to information, the right to privacy, the free flow of information, and preservation. Librarians disseminate information, which is used by people in various ways, and we must advise people about the lawful use of information we disseminate to them. We work with interlibrary loan, copy services, electronic database use, circulation, public performances, and preservation, which are all affected by the Copyright Law.

Librarians must be familiar enough with the Law to be able to refer to it when we have questions. Information is not cost-free. Most creators of works share or publish their works expecting to be compensated for sharing their work. In the U.S. we pay the creators of works to share their work. As librarians we ensure that creators of works shared on our watch are compensated.

Spend time learning about this Law. Take a class, a tutorial or read more about it. The Copyright Law of the United States and related laws in Title 17 of the *United States Code* includes laws about copyrighting works, registering for copyright, ownership, transfer, and infringement. The section of the law that relates most directly to librarians is Section 107 on Fair Use and Section 108 on Reproduction by Libraries and Archives.

USA PATRIOT Act

The Uniting and Strengthening America by Providing Appropriate Tools Required to Intercept and Obstruct Terrorism (USA PATRIOT) Act was introduced less than a week after September 11, 2001, for the purposes of authority of the Federal Bureau of Investigation (FBI) and law enforcement to access personal records such as library records, including stored electronic data and communications. It also expanded the laws governing wiretaps and "trap and trace" phone devices to Internet and electronic communications.

USA PATRIOT Act reauthorization legislation was signed into law by President Bush on March 9, 2006, and differs somewhat from the original legislation. A sunset of December 31, 2009, was established for Section 215 of the USA PATRIOT Act.

Libraries are places where intellectual freedom is exercised, the free and open exchange of ideas and information are practiced, and the freedom of inquiry and the right to privacy are upheld. The USA PATRIOT Act is thought to present a threat to these basic constitutional and privacy rights of library customers. Librarians are concerned about the extraordinary provisions in the USA PATRIOT Act for seeking information from libraries and it is unquestionable that everyone in our profession needs to be informed about this law, know what to do in the face of it, and be positioned to advocate for the freedoms that are at the foundation of our profession.

Sections of the law that particularly affect libraries are:

Title II – Enhanced Surveillance Procedures
Section 214: Pen register and trap and trace authority under FISA.

Removes the pre-existing requirement that the government prove the target is "an agent of a foreign power" before obtaining an order under the Foreign Intelligence Surveillance Act (FISA). The FBI's telephone monitoring authority in FISA investigations includes routing and addressing information for all Internet traffic, including email addresses, IP addresses, and URLs. Law enforcement may obtain orders under this provision if they believe there is a reasonable cause that records are needed for the investigation of terrorism or foreign intelligence matters.

Section 215: Access to records and other items under the Foreign Intelligence Surveillance Act.

Amends FISA to allow the FBI to obtain a court order without probable cause from a secret court for the production of "any tangible things (including books, record, papers, documents, and other items) for an authorized investigation to protect against terrorism or clandestine intelligence activities." "Any tangible thing" can include library circulation records, Internet use records and registration information stored in any medium. FBI agents do not have to demonstrate "probable cause." This information can be obtained without a customer's knowledge and Section 215 forbids persons producing such "tangible things," i.e., library staff disclosing customer records, from disclosing to anyone that the FBI requested the records. This amendment overrides all state library confidentiality laws that protect library records.

Section 216: Modification of authorities relating to use of pen registers and trap and trace devices.

Extends telephone monitoring laws to cover information relating to Internet usage and communication, including email, web surfing, and instant messaging. Libraries that provide access to the Internet including email may become the target of a court order requiring them to cooperate in the monitoring of a user's electronic communications sent through the library's computers, including installing monitoring devices. Law enforcement may obtain orders under this provision if they believe the records are needed for the investigation of terrorism or foreign intelligence matters. The library cannot disclose that communications are being monitored.

Title V – Removing Obstacles to Investigating Terrorism
Section 505: Miscellaneous National Security Authorities

Authorizes the Federal Bureau of Investigation to issue National Security Letters (NSLs) to entities providing wire or electronic communication services. NSLs can be used to compel entities providing wire of electronic services, i.e., libraries, to turn over subscriber information and electronic communication records to the FBI. NSLs are issued by an FBI agent without any review by a court of law, they do not require "probable cause" or the existence of specific facts to support the belief that a crime is being committed or that there is evidence of a crime. Librarians may not disclose the existence of an NSL or that records were produced as the result of an NSL to anyone, including the library customer.

Children's Internet Protection Act (CIPA)

The Children's Internet Protection Act (CIPA) is a federal law enacted by Congress in December 2000 to address concerns about access to offensive content over the Internet on school and library computers. CIPA imposes requirements on any school or library that receives funding for Internet access or internal connections from the Universal Service "E-rate" program or grants disbursed under the Library Services and Technology Act (LSTA). In early 2001, the Federal Communications Commission (FCC) issued rules implementing CIPA.

Libraries subject to CIPA may not receive E-Rate program discounts unless they certify that they have an Internet safety policy and technology protection measures in place. An Internet safety policy must include technology protection measures to block or filter Internet access to pictures that are: (a) obscene, (b) child pornography, or (c) harmful to minors, for computers that are accessed by minors. Libraries subject to CIPA are required to adopt and implement a policy addressing: (a) access by minors to inappropriate matter on the Internet; (b) the safety and security of minors when using electronic mail, chat rooms, and other forms of direct electronic communications; (c) unauthorized access, including so-called "hacking," and other unlawful activities by minors online; (d) unauthorized disclosure, use, and dissemination of personal information regarding minors; and (e) restricting minors' access to materials harmful to them.

Libraries that do not accept federal E-rate funding do not have to install filters. The Supreme Court's opinion has no effect on libraries that are not covered by CIPA (i.e., libraries that do not receive E-rate discounts or LSTA funds for the provision of public Internet access).

Librarians who object to CIPA's imposition of filtering software on libraries view mandatory Internet filtering as a violation of free speech and they consider CIPA a threat to the free access of information. The Library Bill of Rights states, "Libraries should challenge censorship in the fulfillment of their responsibility to provide information and enlightenment."

Deleting Online Predators Act (DOPA) of 2007

This Act amends the Communications Act of 1934 to require schools and libraries that receive universal service support to enforce a policy that: (1) prohibits access to a commercial social networking website or chat room unless used for an educational purpose with adult supervision; and (2) protects against access to visual depictions that are obscene, child pornography, or harmful to minors. It allows an administrator, supervisor, or other authorized person to disable such a technology protection measure during use by an adult, or by minors with adult supervision, to enable access for educational purposes.

Although an earlier incarnation of this bill was overwhelmingly passed in the House in 2006 it eventually died in the Senate. The bill was introduced again on February 16, 2007. As of January 2008, it was still in the House Energy and Commerce Committee, Subcommittee on Telecommunications and the Internet and is expected to fail again.

Social networking technologies are valuable tools for collaboration, business applications, and learning. They are becoming more important as communication tools and necessary for operating in today's work and personal environments. Blocking library customers from using interactive websites would limit opportunities for those who don't have Internet access otherwise, creating an unfair disadvantage for this population.

Laws requiring libraries to use filters or prohibit access to social networking sites have been introduced and passed in several states. Stay informed and be involved.

Recommended Reading

Chapter 1

American Library Association. LibraryCareers.org. www.library careers.org

American Library Association. What Librarians Need to Know. www.ala.org/ala/hrdr/librarycareerssite/whatyouneedlibrarian. cfm

Crowley, Bill, and Deborah Ginsberg. "Professional Values: Priceless." *American Libraries* 36:1 (2005): 52–55.

Curran, Charles. "What Do Librarians and Information Scientists Do? They ODAPCOSRIU in the I&OEM." *American Libraries* 32:1 (2001): 56–59.

Gorman, Michael. *Our Enduring Values: Librarianship in the 21st Century*. Chicago, IL: American Library Association, 2000.

Horrocks, Norman, ed. *Perspectives, Insights & Priorities: 17 Leaders Speak Freely of Librarianship*. Lanham, MD: Scarecrow Press, 2005.

Kniffel, Leonard. "What Turns You into a Librarian" (Editorial). *American Libraries* 35:5 (2004): 29.

McMullen, Haynes. "Library Education: A Mini-History; What Hath Dewey's Daring Venture Wrought? (Melvil Dewey)." *American Libraries* June 1986: 406–409.

Medical Library Association. Medical Librarianship: A Career Beyond the Cutting Edge. www.mlanet.org/pdf/career/eng_cutting_edge_05.pdf

Mulvaney, John Philip, and Dan O'Connor. "The Crux of Our Crisis: We Must Pinpoint What Every New Librarian Must Learn, Lest We Lose Our Professional Way." *American Libraries* 37:6 (2006): 3.

Special Libraries Association. Competencies for Information Professionals. www.sla.org/content/learn/comp2003/index.cfm

Chapter 2

American Library Association, and Information Institute, College of Information, Florida State University. "Libraries Connect Communities: Public Library Funding & Technology Access Study 2006-2007." In *ALA Research Series* 227. Chicago: American Library Association, 2007.

Barnett, Andy. *Libraries, Community, and Technology*. Jefferson, NC: McFarland & Co., 2002.

Basefsky, Stuart. "The Library as an Agent of Change: Pushing the Client Institution Forward." *Information Outlook* 3:8 (1999): 37–40.

Battles, Matthew. *Library: An Unquiet History*. New York: W.W. Norton & Company, 2003.

Bertot, John Carlo, Charles R. McClure, Susan Thomas, Kristin M. Barton, and Jessica McGilvray. "Public Libraries and the Internet 2007: Study Results and Findings." Chicago, IL: American Library Association and The Bill and Melinda Gates Foundation, 2007.

Block, Marylaine. *The Thriving Library: Successful Strategies for Challenging Times*. Medford, NJ: Information Today, Inc., 2007.

Frey, Tom, Jo Haight-Sarling, and Charles Brown. "If a Library Is Bookless, What's in It?" *Talk of the Nation*. NPR, February 27, 2006. www.npr.org/templates/story/story.php?storyId=5235518

Chapter 3 and Chapter 4

Arizona State Library. Collection Development Training for Arizona Public Libraries: Community Needs Assessment. www.lib.az.us/cdt/commneeds.aspx

Consulting Librarians Group (Sandra M. Cooper, Nancy Bolt, Keith Curry Lance, and Lawrence Webster, in cooperation with MGT of America, Inc. for the Library of Virginia). Community Analysis Methods and Evaluative Options: The CAMEO Handbook. skyways.lib.ks.us/pathway/cameo/index.htm

Chapter 5

Balas, Janet L. "Do You Know What Your Mission Is?" *Computers in Libraries* 27:2 (2007): 30–32.

Barker, Joel Arthur, Ray J. Christensen, Brad W. Neal, John R. Christensen, and Corporation Charthouse Learning. *The Power of Vision*. VHS. Burnsville, MN: Charthouse Learning Corp., 1990.

Jacobson, Alvin L., and JoAnne L. Sparks. "Creating Value: Building the Strategy-Focused Library." *Information Outlook* 5:9 (2001): 14.

Johnson, Heather. "Strategic Planning for Modern Libraries." *Library Management* 15:1 (1994): 7–18.

Kennen, Vernita. Our Church Library Needs a Mission Statement? You Must Be Joking. National Church Library Association, 2007. www.lclahq.org/Part%20I%20B.pdf

NcNamara, Carter. Strategic Planning (in Nonprofit or For-Profit Organizations). Authenticity Consulting LLC, 1997–2007. www.managementhelp.org/plan_dec/str_plan/str_plan.htm

Nelson, Sandra. *The New Planning for Results: A Streamlined Approach*. 2nd revised ed. Chicago, IL: American Library Association, 2001.

Penniman, W. David. "Strategic Planning to Avoid Bottlenecks in the Age of the Internet." *Computers in Libraries* 19:1 (1999): 50–53.

Roth, Ginger L. "Write a Mission Statement." Starting a Special Library from Scratch, 2002. www.libsci.sc.edu/bob/class/clis724/SpecialLibrariesHandbook/ScratchIndex_files/ScratchLibrary Index.htm#ms

Wallace, Linda K. *Libraries, Mission & Marketing: Writing Mission Statements that Work.* Chicago: American Library Association, 2004.

"What Is Strategic Planning?" Idealist.org. www.idealist.org/npo faq/03/22.html

Zimmerman, Michael C. "Your Library's Strategic Plan: Plan the Writing Before You Write the Plan." *Information Outlook* 1:12 (1997): 40–41.

Chapter 6

Alabaster, Carol. *Developing an Outstanding Core Collection: A Guide for Libraries.* Chicago: American Library Association, 2002.

Arizona State Library. Collection Development Training for Arizona Public Libraries. www.lib.az.us/cdt

Baird, Brian J. *Preservation Strategies for Small Academic and Public Libraries.* Lanham, MD: Scarecrow Press, 2003.

Baker, Sharon L., and Karen L. Wallace. *The Responsive Public Library: How to Develop and Market a Winning Collection.* 2nd ed. Englewood, CO: Libraries Unlimited, 2002.

Baumbach, Donna J., and Linda L Miller. *Less Is More: A Practical Guide to Weeding School Library Collections.* Chicago, IL: American Library Association, 2006.

Boon, Belinda. *The CREW Method: Expanded Guidelines for Collection Evaluation and Weeding for Small and Medium-Sized*

Public Libraries. Revised and updated ed. Austin, TX: Texas State Library, 1995.

Burgett, James, John Haar, and Linda L. Phillips. *Collaborative Collection Development: A Practical Guide for Your Library.* Chicago, IL: American Library Association, 2004.

Cassell, Kay Ann. *Developing Reference Collections and Services in an Electronic Age: A How-to-Do-It Manual for Librarians.* New York: Neal-Schuman Publishers, 1999.

Idaho Commission for Libraries. Idaho's Alternative Basic Library Education (ABLE) Program: Collection Development. libraries.idaho.gov/able#courses

Katz, Bill, editor. *The How-to-Do-It Manual for Small Libraries.* New York: Neal-Schuman, 1988.

McGregor, Joy, Ken Dillon, and James Henri, eds. *Collection Management for School Libraries.* Revised ed. Lanham, MD: Scarecrow Press, 2003.

Recommended Reference Books for Small and Medium-Sized Libraries and Media Centers. Littleton, CO: Libraries Unlimited, Inc., 2006.

Chapter 7

Arizona State Library. Collection Development Training for Arizona Public Libraries: Acquisitions. www.lib.az.us/cdt/acquis.aspx

Chapman, Liz. *Managing Acquisitions in Library and Information Services.* Revised ed. London: Facet Publishing, 2004.

Eaglen, Audrey. *Buying Books: A How-To-Do-It Manual for Librarians.* New York: Neal-Schuman, 2000.

Fischer, Ruth, and Rick Lugg. "The Acquisitions Tool Belt: Ruth Fischer and Rick Lugg Make Sense of Vendor Systems. (Acquisitions' Next Wave) (Product/Service Evaluation)." *Library Journal* 130:12 (2005): S2–3.

Leonhardt, Thomas W. *Handbook of Electronic and Digital Acquisitions.* New York: Haworth Press, 2006.

Lugg, Rick, and Ruth Fischer. "Acquisitions' Next Step: You've Come a Long Way, Book Selectors. But Technological Innovation Means the Future Will Be Even Better." *Library Journal* 130:12 (2005): 30–32.

Chapter 8

Haynes, Elizabeth and Joanna F. Fountain. *Unlocking the Mysteries of Cataloging: A Workbook of Examples.* Westport, CT: Libraries Unlimited, 2005.

Kaplan, Allison G., and Ann Marlow Riedling. *Catalog It! A Guide to Cataloging School Library Materials.* Worthington, OH: Linworth Publishing, Inc., 2002.

Konovalov, Yuri. "Cataloging as a Customer Service: Applying Knowledge to Technology Tools." *Information Outlook* 3:9 (1999): 25–27.

Miller, Rosalind E., and Jane C. Terwillegar. *Commonsense Cataloging: A Cataloger's Manual.* 4th revised ed. New York: H.W. Wilson Company, 1990.

Mortimer, Mary. *Learn Descriptive Cataloging.* Lanham, MD: Scarecrow Press, 2000.

Taylor, Arlene G. *The Organization of Information.* 2nd ed. Englewood, CO: Libraries Unlimited, 2003.

Taylor, Arlene G. *Wynar's Introduction to Cataloging and Classification.* Revised 9th ed. Westport, CT: Libraries Unlimited, 2004.

Chapter 9

Hart, Lauree G. "RSS Feeds Create Added Value for Special Libraries." *Information Outlook* 11:8 (2007): 26–29.

Chapter 10

Barnett, Andy. *Libraries, Community, and Technology.* Jefferson, NC: McFarland & Co., 2002.

Bopp, Richard E., and Linda C. Smith. *Reference and Information Services: An Introduction.* 3rd ed. Englewood, CO: Libraries Unlimited, 2001.

Brown, Barbara J. *Programming for Librarians: A How-to-Do-It Manual.* New York: Neal-Schuman, 1992.

Honnold, RoseMary, and Saralyn A. Mesaros. *Serving Seniors: A How-to-Do-It Manual for Librarians.* New York: Neal-Schuman Publishers, 2004.

Janes, Joseph. *Introduction to Reference Work in the Digital Age.* New York: Neal-Schuman Publishers, 2003.

Jennerich, Elaine Zaremba, and Edward Jennerich. *The Reference Interview as a Creative Art.* 2nd ed. Englewood, CO: Libraries Unlimited, 1997.

Katz, Bill, ed. *New Technologies and Reference Services.* New York: Haworth Information Press, 2000.

Katz, William A. *Introduction to Reference Work.* Vol. 1. 8th ed. New York: McGraw-Hill, 2002.

Kern, M. Kathleen. *Virtual Reference Best Practices.* ALA Editions. Chicago: American Library Association, 2008.

Mabry, Celia Hales, ed. *Doing the Work of Reference: Practical Tips for Excelling as a Reference Librarian.* Binghamton, NY: Haworth Information Press, 2001.

Owen, Tim. *Success at the Enquiry Desk: Successful Enquiry Answering—Every Time.* 5th ed. London: Library Association, 2006.

Project Wombat. project-wombat.org

Robertson, Deborah A. *Cultural Programming for Libraries: Linking Libraries, Communities, and Culture.* Chicago: American Library Association, 2005.

Ross, Catherine Sheldrick, Kirsti Nelson, and Patricia Dewdney. *Conducting the Reference Interview: A How-to-Do-It Manual for Librarians.* New York: Neal-Schuman, 2002.

Saricks, Joyce G. *Readers' Advisory Service in the Public Library.* 3rd ed. Chicago: American Library Association, 2005.

Schachter, Debbie. "Does Your Perception of Your Service Match Your Clients' Opinions?" *Information Outlook* 11:4 (2007): 40–41.

Weingand, Darlene E. *Customer Service Excellence: A Concise Guide for Librarians.* Chicago: American Library Association, 1997.

Chapter 11

Balas, Janet L. "Useful Resources for Writing Library Policies (Online Treasures)." *Computers in Libraries* 22:6 (2002): 30–32.

Fox, Linda S. *The Volunteer Library: A Handbook.* Jefferson, NC: McFarland, 1999.

Nelson, Sandra S., and June Garcia. *Creating Policies for Results: From Chaos to Clarity.* Chicago: American Library Association, 2003.

Richardson, Ellen. "Four Tests for a Legally-Enforceable Library Policy." State of Michigan. www.michigan.gov/hal/0,1607,7-160-17451_18668_18689-54454—,00.html

Chapter 12

Carson, Paula Phillips, Kerry David Carson, and Joyce Schouest Phillips. *The Library Manager's Deskbook: 102 Expert Solutions to 101 Common Dilemmas.* Chicago: American Library Association, 1995.

Driggers, Preston F., and Eileen Dumas. *Managing Library Volunteers: A Practical Toolkit.* Chicago: American Library Association, 2002.

Fox, Linda S. *The Volunteer Library: A Handbook.* Jefferson, NC: McFarland, 1999.

Giesecke, Joan, and Beth McNeil. *Fundamentals of Library Supervision.* ALA Fundamentals Series. Chicago: American Library Association, 2005.

Gordon, Rachel Singer. *The Accidental Library Manager.* Medford, NJ: Information Today, Inc., 2005.

Katz, Bill, ed. *The How-To-Do-It Manual for Small Libraries.* New York: Neal-Schuman, 1988.

Landau, Herbert. *The Small Public Library Survival Guide.* ALA Editions. Chicago: American Library Association, 2008.

Massis, Bruce E. *The Practical Library Manager.* New York: Haworth Information Press, 2003.

Moorman, John, ed. *Running a Small Library: A How-to-Do-It Manual.* New York: Neal-Schuman, 2006.

Morris, Beryl. *First Steps in Management: The Successful LIS professional.* London: Library Association Publishers, 1996.

Nelson, Sandra S., Ellen Altman, and Diane Mayo. *Managing for Results: Effective Resource Allocation for Public Libraries.* Chicago: American Library Association, 2000.

Sager, Donald J. *Small Libraries: Organization and Operation.* 3rd ed. Fort Atkinson, WI: Highsmith Press, 2000.

Seiss, Judith A. *The New OPL Sourcebook: A Guide for Solo and Small Libraries.* Medford, NJ: Information Today, Inc., 2006.

Smith, Ruth S. *Setting up a Library: How to Begin or Begin Again.* 2nd revised ed., CSLA Guide. Portland, OR: Church and Synagogue Library Association Publication, 1994.

Sutton, Dave. *So You're Going to Run a Library: A Library Management Primer.* Englewood, CO: Libraries Unlimited, 1995.

Tucker, Dennis C., and Shelley Elizabeth Mosley. *Crash Course in Library Supervision.* Westport, CT: Libraries Unlimited, 2008.

Weingand, Darlene E. *Administration of the Small Public Library*. 4th ed. Chicago: American Library Association, 2001.

Chapter 13

Alman, Susan Webreck. *Crash Course in Marketing for Libraries*. Westport, CN: Libraries Unlimited, 2007.

Collins, Kristine L. "Selling Law Librarianship." *AALL Spectrum* 12: 2 (November 2007): 10–11.

Fisher, Patricia H., Marceille M. Pride, and Ellen G. Miller. *Blueprint for Your Library Marketing Plan: A Guide to Help You Survive and Thrive*. Chicago: American Library Association, 2006.

Houston Area Library System. Training for Public Libraries: Plan Target Market. www.hals.lib.tx.us/plan123/3intro.htm

Kassel, Amelia. "How to Write a Marketing Plan." *MLS: Marketing Library Services* June 1999: 13–17.

Kendrick, Terry. *Developing Strategic Marketing Plans that Really Work: A Toolkit for Public Libraries*. London: Facet, 2006.

Lindsay, Anita Rothwell. *Marketing and Public Relations Practices in College Libraries*. CLIP Note #34. Chicago: College Library Information Packet Committee, Association of College and Research Libraries, 2004.

National Library of Medicine (U.S.). *Survival of the Fittest: Strategies to Prove Your Library's Value*. Bethesda, MD: National Library of Medicine, 2007.

Ohio Library Council. Marketing the Library: Web-based Training. www.olc.org/marketing/index.html

Rossiter, N. *Marketing a Library: Promoting the Best Deal in Town*. Oxford: Chandos, 2007.

Schachter, Debbie. "Does Your Perception of Your Service Match Your Clients' Opinions?" *Information Outlook* 11:4 (2007): 40–41.

Siess, Judith. "Marketing Without Much Money: You Don't Need Big Bucks to Get the Word Out. Here Are (More Than) a Few Ideas" (Marketing). *Information Outlook* 8:10 (2004): 28–31.

Siess, Judith A. *The Visible Librarian: Asserting Your Value with Marketing and Advocacy.* Chicago: American Library Association, 2003.

Walters, Suzanne. *Library Marketing That Works.* New York: Neal-Schuman, 2004.

Woodward, Jeannette A. *Creating the Customer-Driven Library: Building on the Bookstore Model.* Chicago, IL: American Library Association, 2005.

Chapter 15

Barclay, Donald A. *Managing Public-Access Computers: A How-to-Do-It Manual for Librarians.* New York: Neal-Schuman Publishers, 2000.

Bolan, Kimberly, and Robert Cullin. *Technology Made Simple: An Improvement Guide for Small and Medium Libraries.* Chicago, IL: American Library Association, 2007.

Huang, Phil. "How You Can Protect Public Access Computers and Their Users." *Computers in Libraries* 27:5 (2007): 16–20.

Jurkowski, Odin L. *Technology and the School Library: A Comprehensive Guide for Media Specialists and Other Educators.* Lanham, MD: Scarecrow Press, 2006.

MaintainIT *The Joy of Computing: A Cookbook for Small and Rural Libraries.* www.maintainitproject.org/files/TheJoyofComputing-1207.pdf

MaintainIT. *The Joy of Computing: Recipes for a 5-Star Library.* www.maintainitproject.org/files/CB2-FiveStarLibrary-0508.pdf

Romm, Diane. "It Pays to Be Thin: New Versions of Thin Clients Can Solve the Many Problems Wrought By "Fat Client" PCs" (Infotech Feature). *Library Journal* 131:2 (2006): 34–36.

WebJunction. You Can Do It! Practical Techniques for PAC, Rural Webinar #14 www.webjunction.org/do/DisplayContent?ID=7569

Chapter 16

Akerman, Richard. "Library Web Services: The Future of Library Catalogs Requires Remixing, Repurposing, and Showcasing Enhancements" (Social Catalog)(Technical Report)(Website List). *Library Journal* 132:12 (2007): S6–8.

Balas, Janet L. "Does Your Library's Web Site Pass the Usability Test?" (Card Catalog Replaced by the Web Opac)(Column). *Computers in Libraries* 25:9 (2005): 36–38.

Breeding, Marshall. "An Industry Redefined: Private Equity Moves into the ILS, and Open Source Support Emerges" (Automation Marketplace 2007). *Library Journal* 132:6 (2007): 36–46.

Breeding, Marshall. "An Update on Open Source ILS: In the Last Few Years, Some Viable Open Source Integrated Library Systems Have Emerged to Challenge the Commercial Offerings" (The Systems Librarian)(Column). *Computers in Libraries* 27:3 (2007): 27–29.

Cohn, John M. *Planning for Integrated Systems and Technologies: A How-To-Do-It Manual for Librarians.* New York: Neal-Schuman Publishers, 2001.

Colorado Department of Education. Basics of Library Automation. www.cde.state.co.us/cdelib/technology/atauto.htm

"Introduction" (Chapter 1)(Library Catalogs). *Library Technology Reports* 43:4 (2007): 5–14.

Kroski, Ellyssa. How to Automate a Small Library. WebJunction. data.webjunction.org/wj/documents/13125.doc

Lamb, Annette, and Larry Johnson. "Open-Source Software in School Libraries." *Teacher Librarian* 33:5 (2007): 55–57.

Leff, Barbara Y. "Planning to Automate Your School, Synagogue or Center Library?" Paper presented at the 36th Annual

Convention of the Association of Jewish Libraries, La Jolla, CA, June 24–27, 2001. www.jewishlibraries.org/ajlweb/publications/proceedings/proceedings2001/leff.pdf

"Next-Generation Flavor in Integrated Online Catalogs" (Chapter 7)(Polaris Library System's Polaris). *Library Technology Reports* 43:4 (2007): 38–41.

Tennant, Roy. "Facing the Not Knowing." *Library Journal* 32:1 (2007): 37.

Waller, Nicole. "Model RFP for Integrated Library System Products." *Library Technology Reports* 39:4 (July/August 2003).

Wayne, Richard. "Helping You Buy: Integrated Library Systems." *Computers in Libraries* 26:9 (2006): 23–31.

Chapter 17

Digital Reference Blog. www.teachinglibrarian.org/weblog/blogger.html

Lipow, Anne Grodzins. *The Virtual Reference Librarian's Handbook.* New York: Neal-Schuman, 2003.

Sauers, Michael P. *Using the Internet as a Reference Tool: A How to-Do-It Manual for Librarians.* New York: Neal-Schuman, 2001.

Chapter 18

Casey, Michael. "Born in the Biblioblogoshere." LibraryCrunch. www.librarycrunch.com/2006/01/post_1.html

Casey, Michael E., and Laura C. Savastinuk. *Library 2.0: A Guide to Participatory Service.* Medford, NJ: Information Today, Inc., 2007.

Chad, Ken, and Paul Miller. Do Libraries Matter? The Rise of Library 2.0. (A Talis White Paper). Talis. 2005. www.talis.com/applications/downloads/white_papers/DoLibrariesMatter.pdf

Farkas, Meredith G. *Social Software in Libraries: Building Collaboration, Communication, and Community Online.* Medford, NJ: Information Today, Inc., 2007.

Library 2.0 Reading List. Squidoo. www.squidoo.com/library20

Maness, Jack M. "Library 2.0 Theory: Web 2.0 and Its Implications for Libraries." Webology 3:2 (2006): Article 25. www.webology. ir/2006/v3n2/a25.html

Miller, Paul. Library 2.0—the Challenge of Disruptive Innovation. (A Talis White Paper). Talis. 2006. www.talis.com/resources/ documents/447_Library_2_prf1.pdf

Web 2.0 and Library 2.0. Squidoo. www.squidoo.com/VBweb2_0

Appendix A

California Department of Education. School Library Policies. www.cde.ca.gov/ci/cr/lb/policies.asp

Connecticut State Library. Sample Policies from Connecticut Public Libraries. ct.webjunction.org/do/DisplayContent?id= 7050

Illinois School Library Media Association. ISLMA Professional Resources. www.islma.org/resources.htm

Indiana State Library. Policies of the Indiana State Library. www.in.gov/library/2453.htm

Massachusetts Regional Library Systems. Sample Massachusetts Library Policies. www.cmrls.org/policies

School Library Media Specialist. Information Access & Delivery: Policies and Procedures. eduscapes.com/sms/access/policies. html

State Library of Ohio. Sample Library Policy Statements. winslo.state.oh.us/publib/policies.html

Washington State Public Library. Public Library Policies and Plans Online. www.webjunction.org/do/DisplayContent?id=6344

Wisconsin Department of Public Instruction. Wisconsin Public Library Policy Resources. dpi.wi.gov/pld/policies.html

Appendix C

Copyright

American Library Association. Copyright. www.ala.org/ala/wash off/woissues/copyrightb/copyright.cfm

Bruwelheide, Janis H. *The Copyright Primer for Librarians and Educators*. 2nd ed. Chicago: American Library Association, 1995.

Kansas State University Intellectual Property Information Center. Copyright Basics. www.k-state.edu/academicservices/intprop/ webtutor/sld001.htm

LibraryLaw.com. Copyright and Libraries. www.librarylaw.com/ Copyright_and_Libraries.html

U.S. Copyright Office. Copyright Law and Policy. www.copyright. gov/laws

U.S. Copyright Office. Reproduction of Copyrighted Works by Educators and Librarians. www.copyright.gov/circs/ circ21.pdf

University of Texas. Crash Course in Copyright. www.utsystem. edu/OGC/IntellectualProperty/cprtindx.htm#top

USA PATRIOT Act

American Library Association. USA PATRIOT Act. www.ala.org/ ala/washoff/woissues/civilliberties/theusapatriotact/usapatriot act.cfm

Colorado Association of Libraries. USA PATRIOT Act. www.cal-webs. org/if_patriot2.html#colorado2

Children's Internet Protection Act (CIPA)

American Library Association. Children's Internet Protection Act (CIPA). www.ala.org/ala/washoff/woissues/civilliberties/cipaweb/cipa.cfm

Caldwell-Stone, D. "Public Libraries and the Internet." *Municipal Lawyer* 44:6 (2003): 16–19. www.ala.org/ala/washoff/woissues/civilliberties/cipaweb/newsarticles/publiclibrariesinternet.pdf

Websites
www.accidentallibrarian.com

Websites are listed by chapter in the order in which they appear. Links to these are available on the website for this book: www. accidentallibrarian.com.

Chapter 1

U.S. Department of Labor, Occupational Outlook Handbook, 2006–07 edition, www.bls.gov/oco/ocos068.htm

American Library Association, www.ala.org

American Library Association, Education & Degrees, www.ala.org/ ala/education.cfm

American Library Association, What Librarians Need to Know, www.ala.org/ala/hrdr/librarycareerssite/whatyouneedlibrarian. cfm

ALA Standards for Accreditation of Master's Programs in Library and Information Studies, www.ala.org/ala/accreditation/accred standards/standards_2008.pdf

Public Libraries in the United States: Fiscal Year 2004, nces.ed.gov/ pubs2006/2006349.pdf

SLA's Competencies for Information Professionals, www.sla.org/ content/learn/comp2003/index.cfm

ALA's Accreditation Draft Core Competencies, www.ala.org/ala/ accreditationb/Draft_Core_Competencies_07_05.pdf

Chapter 2

American Library Association, Public Library Standards, wikis.ala.org/professionaltips/index.php/Public_Library_ Standards

Longshots Podcast, www.sarahlong.org/podcast

Library Garden Blog, librarygarden.blogspot.com

Chapter 3

Arizona Department of Commerce, Community Profile Index, www.azcommerce.com/SiteSel/Profiles/Community+Profile+ Index.htm

New Hampshire Economic and Labor Market Information Bureau, www.nh.gov/nhes/elmi/communpro.htm

Alaska's Division of Community and Regional Affairs, Community Database Online, www.dced.state.ak.us/dca/commdb/CF_ COMDB.htm

U.S. Census Bureau, www.census.gov

Chapter 4

SurveyGizmo, www.surveygizmo.com

SurveyMonkey, www.surveymonkey.com

Zoomerang, info.zoomerang.com

Chapter 5

State Library of Pennsylvania Mission and Vision Statement, www.statelibrary.state.pa.us/libraries/cwp/view.asp?a=2&Q =40190

Madison (WI) Public Library Vision, Mission, and Strategic Initiatives, www.madisonpubliclibrary.org/about/mission.html

Moraine Valley Community College Library Vision Statement, www2.morainevalley.edu/default.asp?SiteId=10&PageId=707

Georgetown University Library Vision Statement, library.george town.edu/geninfo/mission.htm

Albany (CA) High School Library Vision Statement, www.albany. k12.ca.us/ahs/resources/library/vision_policies.htm

Conway (NH) Public Library Mission Statement, conway.lib. nh.us/aboutus/mission.htm

Spotlight on SLA Members: Trudy Katz—Special Libraries Association—Interview, findarticles.com/p/articles/mi_m0FWE/ is_4_5/ai_73280571

Union College, Schaffer Library Mission Statement, www.union. edu/PUBLIC/LIBRARY/about/about.htm

Library of Congress Mission, Strategic Plan, www.loc.gov/ about/mission

Evanston (IL) Public Library Strategic Plan, www.epl.org/library/ strategic-plan-00.html

Glencoe (IL) Public Library Strategic Plan, www.glencoe.lib.il.us/ plan0609.pdf

Parmly Billings Library Plan, ci.billings.mt.us/DocumentView.asp? DID=3787

Morse Institute (MA) Library Strategic Plan, www.morseinstitute. org/PDF/StrategicPlanForWeb.pdf

Chapter 6

NPR Books Page, www.npr.org/templates/topics/topic.php? topicId=1032

Book TV on C-SPAN2, www.booktv.org

Oprah's Book Club, www.oprah.com/obc_classic/obc_main.jhtml

Today Show's Books, www.msnbc.msn.com/id/3041344

Good Morning America's "Read This!" abcnews.go.com/GMA/ Books

The CREW Method: Expanded Guidelines for Collection Evaluation and Weeding for Small and Medium-Sized Public Libraries by Belinda Boon, www.tsl.state.tx.us/ld/pubs/crew/index.html

Chapter 7

WorldCat, www.worldcat.org
Library of Congress, www.loc.gov
BooksInPrint.com, www.booksinprint.com
AcqWeb, www.acqweb.org
Amazon.com, www.amazon.com
Alibris, www.alibris.com
AbeBooks.com, www.abebooks.com
Powell's Books, www.powells.com
BookFinder.com, www.bookfinder.com

Chapter 8

Medical Subject Headings (MeSH), www.nlm.nih.gov/mesh
Art and Architecture Thesaurus, www.getty.edu/research/conducting_
    research/vocabularies/aat/index.html
Thesaurus of ERIC Descriptors, www.eric.ed.gov/ERICWebPortal/
    Home.portal?_nfpb=true&_pageLabel=Thesaurus&_nfls=false
Library of Congress, catalog.loc.gov
Library of Congress Online Catalog Help Pages, catalog.loc.
    gov/help/savemail.htm
Lib-web-cats, www.librarytechnology.org/libwebcats/index.pl
WorldCat, www.worldcat.org
Library of Congress Authorities, authorities.loc.gov

Chapter 9

Bloglines, www.bloglines.com

NewsGator, www.newsgator.com

Google Reader, www.google.com/reader

Blogger, www.blogger.com

WordPress, wordpress.com

Chapter 10

WorldCat, www.worldcat.org

NPR's Book Tour, www.npr.org/templates/story/story.php?story
  Id=10448909

New York Times Book Review podcast, www.nytimes.com/2006/
  10/08/books/books-podcast-archive.html?ref=books

Every Child Ready to Read @ Your Library, www.ala.org/ala/alsc/
  ecrr/ecrrhomepage.cfm

Family Place Libraries, www.familyplacelibraries.org

Prime Time Family Reading Time, www.leh.org/html/primetime.
  html

Collaborative Summer Library Program, www.cslpreads.org

Chapter 13

iContact, www.icontact.com

Constant Contact, www.constantcontact.com

Chase's Annual Events website, www.mhprofessional.com/?page
  =/mhp/categories/chases/content/special_months.html

International Listening Association (ILA), www.listen.org/pages/
  march_psas.html

Healthy Aging Campaign, www.healthyaging.net

Chapter 15

Ubuntu, www.ubuntu.com

Firefox, www.mozilla.com/firefox

OpenOffice.org, www.openoffice.org

NeoOffice, www.neooffice.org

AVG Anti-Virus, www.grisoft.com

ESET NOD32 Antivirus, www.eset.com

Kaspersky Anti-Virus, usa.kaspersky.com

McAfee Virus Scan, www.mcafee.com/us

Norton Antivirus, www.symantec.com

Trend Micro Antivirus, us.trendmicro.com

ZoneAlarm Antivirus, www.zonealarm.com

AVG Anti-Spyware, www.grisoft.com

CounterSpy, www.sunbelt-software.com

Spy Sweeper, www.webroot.com

Spyware Doctor, www.pctools.com

CyberDefender, www.cyberdefender.com

Kaspersky Internet Security, usa.kaspersky.com

McAfee Total Protection, www.mcafee.com/us

Norton 360, www.symantec.com

Panda Internet Security, www.pandasecurity.com/usa

CenturionGuard, www.centuriontech.com

Clean Slate, www.fortresgrand.com

Deep Freeze, www.faronics.com

SteadyState, www.microsoft.com/windows/products/winfamily/
sharedaccess

Chapter 16

Evergreen, open-ils.org

Koha, koha.org

LibLime, liblime.com

LearningAccess ILS, www.learningaccess.org/tools/ils.php

Marshall Breeding's Library Technology Guides, www.library
technology.org/index.pl?SID=20080124926269531

Perceptions 2007: An International Survey of Library Automation, www.librarytechnology.org/perceptions2007.pl

Chapter 17

Selected Internet Resources from the Pasadena Public Library, www.ci.pasadena.ca.us/library/subject_links.asp

Bartleby.com Reference, www.bartleby.com/reference

Best Free Reference Web Sites 2007 ALA/RUSA www.ala.org/ala/rusa/rusaourassoc/rusasections/mars/marspubs/marsbestref2007.cfm

Internet Public Library Reference Center, www.ipl.org.ar/ref

Librarians' Internet Index, www.lii.org

Ready Reference Web Sites from Michigan State University Libraries, www.lib.msu.edu/sowards/home/home2.htm

Refdesk.com, www.refdesk.com/essentl.html

Selected Ready Reference Resources from the New York State Library, www.nysl.nysed.gov/reference/readyref.htm

del.icio.us, del.icio.us

LibSuccess.org, www.libsuccess.org/index.php?title=Online_Reference

AOL's Instant Messenger (AIM), www.aim.com

Yahoo! Messenger, www.yahoomessenger.com

Windows Live Messenger or MSN Messenger, im.live.com

Google Talk, www.google.com/talk

Meebo, www.meebo.com

Pidgin, www.pidgin.im

Trillian, www.trillian.cc

Chapter 18

Internet Librarian, www.infotoday.com/il2008

Library 2.0 Reading List, www.squidoo.com/library20

23 Things Tutorial at School Library Learning 2.0, schoollibrary learning2.blogspot.com/2007/02/23-things_27.html

Five Weeks to a Social Library, www.sociallibraries.com/course

Find Time for Emerging Technologies, unconferencewalibrary. pbwiki.com/Finding%20time%20for%20emerging%20tech

Learning 2.0, plcmcl2-things.blogspot.com

Library 2.0 on Ning, library20.ning.com

SirsiDynix Institute: The 2.0 Meme—Web 2.0, Library 2.0, Librarian 2.0, www.sirsidynixinstitute.com/seminar_page.php?sid=56

Blyberg.net, www.blyberg.net

Information Wants to Be Free, meredith.wolfwater.com/wordpress

LibraryCrunch, www.librarycrunch.com

David Lee King, www.davidleeking.com

iLibrarian, oedb.org/blogs/ilibrarian

Tame the Web, tametheweb.com

The Shifted Librarian, theshiftedlibrarian.com

Librarian in Black, librarianinblack.typepad.com

Walking Paper, www.walkingpaper.org

Library Weblogs, www.libdex.com/weblogs.html

Cleveland Public Library, twitter.com/Cleveland_PL

Lunar and Planetary Institute Library, twitter.com/LPI_Library

Casa Grande Library, twitter.com/cglibrary

MySpace, www.myspace.com

Brooklyn College Library, www.myspace.com/brooklyncollege library

Denver Public Library Teens, www.myspace.com/denver_evolver

Hobbs Public Library, www.myspace.com/booksrcool

Ball State University Libraries, www.myspace.com/brackenlibrary

Barnard Zine Library, www.myspace.com/barnardzinelibrary

Libraries on MySpace, groups.myspace.com/myspacelibraries

Facebook, www.facebook.com

Mills Library McMaster University, www.facebook.com/profile. php?id=7233086835

Regina Public Library, www.facebook.com/pages/Regina-SK/Regina-Public-Library-/7519206045?ref=s

Flickr, www.flickr.com

Lester Public Library, www.flickr.com/photos/lesterpubliclibrary/collections/72157602264429004

North Carolina State University Libraries Special Collections Research Center, www.flickr.com/photos/ncsu_scrc

Library of Congress 1930s-1940s Color Photos, www.flickr.com/photos/library_of_congress/sets/72157603671370361

Newton Free Library, www.flickr.com/photos/newtonfreelibrary

Doucette Library of Teaching Resources Wiki, wiki.ucalgary.ca/page/Doucette

Ohio University Libraries Biz Wiki, www.library.ohiou.edu/subjects/bizwiki

Oregon Library Instruction Wiki, instructionwiki.org

Del.icio.us, del.icio.us

Furl, www.furl.net

Fairfax (VA) Public Library Self-Service Checkout Instruction, www.youtube.com/watch?v=iYwta1lCp8Y&feature=related

Greater Victoria Public Library News, www.youtube.com/watch?v=J9MqhqIZRIM

Brown University Library Video Tutorial, www.brown.edu/Facilities/University_Library/tutorials/gateway_videos.html

UC San Diego Biomedical Library Tour, video.google.com/videoplay?docid=5161576846247354338

Seattle Public Library Virtual Tour, www.spl.org/videos/VirtualTour5-10-2007/VirtualTour5-10-2007.html

Delray Beach Public Library "I Love My Library", www.youtube.com/watch?v=FcNIsWExKEw

The One Minute Critic, oneminutecritic.wordpress.com

Chapter 19

Border Regional Library Association, www.brla.info

Mountain Plains Library Association, www.mpla.us

New England Library Association, www.nelib.org

Pacific Northwest Library Association, www.pnla.org

Southeastern Library Association, sela.jsu.edu

ALA List of State and Regional Library Associations, www.ala.org/
ala/ourassociation/chapters/stateandregional/stateregional.htm

LISjobs Message Boards, lisjobs.com/forum

WebJunction, www.webjunction.org

TechSoup, www.techsoup.org

ACQNET-L, serials.infomotions.com/acqnet

AUTOCAT, www.cwu.edu/~dcc/Autocat-ToC-2007.html

BUSLIB-L, list1.ucc.nau.edu/archives/buslib-l.html

CHMINF-L, www.indiana.edu/~cheminfo/network.html

COMLIB-L, listserv.uiuc.edu/archives/comlib-l.html

DLDG-L, listserv.indiana.edu/cgi-bin/wa-iub.exe?A0=DLDG-L

ExLibris, palimpsest.stanford.edu/byform/mailing-lists/exlibris

GOVDOC-L, govdoc-l.org

Law-Lib, home.olemiss.edu/%7Enoe/llfaq.html

LIBADMIN-L, listserv.williams.edu/archives/libadmin-l.html

LIBJOBS, www.ifla.org/II/lists/libjobs.htm

LIBLICENSE-L, www.library.yale.edu/~llicense/mailing-list.shtml

LIBREF-L, www.library.kent.edu/page/10391

LM_NET, www.eduref.org/lm_net

MAPS-L, www.listserv.uga.edu/archives/maps-l.html

MEDLIB-L, www.mlanet.org/discussion/medlibl.html

MLA-L, listserv.indiana.edu/cgi-bin/wa-iub.exe?A0=MLA-L

NEWLIB-L, www.lahacal.org/newlib

NGC4Lib, dewey.library.nd.edu/mailing-lists/ngc4lib

oss4lib, oss4lib.org/mailing-list

PACS-L, epress.lib.uh.edu/pacsl/pacsl.html

PIJIP-COPYRIGHT, roster.wcl.american.edu/cgi-bin/wa.exe?A0=
PIJIP-COPYRIGHT&X=5D71B90996102E1081&Y=mpalmedo@
wcl.american.edu

PRISON-LIB, lists.topica.com/lists/PRISON-LIB/?cid=2065

PROJECT WOMBAT, www.project-wombat.org/one_list_three_
ways.shtml

PUBLIB, lists.webjunction.org/publib

PUBYAC, www.pubyac.org

SERIALST, www.uvm.edu/~bmaclenn/serialst.html

SYSLIB-L, listserv.buffalo.edu/cgi-bin/wa?A0=syslib-l

TAGAD-L, lists.topica.com/lists/tagad-l

Web4Lib, lists.webjunction.org/web4lib

XML4Lib, lists.webjunction.org/xml4lib

YALSA, www.ala.org/ala/yalsa/electronicresourcesb/websitesmailing.
cfm#discussion

ALA Open Discussion Groups, Forums and Interest Groups,
www.ala.org/ala/ourassociation/discussiongroups/listala
discussion.htm

Links to ALA electronic discussion lists, lists.ala.org/wws

Free Range Librarian, freerangelibrarian.com

iLibrarian, oedb.org/blogs/ilibrarian

Information Wants to be Free, meredith.wolfwater.com/wordpress

Librarian.net, www.librarian.net

LibrarianInBlack.net, librarianinblack.typepad.com

LISNews.org, lisnews.org

Libraryman, www.libraryman.com/blog

OPL Plus, opls.blogspot.com

The Shifted Librarian, www.theshiftedlibrarian.com

Stephen's Lighthouse, stephenslighthouse.sirsi.com

Tame the Web, tametheweb.com

Walt at Random, walt.lishost.org

What I Learned Today, www.web2learning.net

American Association of Law Libraries (AALL), www.aallnet.org

American Indian Library Association (AILA), www.ailanet.org

American Library Association (ALA), www.ala.org

Allied Professional Association (ALA-APA), ala-apa.org

American Association of School Librarians (AASL), www.ala.org/aasl

Association for Library Collections and Technical Services (ALCTS), www.ala.org/ALCTS

Association for Library Service to Children (ALSC), www.ala.org/ALSC

Association of College and Research Libraries (ACRL), www.ala.org/acrl

Association of Specialized and Cooperative Library Agencies (ASCLA), www.ala.org/ascla

Library Administration and Management Association (LAMA), www.ala.org/lama

Library and Information Technology Association (LITA), www.ala.org/lita

Public Library Association (PLA), www.pla.org

Reference and User Services Association (RUSA), www.ala.org/rusa

Young Adult Library Services Association (YALSA), www.ala.org/yalsa

American Theological Library Association (ATLA), www.atla.com

Art Libraries Society of North America (ARLIS), www.arlisna.org

Catholic Library Association (CLA), www.cathla.org

Chinese American Librarians Association (CALA), www.cala-web.org

Church and Synagogue Library Association (CSLA), www.cslainfo.org

Evangelical Church Library Association (ECLA), www.eclalibraries.org

Medical Library Association (MLA), www.mlanet.org

Music Library Association (MLA), www.musiclibraryassoc.org

National Church Library Association (NCLA) www.lclahq.org

Patent and Trademark Depository Library Association (PTDLA) www.ptdla.org

Special Libraries Association (SLA) www.sla.org

Theatre Library Association (TLA) tla.library.unt.edu

AILA (American Indian Library Association) Newsletter, www.ailanet.org/publications

American Libraries, www.ala.org/ala/alonline

American Society for Information Science and Technology (ASIS&T) Bulletin, www.asis.org/Bulletin

Ariadne, www.ariadne.ac.uk

Bates InfoTip, www.batesinfo.com/tip.html

The Cyberskeptic's Guide to Internet Research, infotoday.stores. yahoo.net/cybsguidtoin.html

Booklist, www.booklistonline.com

Charleston Advisor, www.charlestonco.com

CHOICE, www.ala.org/ala/acrl/acrlpubs/choice/home.cfm

Cites & Insights, citesandinsights.info

Computers in Libraries, www.infotoday.com/cilmag

Current Cites, lists.webjunction.org/currentcites

D-Lib Magazine, www.dlib.org

Econtent, www.ecmag.net

E-JASL: The Electronic Journal of Academic and Special Librarianship, southernlibrarianship.icaap.org

EJEL: Electronic Journal of e-Learning, www.ejel.org

Information Outlook, www.sla.org/io

Information Technology and Libraries, www.lita.org/ala/lita/lita-publications/ital/italinformation.cfm

Internet Resources Newsletter, www.hw.ac.uk/libWWW/irn

Journal of the Medical Library Association, www.pubmedcentral. nih.gov/tocrender.fcgi?iid=150885

Library Journal, www.libraryjournal.com

Library Philosophy and Practice, www.webpages.uidaho.edu/~mbolin/lpp.htm

Library Technology Reports, www.techsource.ala.org/ltr

Library Worklife, ala-apa.org/newsletter/current.html

LISNews, www.lisnews.org

MLS: Marketing Library Services, www.infotoday.com/MLS

Multimedia & Internet @ Schools, www.mmischools.com

Search Engine Journal, www.searchenginejournal.com

Searcher, www.infotoday.com/searcher

Smart Libraries Newsletter, www.techsource.ala.org/sln

Teacher Librarian, www.teacherlibrarian.com

Video Librarian, www.videolibrarian.com

Chapter 21

ALA Continuing Education Clearinghouse, www.ala.org/apps/contedu/SearchMain.cfm

Special Libraries Association (SLA) Click University, www.clickuniversity.com

Association of Fundraising Professionals, www.afpnet.org

American Marketing Association, www.marketingpower.com

Library Related Conferences, homepage.usask.ca/~mad204/CONF.HTM

ALA Affiliates, www.ala.org/ala/ourassociation/othergroups/affiliates/affiliateslisting.htm

ALA Conference Calendar, www.ala.org/ala/ourassociation/chapters/planningcalendar/planningcalendar.htm

Information Today Conferences, www.infotoday.com/conferences.shtml

Amigos, www.amigos.org

Bibliographical Center Research (BCR), www.bcr.org/training

National Network of Libraries of Medicine, www.nlm.nih.gov/network.html

NELINET, www.nelinet.net/edserv

Nylink, nylink.org/education

PALINET, www.palinet.org/education_program.aspx

SOLINET, www.solinet.net

Association for Library Services to Children online tutorials, wikis.ala.org/alsc/index.php/Online_tutorials

Basic Tutorial on Searching the Web, University of South Carolina Beaufort Library, www.sc.edu/beaufort/library/pages/bones/bones.shtml

Blended Librarian Online Learning Community, blendedlibrarian.org

Collection Development Training, Arizona State Library, www.lib.az.us/cdt

Copyright Crash Course, University of Texas, www.lib.utsystem.edu/copyright

Copyright Primer, University of Maryland, www-apps.umuc.edu/primer

Free Friday Forums from BCR, www.bcr.org/training

Idaho's Alternative Basic Library Education (ABLE) Program, libraries.idaho.gov/able

Idaho's Supplemental Alternative Basic Library Education (SABLE) Program, libraries.idaho.gov/sable

Infopeople, infopeople.org/training/webcasts/list

Internet Tutorials, www.internettutorials.net

Introduction to MARC Tagging, OCLC, www.oclc.org/support/training/connexion/marc

Librarianship, Texas State Library and Archives Commission, www.tsl.state.tx.us/ld/tutorials/professionalism/lib.html

Library 2.0 at Ning free library-related elearning sites, library20.ning.com

Marketing the Library, Ohio Library Council, www.olc.org/marketing

MORE: Minnesota Opportunities for Reference Excellence, www.arrowhead.lib.mn.us/more/contents.htm

National Library of Medicine Distance Education Resources, www.nlm.nih.gov/bsd/dist_edu.html

Needs Assessment Tutorial, University of Arizona Library, digital.library.arizona.edu/nadm/tutorial

Online Privacy Tutorial, ALA, ala.org/ala/washoff/oitp/email tutorials/privacya/privacy.cfm

PubMed Online Training, www.nlm.nih.gov/bsd/disted/pubmed. html#qt

Online Programming for All Libraries (OPAL), www.opal-online. org/progslis.htm

Professionalism, Texas State Library and Archives Commission, www.tsl.state.tx.us/ld/tutorials/professionalism/prof.html

Reference Excellence on the Web, Ohio Library Council, www.olc. org/ore

Simple Book Repair Manual, Dartmouth College Library, www.dartmouth.edu/~preserve/repair/repairindex.htm

SirsiDynix Institute, www.sirsidynixinstitute.com

WebJunction Courses, www.webjunction.org/do/Navigation? category=372

WebJunction Learning Webinars, webjunction.org/do/Navigation? category=15543

WebJunction Rural Webinars, webjunction.org/do/Navigation; jsessionid=719D88480CF01905D2C862E9AA3D6B0B? category=13496

About the Author

Pamela MacKellar has been a librarian for more than 25 years. She has held positions as a newspaper librarian, library director, assistant librarian, health sciences librarian, cataloger, technology consultant, and independent consultant in libraries of all kinds, including special, school, public, postsecondary, tribal, prison, and state library agency. Pam holds an MLS from the State University of New York at Albany.

Pamela is the co-author of *Grants for Libraries: A How-To-Do-It Manual* (Neal-Schuman Publishers, 2006) and of the article "Wishing Won't Work: 10 Things You Need to Know and Do When Applying for Technology Grants" (*Computers in Libraries*, July–August 2006). She has also written Grant Writing Basics, a web tutorial for the University of North Texas School of Library and Information Sciences, and she hosts the Library Grants blog (www.librarygrants.blogspot.com). Pamela has presented at the Computers in Libraries Conference, the Internet Librarian Conference, and the New Mexico Library Association Annual Conference, and she has taught a class on grants for technology projects at the University of New Mexico Continuing Education Department.

Index